A LOT TO ASK

A Life of Barbara Pym

Hazel Holt

The novels of Barbara Pym

A LOT TO ASK

A Life of Barbara Pym

Hazel Holt

A DUTTON BOOK

DUTTON
Published by the Penguin Group
Penguin Books USA Inc., 375 Hudson Street, New York, New York 10014, U.S.A.
Penguin Books Ltd, 27 Wrights Lane, London W8 5TZ, England
Penguin Books Australia Ltd, Ringwood, Victoria, Australia
Penguin Books Canada Ltd, 2801 John Street, Markham, Ontario, Canada L3R 1B4
Penguin Books (N.Z.) Ltd, 182-190 Wairau Road, Auckland 10, New Zealand

Penguin Books Ltd, Registered Offices: Harmondsworth, Middlesex, England

Published by Dutton, an imprint of New American Library, a division of Penguin
Books USA Inc.
Distributed in Canada by McClelland & Stewart Inc.

Published by arrangement with Macmillan London Limited.

First Dutton Printing, March, 1991
10 9 8 7 6 5 4 3 2 1

The author and publishers would like to thank the following for their permission
to use copyright material in this book: the estate of Lord David Cecil for letters
from David Cecil; Virago Press for an extract from *The Brontes Went to Woolworths*
by Rachel Ferguson; Campbell Thomson & McLaughlin Ltd for extracts from
We Were Amused by Rachel Ferguson; Mrs. Laura Huxley for an extract from
Chrome Yellow by Aldous Huxley; the executors of Philip Larkin's estate for the
Philip Larkin correspondence; the Bodleian Library for furnishing reproductions
from Barbara Pym's papers; Henry Harley for photo of Barbara and Hilary in
Greece, 1966.

 REGISTERED TRADEMARK—MARCA REGISTRADA

LIBRARY OF CONGRESS CATALOGING-IN-PUBLICATION DATA:

Holt, Hazel, 1928–
    A lot to ask : a life of Barbara Pym / Hazel Holt.
        p.   cm.
    Originally published by MacMillan London Ltd. in 1990.
    ISBN 0-525-24937-0
    1. Pym. Barbara—Biography. 2. Novelists, English—20th century—
Biography.   I. Title.
    PR6066.Y58Z68   1991
    823'.914—dc20
        [B]   90-23515
                                                                    CIP

Printed in the United States of America

For Barbara and Hilary

Acknowledgements

I must gratefully acknowledge the tremendous help I have had from Barbara's friends, not only for their kind permission to use letters and documents, but also for many happy hours remembering Barbara. My especial thanks are due to Henry Harvey, Robert Liddell and Bob Smith, all of whom provided so much help, encouragement and delightful conversation.

I would like to thank Helen Gleadow for permission to use extracts from her late husband's letters and to reproduce the horoscope he made for Barbara.

My thanks are also due to Richard Roberts for permission to use Barbara's letters to him and to Honor Ellidge (Wyatt) for her help and support.

I am very grateful to the executors of the late Philip Larkin for permission to use his letters to Barbara, which in such a penetrating and wonderfully funny way increase our perception of her as a writer.

Since Barbara's papers have been lodged in the Bodleian Library, Oxford, the staff of that great library (which Barbara regarded with so much affection) have been immensely helpful in assisting scholars who wish to consult them. I must pay particular tribute to Colin Harris, splendidly friendly and highly efficient, who has made Room 132 an unofficial Barbara Pym Club and general clearing house for information on Pym studies!

I am most grateful to Hilary Hale of Macmillan for all the help she has given to me – for her kindness and patient encouragement and for her marvellous capacity for getting things done.

Finally, I would like to thank Barbara's sister Hilary Walton, without whom this book would not have been possible. She has, of course, been an invaluable source of information and has shown herself to be a true friend by undertaking the thankless task of compiling the index. Not only is Hilary blessed with almost total recall but, having spent the greater part of her life in Barbara's company and having enjoyed such a close and joyful relationship with her, it sometimes seemed to me that I was once more talking with Barbara herself.

Introduction

'So there it stands,' wrote Philip Larkin, 'the world of
Barbara Pym.' Certainly, she created a world that was
entirely her own. 'As we cryptically say "Proustian" or
"Jamesian",' the novelist Shirley Hazzard has noted, 'we may
now say "Barbara Pym" and be understood instantly.' This
world, bounded by English literature, the Anglican Church
and the dustier fringes of Academe, was one that Barbara
Pym herself inhabited and upon which she turned a gaze at
once ironic and compassionate.

There is much that is autobiographical in her novels,
and her letters and diaries give a splendidly vivid picture
of the writer herself. But time passes and what was once
our everyday life is now history, remote and strange to those
of another generation or of another country. It seemed right,
then, to try to put Barbara into her own setting, to define the
manners and mores of the social scene around her (one day her
novels will be a rich source for social historians), to describe
her friends and colleagues, and to show how her books were
moulded by her life, as well as the other way round.

In writing this book I have tried to repeat as little as possible
the material used in *A Very Private Eye*. Some repetition was,
of course, inevitable, but with the help of her friends, I have
been able to add much that is new, so that these two books
will, I hope, complement each other.

Philip Larkin also said that her novels 'exhibit no "development", the first is as practised as the last.' Barbara was not
only a born writer, but also a writer born with a unique view
of life. This view, which only deepened through experience
and suffering, came from her own character and personality:
a complex mixture, as are her novels, of ironic observation
and deep feeling, of frivolity and high spirits and a sensitive

understanding of the unspoken unhappiness, the unformed wish that can never be fulfilled. The stoicism, courage and endurance that she gave to her heroines were qualities that she herself had in abundance. She also shared their vulnerability (to the end her eyes were those of an anxious girl), together with their ability to make the best of things ('not really so bad') and derived great pleasure from 'small blameless comforts'.

In the fourteen years during which her books were not published she was sad and disappointed but never bitter and resentful ('that is not my way'); she simply carried on with her life and with her writing. She continued to watch the world around her, brooded about plots and characters, filling her notebooks with her thoughts and observations, and wrote (in the early mornings, the evenings and at weekends) novels whose publication, she was told by publishers, was 'virtually impossible'. When recognition came at last, and, mercifully, her last few years gave some recompense for all that had gone before, her greatest pleasure came from the reviews, which acknowledged her status as a writer – the most important thing in her life. 'The main thing is to feel that I am now regarded as a novelist, a good feeling after all those years of "This is well written, *but* . . . " '

Above all, as her friend Henry Harvey has said, 'Barbara was a triumphantly good person . . . And her goodness grew. Whatever it was, the moral effect of the exercise of the imagination in Wordsworth's sense, or her Christian routines, she seemed to me more wholly a good person than I would have thought anyone could be when I went to see her a couple of days before she died – we listed people she did *not* want to come and see her, but quite without malice. It was great fun. Her spirit was high.'

Barbara changed the perceptions not only of her friends but of her readers – *our* view of life will never be quite the same again. As Shirley Hazzard said, 'What did one do, pre-Pym, with those observations and imaginings to which she has given a form?' Even now her friends find themselves bereft when they realise that they can no longer pass on to her some overheard remark or observed eccentricity. Returning home from her funeral, Philip Larkin half expected to find a letter from her describing it all.

When we worked in Fetter Lane we often used to have lunch at the Lyons self-service teashop in Fleet Street. Here a jolly woman dished out the food, flourishing a ladle and asking 'Gravy?' or, to regular customers, '*More* gravy?' Occasionally the menu included liver and bacon, a great favourite. The place was rather spartan in its appointments but along two of the walls were upholstered banquettes. 'We don't ask much of life,' Barbara used to say, looking around at the office workers gulping down their stodgy, unexciting food, 'it takes so little to make us happy – just liver and bacon and a seat on the banquette.' As a person, then, Barbara was modest and undemanding, but she fought tenaciously and courageously to establish herself as a professional writer. Sometimes, when she was young, she asked more of other people than they were prepared to give (though in later years her experience lessened her expectations) and of herself she always asked a very great deal, both in her life and in her work. 'Whatever thy hand findeth to do . . . ', whether renewing the Kittylitta in the cat's earthtray or revising, polishing and 'improving' a novel.

In the thirty years that I knew Barbara, I read most of her novels in manuscript and talked with her about them, and we used to joke that I would be her literary executor. When that time came – all too soon – I was heartened (as was her sister Hilary) by the knowledge that her position as a novelist was secure. In the years since her death her readership has grown immensely and her novels and her life have become the subject of much learned comment, which would have amused and, sometimes, appalled her – she was always scornful of the Jake Balokowskys of the academic world. But what would have pleased her most was the fact that she is read with delight and admiration by so many people of all ages in so many countries – a tribute not only to the universal quality of her perception and humour, but also to the comfort her books can bring – 'Good books for a bad day.' So many of Barbara's readers seem to have a personal affection for her and it is for them, most of all, that this book was written.

Hazel Holt
Tivington Knowle
1990

Prelude

A month after Barbara Pym died in January 1980, her sister Hilary had occasion to write to St Catherine's House for a copy of their father's birth certificate. It gave the following details:

> 2nd January 1879, at Poundisford Park Lodge, Pitminster, Somerset, Frederic Crampton Pym, Boy, to Phoebe Pym, a Domestic Servant, registered 30th January 1879 by the Mother.

No father's name was given.

'Somehow,' Hilary said, 'I was not surprised.' Although Barbara and Hilary had known that their father came from Somerset and he would reminisce in a general way about the West Country, he never spoke of his family or relations. 'Why did we never ask? Perhaps it was because we had so many uncles and aunts and cousins on our mother's side and there was plenty going on. Or perhaps we did ask and didn't get an answer.'

Hilary, like Barbara, was a keen and dogged investigator and over the next eight years she set herself to find out who their paternal grandfather had been. The obvious clue was the name Crampton, which Frederic had been given and which he passed on to his daughters (Barbara Mary Crampton and Hilary Crampton) and which it seemed reasonable to suppose had been the name of his father.

The Pym side of Frederic's family was quite easy to establish. Frederic's mother, Phoebe, was the second of the six children of Thomas and Harriet Pym. Thomas was described in the 1871 census as an agricultural labourer and,

1

elsewhere, as a gardener, and his wife may have been the lodge keeper at Poundisford Park at Pitminster, near Taunton, since the family lived in the lodge, a one-storey rough-cast dwelling about a hundred yards from the gates of the Park. It was a hard life, with six children to bring up on very little money and in such confined surroundings, and Phoebe would probably have gone to work up at the Park as a servant when she was in her early teens.

The relevant Crampton was very difficult indeed to identify. After following many possibilities that led nowhere, Hilary had the good fortune to make contact with the widow of one of the present-day Cramptons who had some most useful family documents. Eventually, by a mixture of determination and good fortune, Hilary found that Frederic's father had almost certainly been Fiennes Henry Crampton. This branch of the family was distinguished, well connected, but decidedly wild. An entry in a notebook kept by one of the Cramptons briefly sums up their history:

> Philip Crampton (1707–1792) was Lord Mayor of Dublin and his son, Philip, known as Colonel Crampton, died unmarried, leaving illegitimate issue, amongst others Henry Crampton [1791–1838], afterwards known as Henry Crampton of Fassaroe [Co. Wicklow] – who married a Miss Edwards of the County of Wicklow and had issue by her – Henry [1816–1882] afterwards known as Captain Henry who married a Miss McRoberts and was after Chief of the Police [Chief Constable] in Shropshire – he married secondly a Miss Quartley and afterwards went to ruin.

This Henry Crampton was living in Somerset, with his second wife Blanche Quartley, when Fiennes Henry was born in Wilton, a suburb of Taunton. While the boy was still young, Henry Crampton left his wife and children and 'went to ruin' by marrying for a third time (bigamously) – his housekeeper, by whom he had several children. When he died in Bristol in 1882 neither Blanche nor their son were mentioned in his will. Fiennes Henry was brought up by his mother and his maternal grandmother and lived at Sherford Lodge, a large, handsome house in Haines Hill which was at that time the most socially desirable district of Taunton. The house belonged to Blanche's mother, and another (unmarried) daughter Laura, lived there as well. Blanche's family, the Quartleys, were prosperous farmers, small landowners or clergy and Blanche's mother, widow of the Revd William Quartley who had been Rector of Washfield in Devon, herself owned two farms in North Devon. Blanche had been a spinster of thirty-five when she married Henry Crampton.

Life in a house of middle-aged or elderly women, in the formal and repressive atmosphere of a respectable Taunton suburb must have been tedious to a young boy, especially one with a heritage of Crampton wildness. He was barely sixteen when he met Phoebe, who was then nineteen. There is no evidence that Blanche or Fiennes Henry knew the Bourdillon family who lived at Poundisford Park, but Pitminster is only about three miles from Haines Hill and walking, riding or cycling, the lad may well have met Phoebe quite casually. The Park is surrounded by woodland which would have provided an ideal place for secret meetings. To Fiennes Henry it would all have been an adventure, but to Phoebe, when she became pregnant, at that time and in her situation, it was a disaster.

Since arrangements had to be made for the child, Thomas Pym would have approached Blanche Crampton. We can only assume that he went in person, since he was illiterate (he signed his will with a mark, not a signature) and so could not communicate by letter, and stood in the morning room of that imposing house, determined that his daughter and her child should be properly provided for. It is like a scene from one of the Victorian novels that Barbara was so fond of. Fiennes Henry was immediately packed off to the Royal Military Academy. He had a distinguished army career and retired in 1919 with the rank of Brigadier General. He married in 1901 but had no children and died intestate in 1938.

Phoebe had her baby, but two years later she had gone to Canada, leaving little Frederic with her parents, where, during his early years, he was brought up as a younger brother to their other children. There is no indication of where he received his education, but it must have been somewhere other than the village school, since he is next to be found as an engrossing clerk at a prominent firm of solicitors in Taunton, where a document was found of reminiscences by a former clerk about his fellow employees at the turn of the century. This records that Fred Pym was a fine rugby player (which indicates a rugby-playing school) and a member of the Taunton Operatic Society (where, according to newspaper cuttings, he performed in *Les Cloches de Corneville* and *The Gondoliers*). He was by then signing himself F. Crampton Pym.

Frederic was taken up by Frank White, a prosperous local manufacturer, and his wife Mildred (who became Hilary's godmother). He was almost adopted, in fact, and seems to have been accepted in affluent and important Taunton circles. He was articled to a firm of solicitors in Wellington in Shropshire, and from there moved to Shrewsbury to continue his articles. While he was at Shrewsbury, he went on holiday to Ilfracombe where he met Irena Thomas, also on holiday, and on 26 October 1911 they were married. On the marriage certificate his father is given as 'Thomas Pym, farmer' (his grandfather), the usual way, at that time, of covering up an illegitimate birth.

Irena Spenser Thomas was the youngest daughter of Edward Thomas of Oswestry, who had founded an ironmongery business in the town in 1865. He was rather more than a tradesman since he was also an inventor, some of his agricultural machines being patented and manufactured. He was a prominent figure in the small town and when he died, at a relatively early age, he left his wife Mary in comfortable circumstances, even with ten children to bring up. The Thomas family were originally farmers in the border country around Llanrhaeadr-ym-Mochnant and there were still relatives living on farms near Oswestry.

In 1912 Frederic set up in practice on his own in Oswestry, doubtless having been promised the backing of the extensive Thomas family in and around the town, and very quickly became an established and successful solicitor. Irena must have known about the secret of his birth (although, since she had no father alive to make enquiries about Frederic's circumstances, the couple may not have felt it necessary to tell anyone else). His second wife, Alice, certainly knew about it. But he never, right up to the time of his death in 1966, gave even a hint of it to his daughters.

Barbara died never knowing that there had been a mystery, which is a pity, since it would have been just the sort of investigation that she enjoyed so much.

Chapter One

Barbara Pym had the good fortune to be brought up in the years between the two world wars in an English country town, in comfortable circumstances and surrounded by a cheerful and loving family.

Oswestry is a small market town in Shropshire, near the Welsh border. The population in the 1920s was just under 10,000 and so it was a microcosm of English provincial life, where the social classes were neatly stratified and people knew exactly what their place was in the scheme of things. The family of Frederic Crampton Pym, who was a professional man, had some standing. Not as grand as the gentry – the land-owners and county families, who lived mostly in large houses outside the town itself – but on the next rung down the social ladder. The professional classes, doctors, lawyers and clergy, were equal to (though different from) the manufacturers and wealthier tradespeople. They were not as well off, but their more extensive education gave them a slight social edge in that they were seen to be more 'cultured'.

Frederic Pym soon established himself as a successful solicitor, partly helped, no doubt, by his wife, Irena's local family connections, but also because he was, himself, a charming and sociable man. Barbara was born on 2 June 1913 in lodgings in Willow Street, but by the time Hilary was born in 1916, the family was living in a small house in Welsh Walls, just behind St Oswald's Parish Church in the centre of the town. A few years later Frederic was in a position to buy Morda Lodge, a substantial Edwardian house with an extensive garden, a coach house and a paddock on what were then the outskirts of the town, and next door to Scotswood where Irena's widowed mother lived with her two unmarried daughters.

Morda Lodge was a large, square, brick-built house with an imposing front entrance. As you came into the hall, the handsome drawing room was on the left and the dining room on the right with the nursery behind it. Some steps led down into a large kitchen and the scullery beyond, with the back door opening on to the garden. On the first floor were the family's bedrooms (Irena and Frederic and Barbara at the front, Hilary at the back) together with Frederic's dressing room, a large bathroom and a small room over the front door, known as Johnbar's room after a young cousin who sometimes stayed there. On the second floor, where the electricity didn't reach, were the maids' rooms and the boxroom. A small, separate staircase led up to the attic on the third floor, which had been made into a billiard room. This house was to be Barbara's home for over twenty years.

It was a comfortable and conventional life. Irena and Frederic's marriage was companionable and undemanding; there was a great deal of quiet affection, both for each other and for their daughters. The atmosphere of the household was always equable and cheerful and both Barbara and Hilary remember their childhood as being very happy. The house was large, but there were always a couple of maids, one of whom (Sarah) acted as nursemaid to the girls. Irena Pym did most of the cooking and, when they were older, Barbara and Hilary had their own domestic duties. Little details like these were constantly reflected in her novels.

Although the Misses Bede had a maid they were both domesticated and helped her in various small ways, clearing away the breakfast things, dusting their own bedrooms and doing a little cooking when they felt like it.[1]

The maids – Sarah, Leah, Emily, Dilys and Marjorie – were young Welsh girls from the country, inexperienced and needing to be trained.

Marjorie the new maid (aged 15) came about 6.45. Showed her where we kept things, etc. It was nice to have no washing up, but I felt almost lost without it. . . . How tedious it is showing a new maid but she shapes quite well. I hoovered the bedrooms and did a lot of polishing.[2]

There was also a gardener, shared with Irena's mother and sisters who lived next door, but it was Irena who looked after the chickens, boiling up their mash herself. She also cared for the fat Welsh pony called Mogus who lived in the paddock. Neither Barbara nor Hilary cared much for riding and Mogus was mostly used to pull the governess cart which their mother used to drive. Indeed it was Irena Pym rather than Frederic who drove the car when they acquired one and she even owned a motorbike which she rode with great panache, wearing a workmanlike leather motoring coat. She had been a great tomboy in her youth, with none of the more ladylike accomplishments of her sisters – painting, needlework and arts and crafts. She never did learn to sew and much preferred any sort of outdoor activity. She loved all games and sports and hoped that Barbara and Hilary would share her enjoyment. But, alas, in the perverse way of children, they both disliked sport, rarely attended the tennis parties that were such a feature of social life in the twenties and thirties, and did not even ride bicycles until they became practically the only form of transport in the Second World War.

The one exception to this was golf, which was a family passion. Frederic Pym had been a good rugby player when he lived in Taunton, but now, because of a tubercular knee which had kept him out of the First World War, he turned to the less demanding game and was a keen golfer. Irena played too, with her usual energy and natural athleticism, and so did the girls – though it was Hilary who was the more enthusiastic. They would take the bus out to the Cross Guns Hotel and walk up the lane to Llanymynech, a nine-hole golf course a few miles outside Oswestry. It is an enchanting course, situated on a high plateau and with such spectacular views over the surrounding countryside that only the most dedicated golfer could fail to be distracted by them. Every summer they would exchange one golf course for another and spend several weeks on holiday at Pwllheli in North Wales. This family obsession with golf (their cousin N. C. Selway was a Cambridge blue) inspired Barbara to start the 'Hartley Book', a record of the achievements of Rex and Lister Hartley, two famous golfing brothers. This was not just a simple teenage 'crush', such as a modern girl might have for a pop star, but an extremely detailed and meticulous piece of work and one of the first examples of Barbara's passion for 'finding out' about people, showing the thorough and organised way in which she went about it.

Both Frederic and Irena Pym enjoyed all kinds of music and sang with the Oswestry Operatic Society, mostly Gilbert and Sullivan. He had a good bass voice and she was a contralto with a splendid sense of comedy – a notable Katisha. These dramatic productions inspired Barbara to produce her first completed piece of literature, a very Gilbertian work. It was called *The Magic Diamond* and was written in 1922 when she was nine. It was an ambitious undertaking with a cast of six and was produced with the help of her Selway cousins. The programme (written by N. C. Selway) has a nicely ironic tone. (See Plate 2.)

These Selway cousins were the children of Irena's older sister Nellie and, although they lived at Hatch End in Middlesex, they used to spend Christmas and Easter with the Pyms. They were a lively family and until Barbara went away to Oxford Diana (Betsy) was her closest friend. Barbara and Hilary had few close friends outside the family (although there were a great many Thomas relations, a plethora of cousins) especially when they were away at boarding school and had lost touch with the girls they had known at school in Oswestry. They both enjoyed the company of their grown-up relations and were particularly close to their Aunt Janie, Irena's unmarried sister and the nearest to her in age, who lived next door with her widowed mother and sister May. Scotswood was a large, rather gloomy house, surrounded by tall trees and overhung by laurel bushes. Barbara and Hilary would visit it simply by climbing over the garden wall between the two shrubberies. They would go there for tea – a formal meal.

> Flora got out the best tea service and began to wash the cups and plates, for it was some time since they had been used. Lovingly she swished the pink and gold china in the

hot soapy water and dried each piece carefully on a clean cloth. Tea could be laid on the low table by the fire, she decided, with the cloth with the wide lace border.[3]

After tea the girls would be allowed to look at the special doll's tea and dinner services in the cabinet in the drawing room.

Grandmother Thomas, Northumbrian-born, with a soft accent, was an austere woman dressed in black (she had been widowed at the age of forty-five and left with ten children to bring up), with neat brown hair drawn back in loops and wearing steel-rimmed spectacles. She seemed very remote, since she was already in her seventies when the Pyms moved to Morda Lodge.

May, the eldest daughter, was delicate and sallow and forbidding and not at ease with children. But Janie was far from being a downtrodden spinster daughter at home. She was definitely dashing, full of ideas and initiative, with a passion for painting and a great flair for design. She loved dogs and had two English setters, and she was the first member of the family to own and drive a car. She, like Irena, was athletic and the best of them all at golf: when her mother and sister died she moved from Scotswood to a comfortable house which she had built near the golf course. Although, of course, she had no children of her own, she knew instinctively just what children liked. Altogether she was a splendid example of how it was possible to be unmarried and still have a 'rich, full life'.

Irena and Frederic were affectionate and relaxed parents, loving and humorous. Frederic, according to Hilary, was 'extremely good tempered, undemanding and appreciative'. Surrounded as he was by his wife's family and with no relations of his own, he might well have felt rather overwhelmed. But he had an easy-going nature and was generally liked, with a wide circle of friends. Indeed, after the difficulties and uncertainties of his own boyhood, he may well have been happy to be part of a large, secure family circle. He was gradually building up his professional reputation and the girls enjoyed visiting him in his office at the Cross, looking down from its windows on to the busy centre of the little town. Although he was always there as a solid background presence, a large, handsome, reassuring man, like most fathers at that time he left their upbringing mostly to his wife and she had a very great influence on Barbara's life. Irena Pym was the youngest of the ten Thomas children and always known to her brothers and sisters as 'Baby', even when they were all grown up. Very few people called her Irena and, quite early on, Barbara gave her the nickname 'Links', though no one can remember why. She was slim, with sharp, lively features and masses of curly brown hair. The family was half Welsh and she had much of that nation's liveliness and vivacity. She had a keen eye for eccentricities and was a splendid mimic, especially good at Welsh accents, drawing on her memories of the family farm at Priddbwll and of holidays in Pwllheli. She had a subtle, ironic sense of humour (one of her favourite authors was Saki) and a gift for fantasy, inventing stories about people, and it was Irena who was the instigator of special little phrases and family jokes. It was a family where everyone had a nickname (usually invented by Barbara): Frederic was 'Dor', Janie was 'Ack', later Barbara became 'Buddy' and Hilary 'Poopa', though in early life she was 'little fishy' and 'a fierce drowdle'. There were usually two cats, always considered as part of the family, and when they were lying peacefully together in a chair Irena would declaim from the psalm: 'Behold how good and joyful a thing it is, brethren, to dwell together in unity.'[4] And sometimes, at the dining table, she would snatch up one of the cats, veil its head in a table napkin and quote from Scott:

> When pain and anguish wring thy brow
> A minist'ring angel, thou . . .

At night the cats were put down in the cellar, so that they could get out into the garden. This she would call 'compulsory permanent'. If they wanted to go down into the cellar for any reason during the day, that would be 'temporary voluntary'.

It was Irena who set the tone of the household, with her

feeling for words and her originality of mind, and her influence on Barbara's writing, though not overt, was very strong. She greatly enjoyed the years when Barbara was living at home and beginning to write the novels that Irena, especially, appreciated.

Jane Cleveland in *Jane and Prudence* owes a lot to her. Like Jane she was impervious to fashion and was quite happy to hoist up a sagging petticoat with a safety pin or go out in the old tweed coat that she wore when feeding the chickens. Irena, too, liked to put her feet up in the drawing room in the afternoon, smoking (usually Gold Flake, a cigarette particularly favoured by ladies of her generation) and reading. Once when Mr Passmore, the piano tuner, had left his bowler hat behind on the large plate in the hall, she put it on her head and gave a spirited performance of the popular tango *O Donna Clara*.[5] It was from Irena that Barbara inherited her passion for observing and speculating about people. 'See what you can find out without *asking*,' Irena used to say, thereby bestowing upon Barbara a whole attitude to life.

The Thomas family had always been on social terms with the clergy and the vicar of St Oswald's, Arthur Langford Brown, whose daughter Audrey was Barbara's age, often used to call and the girls went to Christmas parties at the vicarage. There was, too, a succession of curates, one of whom in particular was worshipped from afar by Hilary. When he came to tea on a winter afternoon his combinations, like Mr Donne's, did in fact show, tucked into his socks.[6] 'Can your love stand *that*?' Barbara demanded of her sister. Apparently it could and curates frequently came to supper.

> Were all new curates everywhere always given boiled chicken when they came to supper for the first time? Belinda wondered. It was certainly an established ritual at their house and it seemed somehow right for a new curate. The coldness, the whiteness, the muffling with sauce, perhaps even the sharpness added by the slices of lemon, there was something appropriate here, even if Belinda could not see exactly what it was.[7]

Irena was assistant organist at St Oswald's and Frederic sang in the choir. Like most of their generation, Barbara and Hilary graduated from the afternoon children's service to Matins and Evensong every Sunday. Full participation in church fêtes, jumble sales and church outings was a natural and enjoyable part of their lives from earliest childhood. The year was marked out by the festivals of the Church and they were at home and comfortable with the service, with the beauty of its ancient language and the feeling of unchanging continuity that characterised the Church of England in those less complicated days.

In their early years Barbara and Hilary went to the local private school, Queen's Park. They could have moved on to Oswestry High School, but Irena was determined that they should go away to school. The early 1920s marked the beginning of the heyday of the girls' boarding school. Until the First World War, education for girls was a very hit-or-miss affair. It was considered natural – indeed, essential – that the boys of professional families should be sent to public school, but, unless there were exceptional circumstances, the girls were generally required to have accomplishments rather than learning. But gradually the concept of a proper academic education for girls was evolving, though it took a world war with its upheaval and changing values to bring about real emancipation. Then boarding schools proliferated, some excellent, some merely fashionable, but all giving girls a chance to get away from home and achieve a degree of independence unknown to previous generations. They also provided – as they still do – an opportunity for girls living in more remote areas, where there are few schools, to have a choice in the kind of education they or their parents wanted – provided they could afford the fees.

Irena was very keen that the girls should go to a school where they would have the opportunities for sport that she had always longed for. Perhaps one of them might even become Captain of Games, like the heroine of a school story by Angela Brazil – for the boarding school had by now its own literary mythology. Certainly she realised that the High School in Oswestry could not provide an education that would really stretch two highly intelligent, academically inclined girls whose sights were already set on Oxford. So, at the age of twelve, Barbara was sent to Liverpool College, Huyton, where Hilary joined her three years later.

> My heart sank as I recognised the familiar landmarks. I could almost imagine myself a schoolgirl again, arriving at the station on a wet September evening for the autumn term and smelling the antiseptic smell of the newly scrubbed cloakrooms.[8]

Their parents had to make quite a few sacrifices to send both girls away to school – Hilary remembers that the house was often very shabby during this period – and, since Irena and her daughters were close she missed them very much. Apart from holidays, the girls only saw their parents on the two Long Saturdays each term when they would meet in Liverpool. Irena waited eagerly for their weekly letters.

Huyton was a conventional school, with firm discipline and a strong religious background. Before the building of the school chapel, the pupils went to services at the local church where there was a great deal of interest in and speculation about the clergy since they were the only men on whom the impressionable girls could exercise their romantic imaginations.

> In our day he [the school chaplain] had been a tall good looking man, with whom all of us were more or less secretly in love . . . his visits had been eagerly looked forward to.[9]

Unlike many authors, Barbara does not seem to have been greatly influenced by her schooldays. She was quite happy at school and made friends easily. She was a steady but not spectacular pupil, her only position of authority being chairman of the Literary Society. Her English mistress was Hélène Lejeune (sister of the film critic, C. A. Lejeune), a delightful eccentric who wore long skirts and a djibbah and carried her books in an ethnic cloth bag. She taught English literature well and gave her pupils an excellent and extensive grounding in it, inspiring in Barbara a profound and abiding love of 'our greater English poets'. Barbara contributed to the school magazine, poems and parodies, much as any other reasonably imaginative girl might have done. Her reading was equally conventional: Kipling and Edgar Wallace (both favourites of her father) as well as other detective stories, including those in the *Scout* featuring Frank Darrell, 'the man of many faces'.

In her mid teens she began to read more widely in modern fiction. Irena was very fond of novels, either reading with quiet enjoyment those that appealed to her, or 'tearing the heart out of' those she didn't really like but felt she ought to have a look at. She and Barbara both used that magnificent and ubiquitous institution, Boots' Lending Library. The branch in Oswestry was run by a Miss Lucy Bloomer, an archetypal Boots' Librarian of the period, very refined, with large eyes and a rosebud mouth, dressed in brown with dainty blouses, who would put to one side the most recently published novels for her favoured customers. In 1929 Barbara first read a book that Miss Bloomer might not have thought at all suitable for a girl of sixteen. It was *Crome Yellow* by Aldous Huxley.

> He [Lord David Cecil] told me he had been inspired to write after reading Lytton Strachey's *Eminent Victorians* just as I had been inspired by *Crome Yellow*.[10]

Aldous Huxley was indeed a very powerful influence upon many young people in the twenties and thirties. *Crome Yellow*, his first novel (and perhaps the most classically simple) was published in 1921, followed by *Antic Hay* (1923), *Those Barren Leaves* (1925) and *Point Counter Point* (1928). These brilliant, witty novels about ironic, heartless people typified for many of his more impressionable readers the essence of what was popularly known as the 'Bohemian Set', novelists, poets and painters – 'artists' – who all appeared to live lives in which the brilliance of their intellects mirrored and enhanced the intensity of their emotions. The novels gave their readers the happy illusion that they too, by the very act of reading them, were part of this glittering intelligentsia, even if, on the way, they had to look up some of the more esoteric words in the dictionary. For Barbara, Aldous Huxley's novels seemed to be the height of intellectual sophistication.

I was a keen reader of all kinds of modern fiction, and more than anything else I read at that time *Crome Yellow* made me want to be a novelist myself. I don't suppose for a moment that I appreciated the book's finer satirical points, but it seemed to me funnier than anything I had read before, and the idea of writing about a group of people in a certain situation – in this case upper-class intellectuals in a country house – immediately attracted me, so I decided that I wanted to write a novel like *Crome Yellow*. And so my first novel – unpublished of course – was started in that same year, 1929. It was called *Young Men in Fancy Dress* and was about a group of 'Bohemians' – I must put that word in quotes – who were, in my view, young men living in Chelsea, a district of which I knew nothing at the time.[11]

Young Men in Fancy Dress was written between August 1929 and April 1930. Its 267 handwritten pages constitute a serious attempt at novel writing. The influence of Aldous Huxley is all-pervasive, though the naïvety of outlook occasionally makes it read more like a novel about Chelsea written by Daisy Ashford. But because it was the wit and funniness of Huxley's novel that appealed to her, there is an attempt at irony and humour, still relatively unformed yet giving a hint of what was to come, and there is also that delight in detail, descriptions of clothes, rooms and food, that was to enrich her later novels. Although there are many infelicities and an over-eager, breathless quality about the book, the style is remarkably coherent and totally individual. On holiday, she showed the manuscript to one of the sons of the local pastor at Pwllheli, a young man called Dewi Morgan Griffith, whom she wanted to impress. He was her first critic and, it seems, a perceptive one, since her dedication ran: 'To H.D.M.G. who kindly informed me that I had the makings of a style of my own.'

Like his prototype in *Crome Yellow*, the hero of the book is a poet called Denis, although he also

aspired to be a novelist. He read all the best modern novels and was not ignorant of the classics. . . . This

afternoon he had read *Crome Yellow* and had enjoyed
it immensely. It seemed to him to be about as perfect
as a novel could be. Not actually about anything – of
course not – the best novels never are – but full of witty
and intelligent conversation.[12]

She even opens the novel with a quotation from *Crome
Yellow*:

> 'He took nobody by surprise, there was nobody to take.'
> Denis laid down his pen to consider the words he had just
> written. He said them aloud and meditated upon their
> subtle humour with pride. Then a sudden and horrible
> thought occurred to him. The words seemed familiar.
> Where could he possibly have heard them before? – no
> relative or friend of his was capable of saying anything
> like that.[13]

His family were wealthy Philistines, *nouveau riche*, (his father
'had made money in the sausage trade'), who only cared for
cocktails, nightclubs and bridge.

> Denis longed above all things to be different from
> other people. . . . He attempted to live and dress in
> the Bohemian fashion, but he would never have made
> an ideal inhabitant of Chelsea – he always seemed too
> innocent and unsophisticated. He seemed to get his ideas
> out of books instead of his own head.[14]

Quite soon he becomes acquainted with a very cultured family, rather like Huxley's Wimbushes, full of talk
about Swinburne, Rupert Brooke and – of course – Aldous
Huxley. The son, Peter, is sympathetic to Denis's ambitions
and advises him:

> If you want to be a proper novelist you must get
> to like Town. And develop a passion for Chelsea.[15]

So off they go to visit Peter's cousin, Julian Sabato (half
Spanish and a poet), who is a cross between Huxley's Byronic
painter Gombaud and the multi-talented Ivor Lombard.

Julian Sabato's flat in Chelsea was charming. It was
Bohemian without being aggressively so. . . . The walls
of the drawing room were a very pale green and the
frieze along the top had been designed by one of Julian's
artistic friends. It was very modern and carried out in
shades of green, orange, brown and pale mauve that was
almost grey. The curtains and the cushions were of these
colours and the taffeta of which they were made was shot
with gold and silver. The pictures on the walls were rather
vague-looking landscapes – evidently all painted by the
same hand, for they looked curiously alike.[16]

Already the eye of the novelist is observing and recording,
and we will find echoes of Denis's reaction to this new and
exciting ambience in a later novel when Deirdre admires
Catherine's flat in much the same naïve way. Julian has the
sort of Mr Rochester looks that many girls admire:

Julian was undoubtedly very fascinating. He had wavy
brown hair that was just a little longer than the orthodox
length, and wore elegantly pointed side whiskers. His
eyes were very dark and of course he had long eyelashes.
One eyebrow was a little higher than the other, which
added to his charm. His mouth was rather small and the
expression on his face was one of sulkiness and boredom.
He was clever and conceited and everyone who knew him
at all liked him.[17]

The eye of the novelist is also a humorous eye.

He had no servants. He ate the sort of food that needs
no cooking, such as sardines and tinned fruit salad. He
managed to thrive quite well on foods of this description
and, after all, most struggling poets drink Camp coffee
instead of nectar and find it just as inspiring and much
cheaper.[18]

Julian, however, has some very sound advice for an
aspiring author.

'Nobody here ever seems to get at all famous, and
if anybody does – which is very seldom – you bet he

quits this place as quickly as possible. You'll find that
no proper writer ever lives this sort of life for long –
it's too trying and consequently you've no energy left
for writing. In short, you live the life of novelist or poet
without anything to show for it.'[19]

Later on Denis meets a girl called Gillian at a country house
party and she completes his disillusion with the Bohemian life.

'All my ideas,' she said, 'about being famous and terribly
modern seem to have toned down a little. You see, before
I was sixteen I wanted to do something artistic, write or
paint – and I used to have endless dreams of flats in
Chelsea and queer artistic parties at which I was the
chief attraction, but . . . now I feel differently.'
    'What do you think of these specimens from Chelsea
here tonight?' Denis asked.
    'They're quite interesting – but – oh I don't know –
they're not quite real,' she said rather sadly. 'They seem
like men just dressed up and saying things, almost like a
play or a fancy dress ball.'[20]

She is, in a way, echoing Huxley's Mr Scogan.

'Ah, Denis, if you could only read Knockespotch you
wouldn't be writing a novel about the wearisome development of a young man's character, you wouldn't be
describing in endless, fastidious detail, cultured life in
Chelsea and Bloomsbury and Hampstead. You would be
trying to write a readable book.'[21]

Denis fancies himself in love with several girls, including
an exotic poetess called Marguerite – a fascinating Older
Woman, but Barbara is more interested in describing Gillian's
feelings, which seem to mirror her own. She indulges herself
by creating not only the perfect dress but also the perfect man
for Gillian, who might, also, be the perfect man for the young
Barbara.

Gillian always liked to sit on the window seat, because
from there she could see almost the whole length of
the drive. While she was sitting there Ralph Kingston

arrived. He was very handsome and sunburnt and his hair was dark and curly. At the dance he had been the centre of attraction. He played the ukelele well and danced divinely. He had money and a fascinating way of speaking. Yet Gillian felt that he lacked something.

Gillian liked to think of herself as a young lady of moods. She used to dress to suit these moods and would often appear in unsuitable frocks just because she felt like it. Today she was wearing a frock of creamy chiffon – a dainty creation sprinkled with pale blue and yellow flowers. It was rather long and the skirt fell in points of varying lengths . . .

They walked together down the lane and inside a gate they saw a heap of turnips.

'So "tender-gorgeous",' said Ralph.

'Who said that about them?' asked Gillian. She liked to know the context of everything.

'Edward Thomas,' he replied. 'I think he's almost my favourite poet – after Rupert Brooke, of course.'

Rupert Brooke – how absolutely wonderful that he should like Rupert Brooke. Immediately Ralph became raised on a pedestal above all other young men. At once Gillian realised that he possessed that indefinable something which she had thought he had lacked. . . . She decided that Ralph was the most original person she had ever met. The fact that he was an ardent admirer of Rupert Brooke made him wonderful, but on the other hand he wasn't sickly and poetical. He swore in a manly fashion on the golf links, so Peter had told her, and she remembered his performances on the ukelele and on the tennis court.[22]

Young Men in Fancy Dress tells us a great deal about Barbara at sixteen, about the real world she lived in and the fascinating world of 'writers' that she now aspired to. With the completion of the manuscript, she realised not only that she could write fluently and easily, but also that it was something she wanted to go on doing. She had, one might say, the perception of herself as a writer. The novel also gives us some intimations of the complex, contradictory and generally impossible things she looked for in a young man and explains why she was so often disappointed.

Chapter Two

When Barbara went up to St Hilda's College, Oxford in 1931 to read English she was very naïve by today's standards. Girls grew up more slowly then – they were certainly more romantic, and with a kind of enthusiastic innocence that would be impossible today. She loved the idea of Oxford, revelling in the 'noble' buildings and the poetic Matthew Arnold associations. She didn't take much part in university activities (though she did join the Bach Choir for a short time) but she quickly made friends with her fellow students at St Hilda's, chatting to them late into the night in her room on the top floor, which had a good commanding view of the drive. But after her years at a girls' boarding school, her main interest lay elsewhere and when she was eighteen she began a diary which referred not at all to the beauties of Oxford, but charted her interest in and pursuit of young men with refreshing frankness.

> *1 January 1932.* Beginning the year in an excellently one-sex way. Went to Blackgate [a café in Oswestry where she used to have coffee with her girlfriends] – no thrills there.[1]

In these early vacations she read a great deal, planned her wardrobe, did some dressmaking, listened to dance music on the radio and went to the cinema very frequently – the programme at the Regal was changed every Sunday and Wednesday, so the Pyms often went to the cinema twice a week. Radio and the cinema were still something of a novelty and felt to be rather modern and dashing. Dance band leaders – Jack Payne, Roy Fox, Henry Hall, Geraldo – and film stars, both British and American, brought glimpses of a more sophisticated, cosmopolitan life to young people in the provinces – even to undergraduates.

Flicks in the evening. *Body and Soul* – Charles Farrell
and Elissa Landi. First broadcast of 1932 – Jack Payne
– *Say it with Music*, and a happy new year from all his
boys separately.

Went to Liverpool. Lunch at the Lyceum. *Stand up
and Sing* in the afternoon (1 × 10d!). Very disappointing.
No very hot tunes – typical musical comedy stuff. As for
the wonderful Jack [Buchanan] himself – obviously past
his best – fixed grin – permed hair – and no better dancer
than heaps of others.[2]

Occasionally she went to stay with old schoolfriends,
some of whom had brothers:

I was on pins awaiting the arrival of the devastating
Francis – at about 11 he came – the same fascinating
creature. . . . Francis came in eating a banana – an amus-
ingly dissipated [one of her favourite words at that time]
sight. We tried to put the skin down his neck and into
his pocket and made some noise in doing it! . . . Francis
was actually up before us and looked ravishing in grey
flannels and a yellow polo jersey. We sat in the drawing
room reading in blissful silence. I was reading Maurice
Lane-Norcott [a humorous writer of the period]. Then a
whole herd of people came. We could hear them out in
the hall and devoutly hoped that they wouldn't disturb
our peace.[3]

The adolescent romping and the rather affected prose style
form a strange juxtaposition, but it is typical of Barbara at this
time, when schoolgirlish gush and high spirits were beginning
to be modified by an attempt to find some more complex style
in which to express herself.

Even before she went to Oxford, Barbara had shown a
remarkable propensity to fall in love with people she didn't
actually know. In Oswestry there had been a bank clerk who
was also a lay reader, who had inspired two poems, one of
which, *Midland Bank*, she described as 'a poem dedicated to
J.T.L. [John Trevor Lloyd] with the author's fondest love (but
without his permission)'. Like Flora yearning for Mr Oliver[4]
and the young Mildred for Bernard Hatherley[5] Barbara would

peer into the bank to see if he was on view, hurry past his
lodgings in the hope of catching a glimpse of him and sit
enraptured in church, listening to him reading the lesson.
The most boring and prosaic young man can be transformed
by a young girl's romantic imagination into someone quite
thrilling.

> In church Mr Oliver again appeared glamorous, seen
> in the distance and the dim light; Flora's love came
> flooding back, so that she could hardly bear to look at
> him. . . . She was reminded of a poem she had once read
> somewhere, something about my devotion more secure,
> woos thy *spirit* high and pure. . . . If she could find it,
> she would copy it out into her diary.[6]

Oxford was a richer hunting ground. Barbara's fancy was
caught by several of the moderators, the dons who set and
marked the examination papers for the Honour Moderations
examinations.

> Oh the perfect wife of an Oxford Moderator – that seems
> to be my true vocation. . . . Oxford really is intoxicating.
> I was more than thrilled to be back – in fact quite goofy
> with excitement.[7]

Oxford undergraduates are required to take an examination,
Pass Moderations (P. Mods), at the end of their first term,
and both Barbara and her friend Mary Sharp failed theirs
('De Tocqueville was my downfall'). This inspired Barbara
to further speculations – was the one who had failed her her
favourite, the one she called 'Fat Babyface'? She consulted the
University Calendar.

> Did some research work – I think the one that ploughed
> me may be Will G. Moore of Magdalen. I wonder which
> is my pet!
>   In the afternoon I saw my pet Moderator and that
> seems to be the main event of my day. Really this is
> the queerest crush ever – I think I've got to admit now
> that it's grown as bad as that. He was in a navy blue

suit wearing a rather ancient tie (striped) in which red
and green seemed to predominate. There was a faint
suspicion of a red silk hanky peeping out of his top
pocket. *O lo patetico.*[8]

Brief glimpses of the beloved object are very good practice
for a novelist, since every detail of his appearance must
be registered with photographic speed and accuracy. This
particular passion was quite brief – as soon as she had found
out all she wanted to know about him, she lost interest. By
the time she took P. Mods again in March 1932 she was in
the throes of a new passion for another moderator, Lindley
L. Fraser.

> P. Mods. I felt sick with nerves and apprehension. We
> do our papers in the North Writing Schools, funny little
> places – two rooms joined into one, with a Moderator [as
> invigilator] in the middle. . . . Pliny and Lindley in the
> afternoon. I asked him [Lindley] to lend me a pencil.
> He would have lent me his had he not wanted it for
> correcting papers. I was so thrilled and excited that my
> trembling hands would not allow me to write my paper –
> I had to calm myself down – and turn my attention to
> the source of the Crittumnus.[9]

In spite of these emotional agonisings she passed her
P. Mods.

> I had a card from the Clerk of the Schools with
> the brief but satisfactory message. 'Miss Pym passed
> in four.' Oh . . . inexpressible joy. But like all perfect
> pleasures touched with a marvellous spot of melancholy.
> I wonder if any days will ever be such fun as the P. Mod.
> days – especially those at the end of last term.[10]

But she already had another unknown to dote on and
had, typically, been keeping a timetable of sightings:

> *G. S. Walmsley. Michaelmas Term 1931.*
> 1) Oct. 18th. In St Mary's. With E. C. R. Hadfield?
> 2) Once on a bike riding towards Carfax by Teddy
> Hall [St Edmund Hall] Lane.

3) At Clinkers – Worcester v St Edmund Hall, I saw him smile for the first time.
4) On 2 distinct occasions (maybe more) I remember seeing him walking down the High in his B.A. gown – with others. This was about 11 o'clock.
5) 1.45-ish – a day when we were going to Schools for P. Mods – riding towards Teddy Hall – wearing mac. Looked as if he'd been crying or had a cold!
Hilary Term
1) Sunday 17th. In St Mary's.
2) Monday 18th. – 10.15 p.m. – coming out of St Edmund Hall plus bike wearing mac.
3) Saturday 30th. Walking down the High with E.C.R.H.[11]

The following term she took up the pursuit with continuing enthusiasm.

8 May. Sang in *The Creation* – but that's not the main point. The whole of the past week – ever since last Sunday night – I've thought of nothing but Geoffrey. Though I've only seen him once – rowing on Thursday – I can't help feeling that I must do something about it. Anyway, I'll try a week (a) not going out of my way to see him, (b) not talking of him, (c) not trying to think of him. That will be difficult.
15 May. All these resolutions are little good. I didn't see him at all during the week – but tonight I saw him and it has come back as strongly as ever before. I tried – and succeeded up to a point – to be strong-minded – I hope I shall never forget this.
23 May. I went to Eights [college rowing races on the Isis] – on the St John's barge with Stephen Coppock. I wore my blue costume. . . . I noticed that there was only the Balliol barge between us and St Edmund Hall [barge] Geoffrey came on top of the latter and had tea with 2 or 3 other men. He was amusing – pretending to drink very quickly – he was wearing his macintosh and didn't seem to eat anything.
25 May. The last day of Eights. Saw no sign of Geoffrey after the 5 o'clock race was over. It was on this day that I found that he was taking a Diploma in Theology.

8 June. I paid my first visit to the Rad [Radcliffe Camera library] Saw . . . Geoffrey – who looked heavenly in plus fours. Coming out at about 9.30 I met him coming down the steps. We were all alone – I longed to crash into him or drop my books – but the incident was over, and became one of the many might-have-beens about which it's so lovely to speculate.[12]

It might be assumed that all this emotion for people she never actually met – and it was a very real emotion to her – was a substitute for the real thing. This was by no means the case. Barbara was surrounded by young men. She was a tall girl, not pretty but handsome, with bright hazel eyes and thick wavy brown hair. Her front teeth were rather large – a source of embarrassment to her all her life – and because of this she developed a kind of lopsided smile that was curiously charming. Even by 1930s Oxford standards, where male undergraduates outnumbered the girls by at least ten to one, Barbara had a great many boyfriends. She was obviously very attractive to young men and, equally obviously, revelled in her power over them. There were Stephen and Bill and Harry and Harlovin and Basil and Paul – not surprising, really, that Barbara used to say that of all her heroines, in many ways the one she resembled most was Prudence.

Prudence had her memories too. Laurence and Henry and Philip, so many of them, for she had had numerous admirers, all coming up the drive [of her College], in a great body, it seemed, though in fact they had come singly.[13]

The social life was very rich and full. Unlike their contemporaries, debutantes 'doing' the Season, young women at Oxford had a remarkable amount of freedom. They were not chaperoned in any way (though not so many years before undergraduates had been required to have chaperons if they entertained young men to tea, and even, before the First World War, when they attended lectures) and were not required to be back in College until ten o'clock (midnight, with permission). And even then, if your college was on the river, it was perfectly possible to come back by punt and climb in through the windows of a friend with rooms on the ground floor. She went to cocktail parties and lunch parties:

A delightful lunch party at Trinity. Barbara Flower, Cornelia Wintour, Rupert, Frederic Wells and Hal Summers. Wells is sweet but too intellectual – the girls were too intellectual and didn't have the compensation of being of the opposite sex.[14]

She dined out in restaurants:

Went out to dinner at the George with Harry and had the loveliest cocktail I've ever had – a sidecar, very iced. Also hock and good food. I wore blue lace – with three real red roses pinned on to the front. Also my long crystal earrings and make-up to match the roses. Very nice![15]

Harry was Harry Harker, a tall, good-looking young man reading English at St John's, whom Barbara had met at lectures. He was highly intelligent and was, in fact, supporting himself on scholarships since his father was a railway worker in Bristol. It must have been quite a struggle for him to find the money to take Barbara out to dinner at the Town and Gown and the Moorish, but he was completely infatuated with her and did, indeed, ask her to marry him. Barbara made it perfectly plain that, although she enjoyed his company, she was not in love with him and, accepting this, he continued to be an affectionate friend for the rest of her years in Oxford, selflessly supporting her through various crises and love affairs.

With Harry – and various other young men – she went to the cinema and to the theatre, and just occasionally to a debate at the Oxford Union (as a guest since women were not allowed to be members):

O. C. Papineau 'The ex-Treasurer from Hertford' as he was styled spoke with wonderful eloquence not on the subject at all when one came to think of it. He has wonderful black patent leather hair.

Union debate: 'That this house regrets that the extermination of the Celts was never successfully completed.' Speaking mixed. Prince Lieven rather dull I thought. Bright spots by J. C. Smuts and Freddie Bucher of Oriel and Giles Playfair![16]

Once or twice she went to the Labour Club:

Rather above me – a few superb creatures there including Papineau.[17]

Most of all, like all undergraduates, she went out to tea – often the occasion for romantic exchanges. In later life she remembered them for the buns from Boffins, the honey and the resultant sticky kisses.

After a time the smell of cooking rose up in the quadrangle of Randolph College, rough young voices were heard down below and on the stairs, and a bell began to ring, a loud bell that disturbed the young men and the young women who had come to tea with them. Lights were turned on to reveal the happy lovers blinking like ruffled owls, the honey toast lying cold and greasy on a plate in the fireplace, the tomato sandwiches curled up at the edges, and the Fuller's walnut cake a crumbly mess because it had been cut by inexperienced hands.[18]

She had made a new persona for herself when she went to Oxford. This other self was called Sandra – in those days a rather romantic, East European name, an abbreviation of Alexandra. Her notebooks were labelled with the name, her cushions and evening bag embroidered with it.

In the afternoon I bought an exciting flannel shirt, red, black and white checks – very Sandra.[19]

Also very Sandra was a scarlet satin blouse and tight black skirt. Sandra was, in fact, rather 'fast'.

> Went on the river in the afternoon. Got to know
> Leslie Fearnehough (Queens) and Michael Rabone (Univ.)
> because we wanted to borrow a match. I hope they didn't
> think we were deliberately trying to make a pick-up
> – really I do some unfortunate things – but how can
> you smoke a cigarette without a match? Almost before
> we'd been in conversation 10 minutes Leslie asked us
> if we'd go and have tea with them at the Air Squad-
> ron. We were amazed – there was something so naif
> about it![20]

No wonder other young men 'teased me a lot about my
appalling reputation!' One is reminded of the description
of the young Jane Austen as the 'prettiest, silliest, most
affected, husband-hunting butterfly'. Not that Barbara and
her Oxford contemporaries were hunting husbands. A few
did become engaged while at university, many worked hard in
preparation for careers that were at last being opened to them,
but for others it was simply a delightful interlude in their lives,
when academic pursuits were embellished and enhanced by
rich and varied social activity.

Barbara was, of course, reading English literature and
did work quite hard in spite of all the distractions. While
she enjoyed the reading connected with her subject (though
favouring those poets whose thoughts on Love and Melancholy chimed with hers), she was less enthusiastic about
turning out the required weekly essay for her tutor at St
Hilda's ('Tried to think out an essay on the Puritanism of
Spenser and Milton', 'wrote a bad essay on Bacon's style in
the evening', 'I worked on Old English for about $1\frac{1}{2}$ hours
– Wulfstan's address to the English. Really, it gave me the
pip.' 'Tute [tutorial] in the morning. Morrison couldn't think
of much to say to us'). She did, however, enjoy a wide variety
of lectures – though her reactions to them were more frivolous
than academic:

> Herbert J. Hunt is quite an amusement in himself.
> He has a Lancs accent and one feels that his 'H's' are
> more a matter of luck than habit. He speaks loudly and
> as if he has had rather too much to drink. Anyway, he's
> distinctly good and thorough.

Professor Wylde on the History of the English Language
– he's a sweet old thing – very downright in his views
– favourite habit of condemning most current phrenetic
terms – 'sheer lunacy' – 'means nothing' etc.
Went to Edmund Blunden's lecture. He's nice and
interesting, though very nervous.
Some lectures in the morning. The greatest living
authority on Ben Jonson (i.e. Percy Simpson) tripped
over my legs as he was entering the lecture room.
An amusing lecture in the morning – Professor Tolkien
on Beowulf. After tea I went to Lewis's [C. S. Lewis]
lecture which was deep but interesting in parts.
In the evening the Professor of Poetry gave an
extremely relevant lecture on Shakespeare's sonnets.
He said that there was 'no ignoble sex-perversion' about
Shakespeare's love for Mr W.H.[21]

Lectures, of course, were also fruitful places for observing
the current object of her affection:

Percy Simpson at 12 was singularly amusing – he
read some priceless letters of the 17th C describing
a masque where everyone was tight. Both pale Magd.
and the Headington scholar were there. I was opposite
the latter and had an opportunity of studying his face.
He has a singularly nice expression and smile, and
always looks upwards, so that one never catches his
eye.[22]

'In Oxford in her early twenties,' Barbara wrote, in an
unfinished novel entitled *The Lumber Room*, 'she had been
in love with somebody every spring, not always the same
person, but always somebody.' In the spring of 1932, on
26 May, she went to tea for the first time with Rupert
Gleadow. He was an exceptionally good-looking young man,
a Wykhamist, up at Trinity, academically brilliant, well-
off and very dashing indeed. He was, and continued to
be, a knowledgeable and enthusiastic astrologer and, later
in their acquaintance, cast her horoscope. Barbara was
swept off her feet and could think of little else. On 2
June, her nineteenth birthday, Rupert, 'wearing his purple
subfusc coat' bought her 'a heavenly scarf – royal blue

and orange' and they went to the Super cinema to see
Frankenstein.

> I loved stealing surreptitious glances at Rupert's profile
> and was very thrilled by him.[23]

She chronicles the progress of their love affair most
minutely in her diary:

> . . . we wandered down the Banbury Road . . . in the
> pouring rain. . . . I remember putting my arms round
> him and loving him, because he was very wet and
> shivering and looked at me so sweetly.
> We went into St Hilda's, sat on a seat, and because of
> the ever-present and watchful eyes, behaved very well.
> Rupert was very Theocritean and loving. I got a wee
> bit sick of it – but tried to please him as I was determined
> to treat him as kindly as possible as he'd Schools [exams]
> on the 9th.
> We drank chocolate at the Queener [a café] and
> went on to no 47 [Rupert's lodgings]. This kind of
> *Private Lives* love scene was far better in reality than
> in anticipation.[24]

Rupert's friend Miles Macadam was often with them.

> I remember noticing Miles' voice – which still fascinates
> me – and generally liking him.[25]

Barbara, Rupert and Miles formed a close trio and went
about everywhere together – to the cinema, on the river, dining
at Stewart's and at the Spread Eagle at Thame ('a charming
garden – the flowers seem to grow at random . . . then we
ate a marvellous dinner, at which everything ordinary – i.e.
fish – tasted extraordinarily good. We finished up with yellow Chartreuse – Rupert laughed at me because it made me
cough').
Both Miles and Rupert got Firsts and the term ended
in a romantic haze:

> In the morning Rupert and I wandered about in various
> shops – he bought me some chocolates at Elliston's –

and eventually we arrived at no. 47. Miles came and we went off for lunch, choosing Stewart's because of its happy memories and convenience. In Stewart's they played *Wien du Stadt meiner Traüme* – I heard it for the first time there. At the station I held Miles' and Rupert's hands tightly and gazed into their blue and brown eyes respectively. Then we said goodbye and I settled down to a sober journey home.[26]

Rupert continued to do exciting and glamorous things. In July he bought an aeroplane – a Tiger Moth with a racing fuselage – for £350. In August he wrote to her:

I think that if it [their relationship] had happened a century ago, or even less, we should have been quite admittedly in love. Only we both happen to be hard-headed moderns. I hope you don't dislike the suggestion . . .
    I think your remark that girls have more right to philander than men very provocative . . .
    Anyone reading them [their letters] would say (quite without justification) 'Barbara Pym seems to have been a rather free and easy young woman'. Seeing how charmingly innocent we both are that would be very undeserved.[27]

In September, during the Long Vacation, Rupert went to stay at Morda Lodge. Barbara was nervous at first, partly because seeing anyone on one's home ground is always different, but partly because Rupert came from a slightly higher class and wealthier background and she wasn't quite sure how he would fit in. Rupert, after all, lived rather grandly in London, so she had been decidedly deprecating about Oswestry. After he had left Rupert wrote – with just the faintest hint of patronage:

I'm surprised at how foul you said Oswestry is. . . . I think it's really quite a nice country town, with market and all – quite fit for the honour of your residence.[28]

But after the first slight stiffness wore off they had an idyllic week.

We walked up to Llynclys Hill and made ourselves comfortable in the sun. . . . We laughed out of sheer happiness. . . . Seeing me run down the hill Rupert gave me the name of Atalanta. . . . T. P. [the curate] was coming to supper so we had to change. Rupert and I were still mad. I helped him to dress. I think we managed to behave fairly well through supper, but I was still feeling ridiculous, and drank some beer out of a cup. . . . It was a very cold evening and I felt very tired, but we went down Weston Lane and looked at the stars. I said that the happiness one got out of love was worth any unhappiness it might (and generally does) bring. I can't remember what Rupert said but he wasn't so sure about it, not having had the experience I suppose.[29]

Rupert, too, was a diarist and a romantic – though the letter that he wrote to Barbara on 12 October ends on a splendidly practical note.

I'm enclosing in this letter a tabulated account of our time at Oswestry, which I hope you will return with remarks. Anything without a question mark I am not quite sure of.[30]

and on 14 October:

Thanks for [returning] the chart of our Oswestry week. I feel now I must keep it for ever, because it's a unique document, a document in both our writings! I put my remarks as briefly as possible, for clarity and I'm glad, because it left room for more of yours. I've written up my diary now for the whole week, so if you want to borrow the document to complete yours you may; but when I come to do last term I should like to have the use of yours, or anyway of the information in it.[31]

Their romance continued when they returned to Oxford. He wrote:

On Sunday at 4 o'clock you be at the High end of Queens Lane and I'll be at the Broad end of New College Lane and when four strikes by St Mary's we'll both walk down and meet where the two lanes meet.[32]

She also met Rupert's mother and brother, who were up in Oxford for the degree ceremony.

> [Rupert] persuaded me to have lunch at the Randolph ... I was, of course, terrified, but my fur coat gave me some confidence. Mrs G. is very nice and talkative, not like Rupert in any way. Edmund is vaguely like him – uglier – but he has 'personal magnetism'.... When the ceremony was over we adjourned to Fullers for tea. Edmund was funny and kept putting things in my hand (sugar, pennies) when I stretched it out in my character-istic way.[33]

On 15 October she wrote in her diary:

> Today I must always remember I suppose. I went to tea with Rupert (and ate a pretty colossal one) – and he with all his charm, eloquence and masculine wiles, persuaded ...[34]

Here several pages of her diary have been torn out and there is no entry until 25 October when:

> I went to see Rupert in the morning and stayed to lunch. We had a delightfully domesticated time over the fire and nearly went to sleep.[35]

But on 17 October Rupert had written to her:

> Darling Barbara
>   I've given you time to think over events by not writing.... For over half an hour I'd used every ruse of science and art to plead as beautifully as I was able.... I wouldn't be so unkind as to ask you to do it again; but I expect if (or when) it comes to the point I should merely say 'Well darling, would you like to come to bed?' and you would probably say no, and there would be an end of it.... Since I cannot be with you, angels shall watch over you and Gabriel shall do his best to supply my place.[36]

Barbara obviously did not want a love affair in the fullest sense and Rupert, accepting this, tactfully made a comfortable joke of the whole affair:

It's a difficult art, having a mistress, and Oxford is one of the most difficult places to practise it in. Hence your still lasting immunity.[37]

They continued to see each other frequently and remained friends for the rest of Rupert's time at Oxford – which enabled them both to get their diaries properly written up. On 14 December he sent her a note:

With regard to your diary document, there is just one thing I can't make out, which is where you say that on Sunday June 16 we lay down in some fields near the Botley Road; *that* I can't remember one bit and didn't think there were any fields near the Botley Road where one could lie down – unless – I've just remembered – it was on the slope of Boar's Hill just above North Hinksey wasn't it; below the water-tower and near some cows? Quite close to a footpath up Boar's Hill. Good, I do remember now. The time we walked round the gas-works we had come out into the Botley Road.[38]

When he went down he wrote to her:

How's your own heart? Pining I suppose for some beautiful young man as usual.[39]

And the romance was over, because Barbara was, indeed, already obsessed with a new beautiful young man, someone whom, typically, she had never met, but had observed and tracked down and 'in my own peculiar way' fallen in love with – the young man Rupert refers to in his letter – Gabriel.

Chapter Three

Gabriel, whom Barbara also called Lorenzo, was in fact Henry
Harvey, an altogether more pedestrian name, though he had
a far from pedestrian appearance or personality. He was two
years older than Barbara and in his last year at Oxford, reading
English at Christ Church, although he was tutored by C. S.
Lewis at Magdalen, thus confusing Barbara when she first tried
to track him down. He was born in Evesham in Worcestershire
on 31 May 1911. His father had been a borough surveyor who
also 'painted in oils in the Barbizon style and planned people's
houses for them.'[1] He had died when Henry was eight and
since his sisters were both much older – Jane already at Oxford
and Betty preparing to go there – Henry was not sent away to
school as might otherwise have been the case.

> I was hardly 'forgotten' but shouldn't I stay on for
> a bit at that nice dame school (Greenhill – Gissing's
> sister was one of the dames) and I 'wasn't very strong'
> anyway. And so on to the grammar school [Prince
> Henry's, Evesham] (where we knew some of the staff)
> more or less by default. It was an enjoyable life – I
> recited Keats and Shelley in my canoe, played tennis,
> had girl friends, though (I've much regretted) I wasn't
> made to learn Latin properly, and didn't. I did learn
> Merovingian history and the awfulness of the dissolution
> of the Abbey (the school had been suppressed till the
> end of the Tudors – Henry, who revived it was the elder
> brother of Charles I). It was taken for granted that I would
> go to Oxford and on my part little effort was needed.[2]

So Henry, like Barbara, had enjoyed a pleasant provincial
upbringing, though unlike her he had a more disciplined
mind and one that was not clouded by fantasy and romantic
speculation.

Although he was less conventionally good looking than Rupert, Henry had the kind of thin, sardonic face (memories of Julian Sabato) that Barbara found so attractive. She haunted the Bodleian because he was there and he could not fail to be aware of her scrutiny.

Went to the Bod. [He] was there. Our gazes meet, and he half smiles – but it is a cynical sort of smile. His affectation intrigues me... He has twinkling (but not pleasantly twinkling) hazel-brown eyes, like a duck's I think. And what a mouth! He is able to curl it in the most fascinatingly repulsive sneering smile. He walks swiftly in his effortless yet affected manner. His writing is very small and mingy – the lines sloping upwards to the left. (He uses plain paper)....
I sat nearly opposite him [in the Bodleian] – not on the same row. He doesn't like being observed but often looks at you in his malicious way. He had with him his nice herring-boney grey tweed overcoat – and little brown leather gloves – lined with lambswool . . . in spite of being very conscious of each other nothing seems to happen.[3]

She was very consciously feeding this obsession.

I went to the Dictionary [in the Bodleian] and looked up a word – (an entirely fatuous word) becoz he was there – i.e. *'Pentatremite* – an echinoderm of the genus Pentatremites belonging to the extinct class Blastoidea, allied to the Crinoids' – Is that a definition of me – Lorenzo – or both of us?[4]

Inevitably she turned to writing verse:

Sandra to Lorenzo. Impromptu.
Let Denham's strength and Waller's smoothness join
In verses to the praise of one divine –
Whom shall I sing? Whom can I sing but you
For you alone inspire those things I do –
And I do nothing – sweetly wasting time
I woo my absent Muse – my honied rhyme
May serve the purpose of one little day –
Go gentle gales and bear my sighs away.

and

> *Sandra wishes she had never seen Lorenzo*
> Unhappy day or night –
> When first I saw thy face
> When first that strange delight
> Ennobled all the place –
> Prosaic place of books [Bodleian]
> Not made for loving looks . . .
> Kiss me before I die
> Let me not wish thee harm
> As with a love-lorn sigh
> I curse thy fatal charm
> That charm . . . here followed incoherence – and there
>   had been complete nitwittedness all along.[5]

It was spring and she had to be in love.

> The weather has been perfect – and this is my favourite
> season of the year. It has been very right for all this
> Lorenzo business. . . . Chestnut trees just coming out
> – pale, almost-too-good-to-be-true green – blue skies,
> daffodils and best of all cherry trees in half and full
> flowers. My attitude to Nature is 18th century I know.
> But oh marvellous days![6]

It was an intoxicating mixture of Oxford, spring and our
greater English poets and she revelled, indeed, immersed
herself in it.

On 29 April 1932 Henry Harvey made the first move
and, in doing so, opened a veritable Pandora's Box of
emotion that spilled across both their lives. He imagined he
was simply making advances to one more pretty girl, one with
an 'appalling reputation', considered 'free and easy', a girl in
fact who was perfectly capable of taking care of herself. He
did not know that this was simply Barbara's manner, a kind
of overflowing vivacity and apparent worldliness which hid
an essential innocence, and he could have had no inkling of
the intricate web of romance and fantasy that Barbara had
already begun to weave around him.

Oh ever to be remembered day. Lorenzo spoke to me! I saw him in the Bod. and felt desperately thrilled about him so that I trembled and shivered and went sick. As I went out Lorenzo caught me up – and said – 'Well, and has Sandra finished her epic poem?' – or words to that effect. He talks curiously but very waffily – it's very affected. Something wrong with his mouth I think – he can't help snurging. I was almost completely tongue-tied. I said 'Er – No.' He asked me if I was keeping up the dual personality idea – he had caught me out. 'But you don't know who I am' I said. 'Of course I do' replied Lorenzo. 'Everybody does.' Oh Misery or the reverse! Then I said, 'By the way I hope you don't mind my calling you Lorenzo – it suits you you know.' 'Oh does it – how *awfully* flattering!' He snurged and went on up the Iffley Road while I walked trembling and weak at the knees into Cowley Place.[7]

It would not be possible for an undergraduate of nearly twenty to write in such a way today. But as well as all the gush there was still an observant eye and, somewhere, although submerged, the stirrings of the spirit of irony. Her description of her first evening out with Henry is noted with the precision not only of the lover but also of the novelist.

After tea I went to the Bod. . . . . I wasn't looking awfully beautiful. I was wearing a brown check skirt, yellow short sleeved jersey – yellow suede coat – brown hat and Viyella scarf – flesh coloured fishnet stockings, brown and white ghillie shoes (blue celanese trollies – pink suspender belt – pink kestos – white vest) – brown gloves – umbrella . . . . In a minute or two he came along and sat in his usual place. We took no notice of each other – but of course I couldn't resist staring. At 10 to 7 they rang the bell. . . . I walked out before Lorenzo. We got to the bottom of the stairs – just by the door I felt someone catch me up – I looked up – Lorenzo stood by my side – saying would I like a lift anywhere. I accepted and walked with him to YR 4628. . . . He said he liked me and my sense of humour and thought me quite mad.[8]

Barbara's gaiety and spontaneity must have been refreshingly different from the manner of some of the more carefully

formal girls up at Oxford then. Her habit of plunging into
things without apparently thinking of or caring about the
consequences and her lively way of expressing herself would
have seemed decidedly eccentric. He could not help being
flattered by her obvious interest in him. She had certainly
caught his attention. They went out to dinner at the Trout,
a popular pub by the river at Godstow.

> We ate mixed grill and drank beer – he's fussy so I
> had to pick out all the least greasy of the fried potatoes
> for him. Over supper we talked of general things – but
> everything he said seemed so marvellously significant. I
> think I must have told him quite a lot about how I felt
> for him. Oh cruel Lorenzo. We finished eating – I can see
> the romantic surroundings now – dusk – falling water –
> the wistaria on the Trout. I picked some. Lorenzo said 'It
> will wither'. It did too – although I put it in water . . .9

Barbara remembered the symbolism of that moment years
later when she came to write *Excellent Women* and delicately
noted how a woman (in this case Mildred) will try to keep a
romantic moment – as it might be a piece of wistaria or mimosa
– but that the man (Rocky or Henry), however romantic *he*
might seem, is the one who knows that it will never last.

> Driving back we talked strictly practical things – 18th
> century literature – the Wartons – Young's conjectures
> on original compositions. . . . We got back to Oxford. I
> was still almost in a daze. Outside St Hilda's I kissed
> his bitten cheek [Godstow mosquitoes being particularly
> vicious].
>   And so I began to hope – and what a lot of misery
> was this evening responsible for. But it was wonderful
> while it lasted.10

Henry Harvey took his Schools [Finals] and she wrote
him a good-luck letter: ('Quite prosaic and hearty – but – oh
– what wouldn't I have liked to say – still I knew it would be
a mistake.')
    In the Long Vacation she went to stay with her relations

at Hatch End. They went shopping in the West End, visited Stratford-upon-Avon to see *Romeo and Juliet* (John Wyse's Romeo reminded her, inevitably, of Lorenzo), went to the cinema ('one film had a girl called Sandra in it – who was perhaps even more of a nuisance than I have been to the object of my affections'), and gossiped endlessly with her cousin Betsy about young men.

Back in Oswestry she went specially into the town to get a copy of *The Times* to check the Oxford exam results. Henry had got a Second.

She read a great deal – not only work – *The Revolt of Islam* and Spenser, but also Richard Aldington's *All Men are Enemies* ('rather interesting but intensely depressing') and *Point Counter Point*, for the second time, having disliked it the first time she read it ('This time I loved it – although most of the talk was above my head. He still remains far and away the most interesting modern novelist in my opinion.'[11]) Her first impression of Ivy Compton-Burnett was also unfavourable ('Read *More Women than Men* and saw no point in it – unreal people and not much of a story.'[12]). But Gertrude Trevelyan's *Hothouse* made her 'desperately want to write an Oxford novel – but I must see first that my emotions are simmered down fairly well'.[13]

She also read Burton's *Anatomy of Melancholy* with a certain relish ('I began to read about Love Melancholy – but I haven't got to the part where he deals with the cure. Perhaps I'm suffering from the spleen too – in that case I may be completely cured by taking a course of our English poets.'[14]). What she actually did take were some Yeastvite tablets ('A slightly unromantic way of curing lovesickness I admit, but certainly I feel a lot better now'[15]).

The social life of the small town went on around her, though she was not part of it.

> In the afternoon Hilary went to tennis at the Blakes – I wasn't asked, thank heaven! I dislike tennis parties – here anyway. Too much small talk with people who are generally bores – sometimes one even dislikes them!
>
> At 8 Mrs Wakelam and Maud came to play bridge. I sat in an armchair like a docile donkey and knitted my dark green jumper. I also ate a lot of sandwiches.[16]

She went up to Oxford early, on 1 October 1933, to
settle into her digs, since she was living out of college for
a year.

> I'm terribly enamoured of my new room, and have it
> most artistic and aesthetic. Chaste green cover for my
> bed – check cushions – beautiful pictures [one of which
> was *Winterlandschaft* framed in black oak] – books and
> bookends – bronze golden chrysanthemums on a table in
> the window alcove. I hear Magdalen and Merton clocks
> all the time.[17]

Since Lorenzo had taken his degree and gone down,
she had to content herself with hoping to catch glimpses
of his friends. These were: John Barnicot, his friend Count
Roberto Weiss and, most important of all, Robert Liddell,
who was known as Jock. John Barnicot had spent the two
years after he went down from Balliol in 1929 travelling in
the Balkans on a Lahming Fellowship from Queen's College,
learning the languages and studying the societies there. He
had returned to Oxford to work on the staff of the Bodleian
where he specialised in Old Slavonic books. He could be seen
in the Radcliffe Camera ('They've altered the place and made
a great round enclosure in the middle of the floor – wherein sit
Barnicot and minions'[18]). He was four years older than Henry
and a year older than Jock Liddell, but they formed a close
circle.

Roberto Weiss – in spite of his Germanic name – was
an Italian count and had been in Oxford since 1928. Legend
has it that he had originally gone to Cambridge, taken a
dislike to the place and hired a taxi to take him to Oxford
where he persuaded the startled authorities to accept him
as an undergraduate. By the time Barbara had got to know
Henry, the Count had taken his degree and had gone to live
in the village of Islip, near Oxford, as a lodger with a farmer's
family and in conditions of unbelievable discomfort, doing
bits of research for the novelist John Buchan.[19] He was not
a close friend, but as a foreign count and a notable Oxford
figure, in Barbara's eyes he added to the glamour of the group
surrounding Henry.

The most important person, though, was Jock Liddell, Henry's closest friend. He was born in Tunbridge Wells in 1908 and since his father, a retired major, had a job (something to do with communications) with the Egyptian government he and his brother spent their early years in Egypt. Priscilla Napier, whose father was Sir William Hayter, legal adviser to the Egyptian government, remembers Jock and Donald Liddell among the children of the British community in Gezira in the years before the First World War. It was a nanny-dominated society where the children were dressed in starched muslin dresses or sailor suits in the hot Egyptian sun and were taken for carefully chosen walks along the river to the Pont des Anglais or in the Sirdaria Gardens. In 1914 Jock and his brother returned to England. He went to Haileybury (his father's old school) and then to Corpus Christi College, Oxford, where he read Greats. Henry Harvey describes their first meeting:

> We both happened to be on the deck of a cross-channel steamer from Dover to Ostend in March 1930. I noticed a lonely-looking, curly-haired little boy, very fair, of perhaps 13 and, to be friendly, asked him where he was going. He told me rather primly (Aachen) and let me indulge myself giving him ideas he could use in his school essays ('Tragedy as the Conflict of Goods', I remember, and I assessed Aristotle and Hegel for him too). But this little boy was not 13. He was 21, already at Oxford and reading Greats. He was two years and 8 months older than I was (18) and knew very much more about Tragedy, Aristotle and Hegel than I did (almost nothing). So *he* started talking and didn't stop (neither did I) until we got to Aachen early the next morning.[20]

When Henry went up to Oxford that autumn, they became close friends and in his third year, when he lived out of college, Henry shared lodgings with Jock (who had by then taken his degree and was doing a B.Litt.) at 252 Iffley Road. Soon after Barbara had become interested in Henry, Jock, too, had joined the staff of the Bodleian and was, thus, eminently observable. He was, as we have seen deceptively youthful in appearance, small and slightly built with fair hair and delicate features –

Barbara often mentions in her diary how 'pretty' he looked.
He obviously disapproved of her pursuit of Henry. She saw
Jock in the Kemp Hall cafeteria ('He gave me a poisonous
look but I didn't mind') and Barnicot near St Hilda's ('I smiled
brightly but he took no notice – is he afraid, ashamed or merely
short-sighted?'[21]).

She also sat in the Bodleian reading Dowson's love poems
and 'spent some time in finding appropriate lines and poems.
I'm beginning to enjoy my pose of romantically unrequited
love.'[22]

Barbara had made several good friends at St Hilda's,
especially two like-minded frivolous girls, Mary Sharp and
Rosemary Topping, who were aware of her romantic passions
for young men she had never met and the concomitant looking
up and tracking down that it entailed. They quite entered into
the spirit of the thing and on 7 October Rosemary burst in to
tell her that she had seen Lorenzo.

> I was terribly excited and couldn't eat any tea, although
> it was nice hearty buns which I usually enjoy. After tea
> I prepared to go to Blackwell's to buy some Shakespeare
> books – and to find him. I was wearing my grey flannel
> costume, black polo jersey and no hat. I had an orange
> marigold stuck in the collar of my jersey. I was coming
> away from Blackwell's for the second time when I
> saw [him] and Jockie (of course he *would* be with
> Jockie). There was no escape – we walked towards
> each other and met by Trinity. He took off his hat
> and gave me a marvellous smile – a slightly mocking
> bow I thought. . . . I was horribly nervous and grinned
> I imagine. . . . Then I wandered some more until I came
> upon them by Elliston's but they didn't see me. I tracked
> them down St Michael's Street but I couldn't follow them
> because it was so deserted. And I felt so terribly tired.[23]

Henry Harvey remembers how the Barbara of that period
would contrive a meeting in such a way, and then be
tongue-tied. Almost, the pursuit was more important than
the meeting.

Henry Harvey was staying on at Oxford for another year

to do his B.Litt. and was now sharing a flat at 86 Banbury Road with Jock Liddell. So, with Henry actually in Oxford again, Barbara was able to give her romantic imagination full rein, haunting the Bodleian, trying to catch a glimpse of him in the street and tracking him down, or simply hanging about outside his flat. ('After supper I went on a Banbury Road crawl – in spite of great weariness. There was a light in Lorenzo's bedroom.'[24])

Henry made several overtures to her, asking her to tea. Barbara longed to go but refused. ('I think I should love to go – but probably it mightn't be wise.'[25]) She was, perhaps subconsciously, trying to keep the relationship in the realm of fantasy, partly because she felt that it would lead to something more than she was ready for, and partly because she found the preliminaries to a love affair – the speculation, the pursuit, the 'finding out' – almost more exciting than the reality of the affair itself.

As well as the ever-faithful Harry Harker, other young men were interested and invited her out.

> Roland Rahtz approached me and asked me to tea – I couldn't very well refuse. We went to Elliston's – I can't see any prospect of being interested in him – what shall I do, I don't want to be unkind. Still there's all the vac for him to simmer in.[26]

She managed to have a very enjoyable Christmas vacation, staying first with the Selways at Hatch End, going to the cinema (Mae West in *I'm No Angel*: 'Fat and not attractive – at least I didn't think so – a purely physical appeal and crude technique'[27]) and shopping ('I saw the divinest black velvet dress in one shop which makes me determined to have one.'[28]). Her time at Oswestry was made happy by the arrival of a card, a reproduction of a picture of St Barbara, inscribed by Henry 'Sandra from Lorenzo' – though she noted that the address on the envelope was in Jock Liddell's handwriting. Reassured by that, she had a happy family Christmas – church at 8 a.m., breakfast and presents, an 18lb turkey for Christmas lunch, tea, then (extraordinarily) a visit to the cinema to see Leslie Howard in *Smilin' Through*, ending up with an evening listening to Henry Hall and the BBC Dance Orchestra playing tunes 'full of memories sweet and poignant – *Stormy Weather* and *Won't You Stay to Tea?'*.[29]

Back in Oxford she continued her pursuit of Henry with renewed enthusiasm.

> I followed Lorenzo to Balliol – then Jockie down the snicket and we all of us met at Kemp Hall [cafeteria]. Poisonous looks from Jockie, and amused ones from Lorenzo.[30]

Barbara had now been to tea several times with Henry, and was taking the love affair very seriously indeed. Henry was deliberately trying to keep things on a casual basis. He flirted with a girl called Alison West-Watson and Jock reported the details to Barbara:

> It seems that Lorenzo is really in love with Alison West-Watson, because she has not fallen into his arms straight away as he expected she would.[31]

The affair was becoming more a matter of pain than pleasure.

> Lorenzo and I were left alone. We sat in silence and I felt miserable, then into his room. He was not kind to me and his attitude to me was made so cruelly obvious. . . . All the time I was getting more and more unhappy, until suddenly I burst into tears and cried more than I'd done for years. It was as if I'd felt it coming for days – my love for him, his indifference to me, the mess I'd made of my affair with him, and the fact that I was leaving him probably for another woman to have, was simply too much for me. When he saw my tears he was quite nice to me – and promised that next term we should be good friends and go on the river together. By the time I was more or less clothed and in my right mind Jockie came in.[32]

Jock Liddell had by now accepted Barbara, not only as 'belonging' to Henry, but also as a friend in her own right.

He could see that she would never be a threat to his own
friendship with Henry and it would have been very difficult
to resist Barbara's obvious desire to be his friend too. He must
have been flattered that she also observed and followed him
as well as Henry and was deeply interested in everything that
he did. She, in return, was grateful to have someone close to
Henry to discuss him with, especially someone like Jock who
was highly amusing, with a waspish wit. They soon established
a cosy relationship and never tired of talking of Henry while
they performed domestic tasks around the flat, Jock cooking
and Barbara mending a pile of socks.

> [Jock] and I went and cooked the supper and talked
> a lot. . . . He told me a few things about Lorenzo which
> made me realise even more than I had hitherto done,
> what a terribly difficult person he is.[33]

Though after seeing a performance of Coward's *Design for
Living* Barbara wondered if one day she, Henry and Jock
might set up a similar ménage. Henry was also one of the
main subjects of the correspondence between Barbara and
Jock, which started at this time and continued until Barbara's
death.

> Society [Jock wrote in an early letter] keeps Henry
> happy and tolerably well-behaved – as soon as he is
> alone with me he begins to groan again. When he is
> quite alone, I suspect he goes to sleep.[34]

Her affair with Henry continued on its uneven way, each
wanting what the other was not prepared to give.

> I had a most touching meeting with Henry on the steps
> of the Radcliffe Camera. I always think that Providence
> must arrange little incidents like that. He tried hard to
> persuade me to come to tea – but I would not, although I
> felt very tempted. He swore that he would not even touch
> me – but how can I believe him after all the other times
> he's sworn and promised? When I met him I was moved
> instinctively to put my hand out towards him. Deep down

> in my heart I know I love him, although I hardly dare
> admit it to myself. As it is – although I didn't go to tea
> – I am thinking of the happy time we might have had –
> and am loving him far more than I probably should do if
> I had actually gone.[35]

She was accepting the fact, later stated by Miss Doggett in more comic circumstances, that 'men only want *one thing*'.[36] Henry had been initially misled by her manner and reputation.

> Just before going he said 'Oh you're common property'.
> He tried to be nice to me when he saw he'd hurt me.[37]

Barbara, looking back at the affair a few years later when she wrote *Crampton Hodnet*, drew, in Barbara Bird a girl whose feelings, although heightened for the purposes of fiction, were not too dissimilar to those that she herself felt at this time, a girl who was coaxed and persuaded to accept 'the right true end of love' and the poet John Cleveland's dictum: 'Love that's in contemplation placed is Venus drawn but to the waist.'

But Barbara Bird's passionate glances didn't mean what Francis thought they did. To her, passion was cerebral and romantic, the *idea* of Love rather than the actuality.

' "You look so amorous and really you're just a cold fish," [Francis Cleveland] said shortly.'

The phrase comes through as one that someone had actually used. Barbara Bird brooded over it as Barbara must have done and, goaded by it, actually agreed to go away to Paris with Francis. But what she really wanted was to keep her love within the pages of Literature, as it were. When Francis sent her the lilies with a loving message, 'she was conscious of a slight feeling of disappointment. She wished he had put a quotation from some 17th century poet on the little card.'

Barbara herself was seduced not by Henry, the actual young man, but by Lorenzo, her own creation, who might have stepped out of a seventeenth-century poem or play. Rupert Gleadow (with whom she still corresponded) seemed surprised to find that Henry did indeed exist: 'I always imagined him a *painted* god, not real.'[38] As long as the affair could be swathed in the drapery of Literature Barbara was able to accept it – even to laugh at it.

> Henry wrote in German on some of my Milton notes 'Kommst Du – Ja?' and a few other things. I went and he was extremely nice – but Jockie came in and caught us reading *Samson Agonistes* in bed with nothing on. Really rather funny. I stayed to supper. Jockie forgave me as I was penitent and was very sweet.[39]

In his talk to the PEN Club in 1985 Henry Harvey said:

> In spite of chasing people who took her fancy and having no apparent inhibitions, Barbara was no *houri*, she wasn't voluptuous. She was without sensuality. Her passions, in so far as they were not kept back to being pretend play passions, stayed in her head and heart.[40]

With hindsight, he is very perceptive about the young Barbara:

> I think the chief strand in my picture of her in the early days is the alternation in her between pretend play on the one hand . . . and her trying or pretending to make her pretend play real. And she had some damn good goes at that, at turning pretend play into real, bouncing and bouncing along did our Barbara go and having some bumps too, which she was philosophical about. It didn't work. 'Being-in-love' and 'being-in-Oxford' were better kept as pretend play. That way they could be turned into art.
>   She was tempted I think sometimes though. Oh the luxury of giving up, of giving up pretend play with all its elaborations, of becoming just a participant, an actor in life, in mere lazy undemanding life.
>   But the other side of Barbara won, the observing, creating Barbara doing her pretend playing in her writing and doing it so well.[41]

Henry Harvey also says:

One thing I can say about our thirties Oxford. We tried to be, and largely were, private. Auden describes the ethos in

> Private faces in public places
> Are wiser and nicer
> Than public faces in private places.

Exactly. When I read that I thought Auden must have been hiding on the stairs.[42]

The concept of strong friendship is now out of fashion, one of the penalties of a too-strenuous analysis of relationships, but in the 1930s it was still very real. 'The fact was,' Henry Harvey explains, 'that friendship was stronger than romance for all of us in those early days – *and* whether or not we got married – *and* without denying that romance was strong too.'[43]

He also emphasises the importance, right from the beginning, of Barbara's attitude towards that fascinating, rather esoteric circle of friends. Henry was the centre, not only for Barbara, but for the whole group. 'I think what mainly happened in Barbara's relationship with me . . . was simply that she was co-opted into the group of friends, of whom I was one, right at the beginning of the relationship between us in 1933 in Oxford.'[44]

'Co-opted' is perhaps not quite the right word, she did rather insinuate her way in, not only by her pursuit of Henry, but also by her wooing of Jock Liddell and her great desire to be accepted by them all. There were times, though, when she felt she was tagging along behind them, like a kind of intellectual Violet Elizabeth Bott and sometimes she got 'a bit fed up' with it all:

On this day H, J, Mr B[arnicot], and I went out in the car for the day. But somehow I didn't get on very well with them. It was largely my own fault as I was inclined to be rather aggressive in my 'lowness', talking about dance music etc. I think I did this because I felt intellectually inferior to them all, especially Henry, who always makes you feel it more than the others. I felt that they were all against me and I made things worse by my obstinacy. But I felt resentful of being dominated by them and not being allowed to be myself at all.[45]

Not being able to relax and be her frivolous self was the price she felt she had to pay in order to belong to this charmed circle. She still had her friends at St Hilda's and she chatted ('I raved and soliloquised as usual'), smoked, drank coffee, listened to the gramophone and went to the pictures. She went out with other young men, she even did some work. 'A helpful Spenser revision class with Rooke [her Tutor]. Very funny too, as she had a great cauldron of marmalade boiling on the gas ring.'[46] But life was centred for her at 86 Banbury Road.

Her final exams, Schools, were fast approaching and she did some panicky last-minute revision. She was supported greatly by the faithful Harry Harker, who took her to the Bath and West Show, where 'the fine bulls and pigs took my mind off Schools for a while' – though 'among those present (also looking at the pigs) were Mr Barnicot and Count Roberto Weiss'.[47] She sums up this period:

I enjoyed the experience of Schools and the papers were quite nice, if dull at times. I always did the morning ones best. Henry, divinely beautiful in B.A. gown, white fur etc., was taking B.Litt. papers – but I saw very little of him.

Every afternoon I had tea with Harry and sometimes we would wander about until 6, and then have a sherry in the Bijou.

At nights I used to stay up late, working and talking, and I always worked after breakfast and in the lunch hour.

It was a good time, especially as I got my second.[48]

Henry was successful, too, and in July got a job as a lecturer at the University of Helsingfors in Finland, starting in September.

After Barbara took her viva she had tea with Henry.

He said I was part of his background, like Jock and Barnicot, which pleased me. It is what I have always wanted – I love him too, but don't want him for my very own yet awhile.[49]

In July she began 'writing a story about Hilary and me as spinsters of fiftyish. Henry, Jock and all of us appear in it. I sent it to them and they liked it very much. So I am going on with it and one day it may become a book.'[50]

Back in Oswestry it was arranged that she would stay at home and not take a job. This was not an unusual arrangement for a girl of her day and class. As long as her parents were able to support her there was no pressure on any girl to take up a career. It is true that a few years later Irena was very keen that Hilary should apply for a job at the BBC and did a lot to encourage her, but that, Hilary says, is because their mother appreciated the difference in temperament between her two daughters and felt that Hilary, the more restive of the two, needed the discipline of a career. Barbara had her own discipline. She worked steadily at her 'novel of real people' and already saw herself as a professional writer.

In December she went back to Oxford to take her BA degree and decided, after some indecision, to stay on and see Henry when he returned to Oxford for the Christmas vacation. She derived much comfort and amusement from her friendship with Jock Liddell, which was now strengthened since they were both missing Henry very badly. The short time she spent with Henry was as unsatisfactory as ever but she was fairly philosophical about it.

In spite of unhappiness it has brought me Jockie and other friends – and a little of Henry which I shall never forget.

How small a part of time they share
That are so wondrous sweet and fair!

as I am always quoting in my novel.[51]

In the winter in Oswestry, with Hilary away at Oxford, she notes in her diary: 'Actually I miss Jockie more – his company and conversation.'[52] So she remained at home, writing her novel, doing a lot of reading, some housework and some dressmaking, until the spring. Henry, on leave from Finland (he had over five months' vacation to work on his thesis in Oxford), took temporary lodgings in Pusey Street. Henry was as fascinating as ever, with the added attraction of now being able to speak Swedish, and Barbara was still endlessly analysing her feelings about him. Henry, who now had a life elsewhere, was more noncommittal than ever.

> He will never talk about him and me and always gives evasive answers that are unsatisfying to me, as I want so much to know how things *really* are between us. Is it any use hoping even for his friendship – and is that enough? ... Barnicot thinks I have no hope at all and that his friendship would be of no use to me. But I think somehow that I'd like it. I don't mind being part of the furniture of his background, or even hanging over him like a gloomy cloud, as he said at tea one day. He himself has admitted that I have a special place in the little world he has built for himself and of which presumably J. is the centre.[53]

In the August Henry and Jock and John Barnicot visited Barbara in Oswestry. They obviously enjoyed themselves and were greatly taken with Irena. A photograph of them all in the garden of Morda Lodge captures an especially happy moment in time, when everything went right.

> Henry was absolutely at his best. He wore his grey flannel suit, a bright blue silk shirt with a darker blue tie and blue socks. He wanted me to return to Oxford with them, but I feel it is better that I remain here, thinking lovingly of him, with more real fondness than before. He goes to Finland on the 11th of September. I don't know when he comes back or when I shall see him again.[54]

Chapter Four

Barbara was making good progress with her novel, which she finally decided to call *Some Tame Gazelle* (having rejected *Some Sad Turtle* as being too reminiscent of soup). It was, of course, 'for Henry' and as Archdeacon Hoccleve he displayed all the selfishness, insensitivity and arrogance that Barbara felt she saw in the original. But, because Barbara was still fascinated by Henry, the Archdeacon comes through triumphantly as a marvellous eccentric, with great charisma and one who, in spite of his faults, the heroine Belinda/Barbara could not help loving faithfully even after he had been married to another woman for thirty years. She deliberately took all the main characters directly from life, since this was to be a *roman à clef* for her own particular circle. Thus she herself was Belinda, Hilary was Harriet, Henry was the Archdeacon, the hated Alison West-Watson was Agatha, Jock was Dr Nicholas Parnell, Honor Tracy was Edith Liversidge, Count Roberto Weiss was Ricardo Bianco and Julia Pakenham (because of a rather matronly figure) was Lady Clara Boulding. She circulated chapters among her friends as she wrote them and they were all enthusiastic. Quite early on, in July 1934, Jock had written:

> Henry and I think you are a very great novelist and implore you to continue your story – we long to know more about Barbara and Hilary and the Archdeacon's family and Miss Tracy and Dr Liddell. Henry thinks you are far greater than Miss Austen. I don't quite agree, though I place you well above the Brontës. We have read your story aloud to each other, to West-Watson, to Mr Barnicot and to Henry's sister Betty. Henry's mother, present on the last occasion, thought it very clever of the little girl Barbara to think of all that.[1]

This frivolous comment was, however, followed some months later by a more thoughtful comment from Jock:

I think you have a genius for quotation which has probably never been equalled – not only have you put the culture you have acquired here to extremely effective use, you have also permanently increased your readers' knowledge of English Literature.[2]

Barbara worked away diligently, not only at her novel but also at a couple of short stories – 'Unpast Alp' and 'They Never Write'. She was never very happy with the short-story form. 'How bad mine are,' she wrote to Jock, 'and how I hate doing them.' But she felt that this was the quick way into the literary world – to get *something* published, to make some sort of name for herself until she was established as a novelist.

Her correspondence with Jock – Henry hardly ever wrote, or, if he did, his letters were unsatisfactorily 'written in Latin, German, French, Swedish, Finnish and the English of James Joyce and I could not well understand it'[3] – was her lifeline at this time, living as she was, in Oswestry where no sort of literary conversation was available. She thought enviously of Hilary who, three years younger, had just gone up to Oxford herself. It wasn't only thoughts on the novel and Our Greater English Poets that she missed, but the cosy world of Oxford chat and gossip and – of course – news of Henry. This Jock supplied in his own elegant and amusing style.

We had a pleasant jaunt in East Anglia – Mr Barnicot's motor car behaved excellently, except one day when Henry forgot to give it enough petrol. Though it carried us to Mass (being Sunday) and we heard a short discourse on Hell.
    Henry has bought a book about neuroses and is relieved to find that his neurosis differs in kind from psychosis and madness . . . he is also taking yeast which I hope may help. [One is reminded of the younger Barbara taking Yeastvite tablets as a cure for lovesickness.]
    Henry said it was uncivilised and Matthew Arnoldish to walk in Oxfordshire – in the Lakes (which are remarkably fine) it was justified by Wordsworth. He also gave

me a long discourse on the psychology of persons who
voluntarily went for country walks – you can imagine
how improving it was. Poor Henry was prostrate after
it, but managed to keep Mr B and me up until 1 o'clock
last night. He has tried to teach me to roast mutton in
the Finnish style. You pour a cup of coffee over it halfway
through – it makes no appreciable difference.

Henry and Mr B every evening last week either
arguing about money or philosophy or reading plays
or writing surrealist compositions. We read *The Country
Wife* and *Venice Preserved* (remarkably fine) and Mr B
and I vainly tried to lay the foundation of poor Henry's
philosophical studies by persuading him to accept the
principle of non-contradiction. . . . Poor H. much con-
temned our little systems and holds himself (unlike us) a
real original thinker untrammelled by Aristotle. I do not
think you would be so tiresome.[4]

He also wrote of his life in the Bodleian, thus providing
splendid material for Edward Killigrew in *Crampton Hodnet*:

I now sit in Mr Dubber's chair at the entrance to
the arts end [of Duke Humfrey] and am exposed even
more to draughts and readers. I have bought a leather
jacket as protection against the former and hope it may
not unduly amuse the latter.

Our great Library is damping to the spirits and a trial
to the temper and stupefying to the intellect. I spent
most of today reading letters in which Anthony Trollope's
grand-daughter describes the affectionate disposition of
her dog.[5]

and prophetically

How immensely valuable our correspondence ought to
be to the Department of Western Manuscripts – only we
don't leave enough margin and I can't think how it will
ever be bound, even though my successors should set it
in chronological order and Mr Field's successors should
stamp and foliate it.[6]

She too had thoughts about her correspondence:

All my love letters – no young woman should be without 50 of these. Could I deposit them in Bodley and order them when I felt inclined to reread them?[7]

Most of all Jock gave her encouragement – as one novelist to another, equal to equal.

We are, I think, entirely right-minded authors – we write, not perhaps because we like it, but because we are not satisfied if we don't. We should probably (given the materials) write on a desert island if there were no possibility of publication. But when there *is* a possibility of publication we have the sense to see that it is absolutely essential to publish – and Henry's consolations drawn from the period before the invention of printing are quite useless. I think in time we must succeed – but it is fearfully discouraging, especially when writing is such an effort as I generally find it, and perhaps you do as well.[8]

He sent her a detailed chapter-by-chapter criticism of *Some Tame Gazelle* ('Why do you not keep your Crashaw title *The Well Tam'd Heart*'?) as well as some general observations:

Literary allusions: Some cutting is essential – but cultivate, even more, the practice of using them as recurrent themes – e.g. 'sentiments to which every bosom returns a echo'. And each character could have his *leit-motiv* I daresay. But do not be too ruthless, as much of the beauty of the style derives from the frequent reminiscences of our greater writers. The following notes, mainly on style, were taken while I was reading. They are not all of equal importance and many recurrent blemishes have not been mentioned every time they occur, e.g. *somewhat*. You will I hope not expect me, as Mason expected dear Gray, to think everything you write the most perfect thing in nature – so I venture a few little recommendations.[9]

A few months later he sent her the manuscript of his novel *Kind Relations* for her comments.

Observations of a more general literary nature were also exchanged. Barbara, who had immersed herself in words – her

own and other people's – and who read at least two novels a
day, wrote:

> If only I could write as well as Aldous Huxley and
> Elizabeth [von Arnim] combined! I consider the Francis
> Chelifer part of *Those Barren Leaves* one of the finest
> things in all literature.[10]

Jock wrote:

> Henry thinks Miss Compton-Burnett remarkably fine I
> am glad to find – he is usually so arrogant about our
> less great novelists that I do not know how you or I dare
> to write.[11]

He recommended to her Stevie Smith's *Novel on Yellow Paper*
and also wrote: 'I have suspended my circulating library sub-
scription [at Elliston and Cavell] since Henry rightly says I
read too much trash.'[12]

So Barbara continued to work on her novel, with only the
occasional feeling that she should be 'out in the world'. She
wrote to Henry in January 1936:

> Periodically I think that my life here is too pleasant
> and lazy and that I ought to earn some money or go
> to Budapest tomorrow, or get a job in Selfridge's or the
> Times Book Club. But I salve my conscience by reminding
> myself that my parents really do like having me here (or
> so I think) and that it would be very feeble not to struggle
> on with my writing.[13]

Life was peaceful and agreeable and unchanging – a most conducive atmosphere for writing a novel like *Some Tame Gazelle*:

> My mother is in the drawing room practising psalms as
> she is playing the organ for this evening's service.[14]

In fact she could have changed her life if she had chosen.
Brian Mitchell, the brother of one of her Oxford friends, had
been very attentive. She had been on holiday with him in
Scotland and in 1935 he had taken her several times to meet his
parents.

Went to Brian's dance. We kept getting lost . . . but
eventually arrived at Petersfield about 6. We changed
hastily and had a magnificent dinner at the Red Lion. We
had a good start for the dance with cocktails, champagne
and port, so that I felt quite dizzy! The dance itself
was great fun although having to dance and make
conversation with so many different people was rather
a strain.[15]

Brian proposed to her and would, indeed, have been an
excellent match, in worldly terms, but Barbara (unlike many of
her contemporaries) did not want simply 'to be married', and
so, since she was not in love with him, she refused him. She
was at this time trying to sort out her feelings for Henry. She
wrote him a long letter analysing the pretend-play element of
their love affair:

As you said, we have never been real to each other.
This may be because of the way Jock has treated us
by refusing to take anything seriously – but it is really
because you haven't been sufficiently interested in me to
make much effort about it. . . . But however much Jock
may be responsible for the state of affairs between *us*, I
can never forget that he saved me a great deal of unhappiness by his way of looking at things, which I adopted
too, at least in our correspondence and conversation. It
is an amusing game and I don't see why it should affect
one's real self unless one wants it to. I know that as far
as I'm concerned, although I've learned to treat things in
his way, the other side of me is still there to be brought
out when necessary. I have no wish that it should be
annihilated altogether because I know I couldn't find
any happiness unless I were a real person as well as
a 'flat' one.[16]

She told John Barnicot that she wouldn't marry Henry at
any price, as once she thought she would.

But in the summer vacation of 1936 Barbara went back to
Oxford to help Henry with his thesis on Gerard Langbaine.

We've been together day and night for the past three
weeks and yesterday he and Mr B. brought me home

and now I'm wretched and missing him terribly. I've typed and taken dictation and copied pieces out of the *D.N.B.* for him – worked all night for him – made tea – and received 30/– a week. . . .

I remember . . . typing Chapter III, all that complicated stuff about the 1680 Catalogue, which I didn't very well understand. . . . The last day of all I worked all through the night. . . . And at about six o'clock in the morning, I tucked him up in an armchair with a rug, while I went through one of the copies marking in notes. Without me he couldn't have done the thing at all. I can say this knowing that it is true. Between seven and nine . . . he dictated the last pages of the chapter on the Account. I have been given a taste of how lovely things *could* be with Henry.

He will be back in Oxford today and I shan't be at the flat to make tea for him. I can't help hoping that he will realise this, but naturally he will only look upon it as a fact, it will have no sentimental significance.[17]

A letter from Jock deplored Henry's lack of appreciation and wished for

an occasional careless admission that no one else could or would have done what you did and praise of your silence contrasted with Mr B's argumentativeness.[18]

The theme of the woman – the girlfriend or the wife – typing the thesis, reading the proofs, making the index, doing all those thankless tasks and being taken for granted, is a recurring one in Barbara's novels.

'Perhaps you could help me with the index too? Reading proofs for a long stretch gets a little boring. The index would make a nice change for you.'

'Yes, it would certainly make a nice change,' I agreed. And before long I should be certain to find myself at his sink peeling potatoes and washing up; that would be a nice change when both proof reading and indexing began to pall. Was any man worth this burden?[19]

Henry and John Barnicot went off to Scotland for a holiday and Barbara went home, finding Oswestry 'so awful after Oxford'.

Now her writing was the mainspring of her life. She wrote in her diary:

I must *work* at my novel, that is the only thing there is and the only way to find any happiness at present. . . . I want *Liebe* but I would be satisfied if my novel could be published.[20]

And in a letter to Jock:

Would one rather be loved by Henry or have a novel accepted?[21]

She had had *Some Tame Gazelle* professionally typed and bound ('very nicely with green backs and soft yellow covers') and sent it to various publishers. It was rejected by Chatto – they found it too long and the character drawing too detached, but noted that she had 'a style of my own which is a pleasure to read'. She found that she wasn't too depressed by this 'and even looked forward to cutting and improving it'. Gollancz rejected it too, with a polite note, and so did Macmillan and Methuen. Her short stories were not accepted either. But in August 1936 her hopes were raised by a letter from Jonathan Cape saying that he was interested in her novel and thought that he might be able to publish it if she would make some minor alterations. She made the alterations and returned the manuscript, but, alas, the following month it was returned to her with a letter from Jonathan Cape which expressed regret and said:

There is not here the unanimity of appreciation of the book's chances that I feel is essential for successful publication. Personally I like your novel, but I fear that if I were to offer to publish it, we should be unable to give it all the care and attention which I feel are necessary if it is to be successfully launched.[22]

It was a very bitter blow. Later in her life she would have an equally inexplicable rejection from Cape that would distress her even more – though she did shed many tears over this one.

She put *Some Tame Gazelle* aside and resolutely concentrated on the new novel that she had already started. It was provisionally called *Adam and Cassandra* [later retitled *Civil to Strangers*] ('I can't feel it's really as good as *Some Tame Gazelle*, but it may stand a better chance of getting accepted'[23]).

Jock said of it:

> I have not yet examined it critically for style, but I am very glad to hear what you say about *rather* and *somewhat*. I should suggest emending one or two sentences which lay you open to the charge (unjust though it would be) of being philistine about our greater modern poets – the insertion or deletion of a word or two would just make the difference. *Adam and Cassandra* is, I think more mature than *Some Tame Gazelle* but without something of its peculiar charm.[24]

Henry was once again the hero – or anti-hero, rather, since Adam was an even greater monster of egotism than the Archdeacon. Barbara told Henry about the novel in a letter:

> Adam is sweet but very stupid. You are sweet too, but not as consistently stupid as Adam. But I wish you were here to show me where to put the commas. . . .
>
> I am all alone in the house, except for the wireless, which you despise so much. I am writing rather slowly and laboriously and every time I think of something nice to say I stop and consider it well before I put it. . . . I wish I knew something about the modern poets. . . . I wish you would teach me about them and tell me which ones to read and how to understand them. Even the Finns know more than I do. You ought to try and educate me in things I don't know about. . . .
>
> Just such a letter might poor Elsie Godenhjelm write to you, only perhaps she has more respect for you than I have.[25]

In September 1936 Henry, Jock and Barnicot paid one more visit to Oswestry. They collected Barbara and all spent a delightful day at Port Meirion, a

> very Henryish place with pink and blue and yellow Italian villas and statues all about in odd corners. He goes back to Finland on Tuesday. I envy Elsie Godenhjelm – after all I love him too![26]

Jock Liddell had already told Barbara about Henry's interest in Elsie Godenhjelm, a young girl he had met in Finland. 'A tall, fair creature, nice mannered and quite pretty' he had reported. She was actually more than pretty, with a 'delicately modelled face and long straight flaxen hair'[27]. Jock sent Barbara a photograph and she replied:

> My dear sister has a sweet little face, I think. What nice people Henry seems to get hold of! Because *I* have a beautiful nature, although opinions vary about my face.[28]

The phrase 'my dear sister' was part of her epistolary style to Jock, since they had started to write to each other in the style of Ivy Compton-Burnett. Henry Harvey says,

> Raymond Mortimer's review of *A House and its Head* had put Jock onto Ivy Compton-Burnett in 1935 and he relished her worse-than-Samuel-Butler family-hating as well as her dialogue. And Jock put Barbara onto Ivy Compton-Burnett [actually, he made her revise her original opinion of the novels]. And Barbara and Jock's conversation was full of 'what could be my meaning' and 'I would not tolerate it'. 'It seems to me that the young nowadays don't have anything like as much fun in their communes.'[29]

So Barbara wrote to Jock, 'I think Elsie should accept my offer of being a sister, as I am really quite a good one.'[30] There was even some talk of them making a trip to Finland – Jock and John Barnicot had already been to visit

Henry there – but it came to nothing. 'Although we have lost a dear sister we have saved at least £20,' Barbara said succinctly.[31]

She made several references to marriage in her letters. To Henry she wrote quite frivolously:

> I am looking for a nice suitable husband – preferably a clergyman. It's always much nicer not to see you and imagine how it might have been, than see you and be disappointed.[32]

To Jock she wrote more gloomily:

> I'm not yet much of a catch. Definitely *not* the top (a frog without a log on which to hop).[33]

Jock replied bracingly:

> Why is your future any worse to contemplate than anyone else's?[34]

and unhelpfully, though prophetically:

> Surely Henry will wear out more than one wife.[35]

Marriage had never been mentioned by Henry. He has said that the question never arose – they were too young and it was not that sort of relationship. The fact is that – quite simply – he was not in love with Barbara. She it was who 'hung over him like a gloomy cloud' and 'sprawled all over him'. He certainly encouraged her to do so and could not bring himself to make a clean break to give her a chance to find someone else.

> 'But have we ever been more than friends?' he asked. 'Very good friends, I admit, but not more than that.'
> 'You don't understand,' said Flora desperately. 'I can't ever make you understand. I can see that. You're too afraid of facing any sort of finality, even if it doesn't touch you. You haven't the courage to put me right out of your life as I would put you out of mine.'

'But Flora,' said Gervase in a puzzled, exasperated tone, 'it isn't necessary. Why should I face things I don't have to face? All this putting each other out of our lives,' he added with an indulgent smile. 'We can always be friends.'[36]

Barbara must have been aware of the situation. In one of her letters to Jock she had envisaged embroidering a Jacobean screen for Henry and Elsie. And about this time, Henry Harvey relates

I'd started a bad mock-heroic poem to Elsie Godenhjelm, a few lines at the top of a blank sheet of paper on my desk [on leave in Oxford], and gone out. Barbara comes while I'm out, sees what I'd been doing, and finishes my poem for me in *good* mock heroic.[37]

She had also, as a kind of literary *jeu d'esprit*, begun a novel set in Finland and had sent chapters of it in letter form to Jock and to Henry. The hero, Gervase, was Henry once again, a young lecturer at the University of Helsingfors, who, although pursued by his old love (lively, bouncing Flora, who has followed him from England), finds himself drawn to the beautiful and enigmatic Swedish girl, Ingeborg. It began quite frivolously as the adventures of Herr Lektor Harvey in Finland, with references to the country and the language, all carefully worked up, but soon, real feeling breaks through and Barbara knew that she was describing the ending of an actual love affair.[38]

In the summer of 1937 Jock went on holiday with Henry and Elsie to France and Italy. He wrote to Barbara several times, sending her a Compton-Burnett account of their travels.

Ladies and Gentlemen

'I should prefer to drive in the right direction,' said Henry. 'I should not like to be driving at random. You had better find the map.'

'Drive on Henry,' said Elsie, 'and as we pass Jock may call out and ask the way. If it takes too much time, we need not wait to hear the answer.'

'See,' said Jock, 'it is raining. As the car is open at the sides perhaps we may get wet' . . .

'Here is an hotel,' said Henry. 'Shall we stop here?'

'It is well recommended,' said Jock, 'that is something.'

'It is not very much,' said Henry, 'perhaps it is really nothing.'

'Let us drive round and look at other hotels,' said Elsie. 'Let us choose after full consideration.'

'Let us make haste,' said Jock, 'there is thunder and lightning and much rain.'

'Ah thunder is so dangerous,' said Elsie.

'We have driven twice round the town,' said Jock. 'It would hardly be self-respecting to drive round a third time.'

'Do not be hurrying us,' said Henry. 'I am ready to drive round all night.'

'Which hotel do you prefer?' said Jock.

'Do not ask me which I like,' said Elsie. 'I say only what I think others would like.'

'Then do you choose, Henry,' said Jock, 'a choice must be made.'

'So the burden of responsibility is to be mine,' said Henry.

'Yes,' said Jock and Elsie.[39]

On 6 December 1937 Jock wrote a letter to Hilary, typewritten so that Barbara should not recognise his very distinctive handwriting on the envelope.

Will you please break the news to your sister that the marriage has been arranged and will take place in about a week's time (quietly in the English church at Helsingfors) between Lektor Harvey and Fröken Elsie Godenhjelm? I had not the courage to tell her – besides I thought it would come better from you, and in Oswestry.[40]

On 11 December he wrote to Barbara:

They [Henry and Elsie] are both tired and depressed and want to have other people to amuse them and won't be amused by anything. I suppose they will gradually settle down. . . . It's really very hard to write about these Harveys because one is likely to give a false impression and I don't know what you want me to say – I don't think you need at all envy Elsie, but I don't suppose you do.[41]

Flora often wondered what would become of her. She had been in love with Gervase for so long that she could not imagine a life in which he had no part. Nor, on the other hand, could she imagine a life in which he returned her love. That would somehow spoil the picture she had made of herself, it was an interesting picture, very dear to her, and she could not bear the idea of it being spoilt. Noble, faithful, long-suffering, although not without its funny side, it was like something out of Chekov, she thought. The first two years were the worst, she reflected calmly. She could tell any young woman that. But it was really no use entering upon an unrequited passion unless you were prepared to keep it up for at least five years. Seven years was best. There was something very noble about loving a person for seven years and getting nothing in return.[42]

So it was back to pretend play. And Elsie, joining in the game wrote (on black-edged paper): 'Barbara has written me such a brave letter. . . . I hope she shall be a sister to me.' And the pretend play turned itself into art and Barbara wrote about Flora/Barbara:

Perhaps if she put her misery away at the back of her mind and left it there she might one day be able to bring it out into the light and smile at the idea of its ever having had the power to hurt her.[43]

Chapter Five

Barbara went on several tours of Hungary and Germany with the National Union of Students and on one such visit to Cologne in 1934 she had met Hanns Woischnick and Friedbert Gluck who were officially entertaining the party of students. Both young men found her attractive and she was very happy to flirt with them. Her German was quite good and she enjoyed speaking it, and she was greatly drawn to German literature, especially the poetry. Her diary entries for this trip are full of ecstatic exclamations about the romantic beauty of the country and the charm of the people – especially the gallantry of the young men. 'The Germans are glorious to flirt with.' All of which provided a beguiling contrast to Henry's uncaring attitude. Back in Oxford she corresponded with Friedbert, showing his letters to Henry ostensibly for help with the translation, but obviously to try and make him jealous. 'The Germans appreciate me,' she wrote defiantly, 'if the English don't.'[1]

She went back to Germany later in the year, this time to Hamburg, arriving there on the same day as Hitler, who impressed her as looking 'smooth and clean'. She noted that the elections were held while she was there: 'There was plenty of publicity etc. urging voters to say "*Ja*" for Hitler.'[2]

Rupert Gleadow received an enthusiastic letter about it all and struck a note of caution: 'It's good that you have been to Germany and can talk it. Oh but *please* don't admire those *filthy* Nazis in their beautiful (sic!) uniforms.'[3]

She was, though, quite uninterested in politics of any kind. Her father was the sort of professional, middle-class man who would naturally vote Conservative and although Barbara occasionally went to Labour Club meetings in Oxford it was, as we have seen, more for the young men than for the

politics. She also joined other students in feeding the Hunger
Marchers as they passed through Oxford on their way from
Jarrow to Westminster, but the motive was humanitarian rather
than political. In those early days of National Socialism she,
like most of her contemporaries, had only the vaguest idea of
what it was all about and she did not care enough to question
things she was not interested in. Perhaps she was more naïve
than most. She had no idea of what was involved during the
students' visit when

> There was much merriment – shouting and singing
> too – English and German songs. We sang *God Save the
> King* and *Deutschland Über Alles* – that rather worried
> Friedbert, although I couldn't understand why. He and
> Hanns had an animated talk about it in German.[4]

She went again in 1935 and continued her love affair
with Friedbert, who 'was angelic to me. Such kindness as his
one can never forget.'[5] This time she was more aware of the
political scene, but for Barbara, as always, it was the human
relationships that were important.

> After Germany I was in love with Friedbert *in a way*.
> I put it so because I realised even at the time that most
> of it was probably glamour. His being a foreigner – the
> little Americanisms in his speech . . . and the way he
> said 'Barbara' – it being in a foreign country with the
> Hohenzollern Brücke by moonlight and *zwei* Manhattan
> at the Excelsior and his Nivea Creme that I rubbed on my
> arm to remember the smell of him – for all these things
> I loved him and yet I hardly knew him as a person and
> didn't at all agree with his National Socialism, although
> I tried to read Feuchtwanger's book *The Oppermans* and
> a lot of German poetry after my stay in Cologne and my
> interest in the language was reawakened with the result
> that really I learnt a good deal more.[6]

They corresponded quite frequently (in German), as she
wrote reproachfully to Henry Harvey in 1936, 'Even Friedbert
has spared a moment from the organisation of the Olympic
Games to send me a beautiful postcard.'

In early 1938 she wrote one of her pastiche Compton-Burnett pieces for Jock, then staying with the Harveys in Helsingfors, which contains the following passage:

> 'What do you think about Austria and Germany?' asked Aunt Helen.
> 'Well, I always like the Germans,' said Barbara.
> 'Oh, Barbara, surely you do not like the Germans,' said Aunt Helen.
> 'The ones I have met have been very nice,' said Barbara in a firm, level tone. 'I have a friend in Dresden . . . '
> 'I expect it is a young man,' said Aunt Helen in a triumphant tone, 'that is what it is.'
> 'Well, yes,' said Barbara, 'it is a young man but that is not why . . . '
> 'Oh, Barbara, you surely would not marry a German?' persisted Aunt Helen.
> 'No, I have no intention of marrying a German,' said Barbara firmly.
> 'Well, it would be something to talk about if Barbara married a German, would it not?' said Aunt Helen brightly. 'Personally I could not marry a foreigner.'
> 'Neither could I,' said Barbara in a hopeless tone.[7]

In May 1938 she went to Dresden to see Friedbert and took lodgings in the Strehlererstrasse. Friedbert worked at the Büro in Dresden, and, since Barbara refers to his black uniform, it seems he must have been in the SS, though she never mentions this in her brief diary entries, being totally absorbed in her romantic view of Germany and the glamour of Friedbert himself. She wrote to Jock from

> a beer garden and the sun is shining and the birds are singing and the chestnut trees are in blossom and the band is playing . . . a sad Volkslied thing that I am very fond of. . . . I find this atmosphere has on me the same effect that the meanest flower that blows has on Wordsworth. . . . Friedbert is being educated to enjoy the poems of John Betjeman. . . . I make him read them aloud . . . he has a disconcerting habit of asking me things which I feel I ought to know and don't.

F. Let us talk about Cromwell.
B. (in an interested condescending tone) Cromwell?
What about Cromwell?
F. (in a firm direct tone) What was the influence
of Cromwell on Milton? I needn't say any more, you
know that Cassandra is familiar only with the more
sympathetic parts of *Paradise Lost*, *Comus* and of course
Samson Agonistes.[8]

During the day while Friedbert was at the Büro she
had coffee at the Eden and tea at Rumpelmayers, went
around the galleries and the churches (she quickly found
the Anglo-American one) like any tourist. In the evenings
she and Friedbert went out to the Regina Palast 'where we
had champagne and danced till nearly 3', or had Manhattans
at the Eden and visited little cafés for more cocktails, food
and music.

They spent the weekend of 13 May in Prague, just two
months after Hitler had marched into the city, but Barbara
doesn't mention the German presence at all, though there
are casual references to several Sudetan Germans she met.
She and Friedbert stayed at the Hotel Beranek ('*Doppelzimmer*')
and for her everything was magic, though she seems to have
irritated (and perhaps alarmed) Friedbert by her frivolity and
her inclination to get into conversation with various Czech
young men. To her Prague was

the Golden City, I kept saying, the Golden City. No, I
do not think it is Golden, he said. To me it is Golden,
it will always be Golden.[9]

Back in Dresden she continued her sightseeing and waited
for Friedbert.

F came very late for lunch. Went to Rumpelmayers and
read the papers and then met F by the station about 5.30
and had a lovely walk in the Grossergarten until 7. Met
him again at Alt Bayern at 9. Walked down Pragerstr.
and had more food and beer and looked at the Elbe.[10]

Sometimes Friedbert came to her lodgings for supper:

Supper has been brought in and I am waiting for
dear Friedbert to come; it is all so domesticated. I feel
I should say 'The Master has to go to Pirna today – he
will not be here for lunch'. And then in he comes – the
hasty, husbandly kiss . . . [11]

On her last day:

F came to supper. Went to his room in Jedensstr, where
he typed a letter, then to the Wendorf. Very nice. Then
mock turtle soup at the station, then home. I chased my
hat down Uhlandstr. at 4 a.m.[12]

She never saw him again. Sometimes, during the war, in
the middle of all her Home Front activity, she would think
of Friedbert and wonder what had happened to him. And on
6 May 1940 she wrote in her diary:

Day of National Prayer. Church packed morning and
evening. Two fine services. I thought – Friedbert, against
this you haven't a chance.[13]

There are two more rather mysterious entries about him
in her diaries. On 13 December 1941 she wrote:

Poopa [Hilary] hears from Nora Wahn [who had written
several books on Nazi Germany and was then working at
the BBC] that Friedbert has gone anti-Nazi. *Ach wenzig
das treue wäre.*[14]

It is hard to imagine how an SS officer could have done
this and survived. But Friedbert did survive and Barbara's
diary entries for 31 July and 24 September 1946 both read 'A
letter from Friedbert'. By then Barbara was living in Pimlico
with Hilary, who has no memory of these letters, so perhaps
Barbara never mentioned them to her. She never mentioned
him again in her diaries or in conversation.

Chapter Six

On 3 December 1937 Barbara was having lunch in Oxford
with a young friend, Denis Pullein-Thompson. As she sometimes did, when she was feeling exuberant, she had assumed
an accent and was pretending to be a Finn. A young man
approached their table and Denis, entering into the spirit of
the game, introduced her as Päävikki Olafsson. The young
man was

> about my height, slight and dark with a quizzical,
> rather monkey face. He wore a camel hair coat and
> a spotted tie and looked sleek and neat.[1]

His name was Julian Amery. He was eighteen, the younger
son of Leo Amery, a distinguished political figure who had
been First Lord of the Admiralty in 1922 and Colonial Secretary
and Dominions Secretary from 1924–9. The Amerys' house in
Eaton Square was thus a meeting place for influential people –
politicians and diplomats – and Julian was at home and happy
in this world and eager to make his mark in it. He had been at
Eton and was now at Balliol, a college notable for producing
eminent political figures. He often spoke at the Union and
was writing for a newspaper called *Oxford Comment* which
was edited by Woodrow Wyatt.

They went back to his rooms in Balliol – Barbara had
stopped pretending to be a Finn – and he played German
and Hungarian records on the gramophone. When he kissed
her she was surprised:

> It was the first time anyone so much younger than I
> was had done such a thing, for he was only eighteen
> and I was twenty-four.

He had so much charm and a kind of childish sim-
plicity, combined with Continental polish that was most
appealing.[2]

In the vacation he wrote to her to say that he had been
to a ball at the Austrian Legation and was just about to go
to Kitzbühel. It was a glimpse of another world and Barbara
was fascinated. Back in Oxford he wrote that he couldn't get
her out of his mind: 'I simply can't believe that I've only seen
you once for an hour and a half. Budapest is on the wireless,
the songs have all been very melancholic so far – I feel very
Hungarian.'[3] Leo Amery's mother was Hungarian and had
had a considerable influence on his life, so Julian enjoyed
assuming a Continental manner and a kinship with all things
Mitteleuropean.

Barbara was enchanted by the glamour and admitted quite
honestly that she had been unhappy and lost after Henry's
marriage and 'thankful for any interest to be taken in me'.[4]
The Hungarian motif, too, struck a chord with her, since
she had visited Budapest with Hilary in 1935, had been
delighted by its charm and *Stimmung*, and had, indeed, used
it as a setting for the climax of her novel *Civil to Strangers*,
which she wrote in 1936. She went back to Oxford in
February 1938 and met Julian again. They talked about their
ambitions, her writing and his place in the great world of
events.

He said he couldn't bear to die without having done
something by which he could be remembered.[5]

Julian was very brilliant – Chips Channon said in 1943
that he was the cleverest young man he had ever met – and
had gathered around himself a circle of likeminded, clever,
ambitious, upper-class young men – all of whom looked rather
alike to Barbara.

The entrance to the front quadrangle of Randolph
[Balliol] was blocked by a group of rich young men newly
arrived from town. Suede shoes, pin-striped flannels,
teddy bear coats and check caps – Anthea knew the uniform well.[6]

They had tea together, went to the theatre and one day they lunched in his rooms in Balliol ('eggs with cream on top, chicken and chocolate mousse. And Niersteiner, of course') and then walked about Oxford and into the Botanical Gardens, where Julian plucked a spray of orchids – pinky-mauve with purple centres like velvet – and presented them to her with a romantic flourish. On 11 March she went to lunch in Balliol again ('fish, duck and green peas, peaches and cream, sherry, Niersteiner and port') and spent the afternoon with him until five o'clock when he had to go and see his tutor.

> I knew it would have to be goodbye. . . . Julian stood in front of his mirror and combed his hair and put on his coat. Then he came up behind me and said '*Servus*'. That was the last time I saw him.
> I inscribed a card of Boecklin's *Die Insel der Töten* with our initials and the dates of our first meeting and our last and added a line from my favourite poem by Heine . . . *Neuer Frühling gibt zurück.* . . .
> I took a red anemone from my buttonhole and left it on top of his pale blue pyjamas. I walked round the room touching things. Then I walked slowly down the stairs.
> I walked out of the St Giles' gateway in a happy daze and then went into Elliston's for tea. I was so happy I could hardly speak coherently to Ruth Brook-Smith and Alison Ross whom I met there. Still in the same state I went back to change to go to dinner at St Hilda's. Just as I was ready to go out I saw that there were some flowers in the hall. Two dozen of the loveliest daffodils and with them a card from Julian saying in German that although he had to go away I knew that he had thought of me. I felt it was a perfect ending to what had been one of the happiest episodes of my life. I was so glad that I didn't see him again in Oxford.[7]

They had spent only twenty hours together – Barbara carefully noted the amount of time of each meeting – but they provided, as she wrote later, 'twenty years of memories'.

In March Julian went to Spain to report on Franco's

movements, as a war correspondent for the *News Chronicle*. He wrote to Barbara from the Lord Warden Hotel in Dover, having two hours to wait for his boat, and mentioned casually that he had forgotten to go to the Examination Schools to do a French Unseen paper for his Pass Moderations. This upset her so much that she rushed off to see his tutor in Balliol to find out what could be done about it. But, as Julian Amery writes in his autobiography, when he got back from Spain, no one seemed to mind too much and his career was not affected.

A year later Barbara met him in London. Her diary entry is very succinct:

> Met Julian by the traffic lights at Portman Square. Went back to 112 [Eaton Square] and met Mrs Amery.[8]

Later she wrote more fully:

> On the 4th of July I met one I had loved and not seen for·more than a year. Such meetings should be avoided if possible. On this same day I went inside that curious house in Eaton Square with its paintings and smell of incense and met his mother, a splendid character for a novel.[9]

Mrs Amery, whom Chips Channon remembered at a party at his house in 1943 'wandering sad-eyed like a ghost' did indeed appear in several of Barbara's novels. Most notably she was Mandy Wraye in Barbara's Home Front novel, a politician's wife, happy to be relieved by the war of the burdens of public life and able to be herself at last in the country (the Amerys also had a country house in Sussex). She appears again in *Crampton Hodnet*, this time as Lady Beddoes, the wife of a diplomat and the mother of the irrepressible Simon, a vague and charming woman who is liable to make unsuitable remarks when opening a garden fête. She also appears as Mrs Lyall in *Jane and Prudence*, again the mother of a politician, again vague and pleasant and apt to make unexpected remarks which embarrass her more conventional son.

In the Home Front novel, written in 1939, there is a scene where the vicar's daughter, Flora (usually Barbara's name for herself) visits Edward Wraye at his house in Eaton Square. He is bored and thinking of another, more 'suitable' girl.

> His bright hazel eyes were looking out over Flora's head, while one hand played absently with her golden hair, at a coloured print of Lake Maggiore which hung over the mantelpiece.[10]

Flora feels that she will never visit Edward's study again and wants to remember it all, from the view of the trees outside in the square to the red curtains with their design of white horses.

> It would be a grand thing to cry, to rush sobbing down the three flights of stairs, past the sepia photograph of Lyall Wraye as a young man and the Indian oil paintings, and the golf clubs and shooting sticks in the hall, out of the front door and into the hall.[11]

Flora, of course, being a clergyman's daughter, did no such thing, but made polite, stilted conversation with Mandy, whose curiosity had brought her out into the hall.

In her spy novel *So Very Secret*, written in 1941, Barbara again used the house in Eaton Square. It is the home of the heroine's 'lost love', again a politician, and as she takes refuge there when pursued by The Enemy, she notices the door knocker in the shape of a fish and the smell inside like incense or Turkish cigarettes. Barbara never wasted anything.

Certainly, after Henry Harvey, Julian was to be one of her richest sources of inspiration. He was the young Simon Beddoes in *Crampton Hodnet*, and Edward Wraye in the Home Front novel and Edward Lyall in *Jane and Prudence*.

In *So Very Secret* he appears twice. First, he plays his younger self, as Hugh, the charming but self-centred young man who helps the middle-aged heroine, Cassandra, in her quest. But Barbara also projects him into middle age (as she had done with Henry) as Adrian, Cassandra's lost love, now a successful politician who does not recognise her after twenty-seven years. He has become pompous and platitudinous, with only a brief glimpse of his old charm when he responds to Cassandra's careful flattery.

> A rather charming smile had now appeared on the wooden face. He looked quite like the old Adrian. I imagined him in his constituency asking after the old people's health.[12]

In her unfinished novel *The Lumber Room*, written in 1938, Barbara explores the relationship of Beatrice Wyatt, an Oxford don in her middle thirties, who is attracted to a handsome and brilliant young undergraduate, Gerald Cleveland, this time only a clergyman's son, but one who has acquired sophistication and a cosmopolitan polish after three months in Vienna. He tells her that she has 'Russian cheekbones' and kisses her hand and they have an idyllic term in Oxford until Beatrice forces herself to withdraw from a hopeless relationship and Gerald goes cheerfully off on holiday to Spain. Beatrice is rewarded, however, with the attentions of her old love, Henry Grainger, whose wife (chosen in preference to Beatrice) has conveniently died. Barbara herself did not have this particular consolation. Instead, in 1941, she wrote what is probably her best short story, 'Goodbye Balkan Capital'.

This was inspired by the scraps of news she had of Julian during the war. He was to have a very distinguished war record, quite as romantic as anything he (or she) could have imagined in those consciously romantic days of 1938. He was attached to the British Legation in Belgrade and went on special missions to Bulgaria, Turkey, Rumania and the Middle East. He later saw active service in Egypt, Palestine and the Adriatic and was Liaison Officer with the Albanian Resistance Movement in Albania in 1944. On 27 March 1941 Barbara wrote in her diary:

> Julian's 22nd birthday. Daffodils by his photograph and a Yugoslav revolution as a present. I heard the exciting

news [on the radio] at 1 pm. I hope J. *is* in Belgrade – it seems so right that he should be.

29 April. Heard the 6 o'clock news that Mr Ronald Campbell and the staff of the Belgrade Legation are nowhere to be found! I wonder if J. is with them?[13]

'Goodbye Balkan Capital' is about Laura, an English spinster who lives on her memories of one wonderful evening at a Commemoration Ball at Oxford with a dashing young undergraduate who then went out of her life and into the Diplomatic Service. She follows his career and pictures him in all the romantic places his job had taken him to. Now, in the war, 'doing her bit' in the ARP and at the first-aid post, she imagines him burning papers and codes, leaving *his* Balkan capital and rattling in the train through the night across Europe, encountering amazing dangers and adventures. But when she comes across his obituary by chance, she finds that he had retired from the Diplomatic Service some years before and had died peacefully in an Oxfordshire village, 'his life as dull as hers'. So Laura grieved 'not so much for his death . . . but for the picture she had had of him.' And yet, she decided, 'In life or in death people are very much what we like to think them.'

Barbara thought about Julian for most of her life and she refers to him often in her diaries, strangely, perhaps, since she had known him for such a short time and he had long since forgotten her. But the power of this memory and the feeling she had deliberately generated from it was simply *because* the incident had been so brief, so perfectly rounded – and she had ended it herself. Because they had both been consciously playing at Romance, there was no pain, only a pleasurable memory. It was as if Julian was more or less her own creation – certainly the figure she carried in her mind and imagination was – and that gave her the freedom to have these deep and continuing feelings about him, the sort of feelings that she could not have had for a real person and a real relationship. He had become like something out of a novel – as Henry never would, in spite of *Some Tame Gazelle* and *Civil to Strangers*, because there the pain was real. She kept her 'relics' of Julian – his photograph, the pressed orchid from the Botanical Gardens and a handkerchief he had bought to replace one he had 'stolen' from her.

> The photograph of him at the Union stands on the mantelpiece and in front of it a spray of red roses – but they are artificial ones from Woolworth's.[14]

The novel was, of course, a comedy.

Chapter Seven

A combination of a certain restlessness – a feeling that she really ought to be *doing* something – and an appetite for travel inspired Barbara to go as a kind of governess to Poland. It says a great deal about her political naïvety that she chose to go there in August 1938 to live with the family of Dr Michal Alberg in Katowice, to teach English to his daughter Ula. Her parents, too, like so many of their countrymen, did not really appreciate the worsening political situation in Europe since they did nothing to dissuade her. As it was, Barbara made a list of clothes she needed to buy or to make: 'smart day or afternoon dress, tan gloves, comfortable but not too hearty tan shoes, blouse or jumper to go with grey suit'. Shopping in Liverpool, she bought 'dull turkis [turquoise] wool material, black lace for evening blouse, white lace blouse, 6 silver buttons, white and gold evening bag, pale blue jumper, golden bracelet, gingham for lining waistcoat'. Thinking of the cold Polish winter, her mother bought her a new fur coat 'golden brown musquash, quite long'.[1]

Thus equipped she set off for Poland with Ula, who had been staying in England. After a brief bout of sentimental nostalgia as they passed the Lord Warden Hotel in Dover, Barbara managed the travel arrangements quite well, though after breaking their journey in Holland with some friends of the Albergs, they missed a couple of connections and had to pay extra money on their tickets. But

> All my guilt vanished when the marvellous train came in – dark blue *voitures-lits* going to Bucharest, Warsaw and such glamorous places. And when we got in I didn't know we were to have real beds, and there

was a private washing place too. Oh the *Stimmung*
of sleeping comfortably, in a nightgown, of not waking up at every station and at Aachen, of having
the customs officer come in and sitting up indicating
with languid arm my *gepack* – oh wonderful, not to
know where we were until we got up at 7 for breakfast.[2]

They arrived in Katowice on 29 August at 4.30 ('country
flat with factories – poor looking'). She settled in quite
happily and got on well with the family, the doctor, Mrs
Alberg, Ula and her sister Zuza, and began to give Ula
and Mrs Alberg English lessons. She made only brief diary
entries for the next few weeks, but they are very vivid. She
saw only what her own idiosyncratic vision showed her
and she seems not to have noticed the signs of tension
and unease that must have existed in that Polish town
in 1938. Although she notes without comment that the
Germans had entered Prague she gives equal space in her
diary to the fact that she had been served fried potatoes with
yoghurt.

31 August. Saw a large animal like a wolf hanging
up outside a provision shop [presumably a wild boar].
After supper a cavalry officer and his wife came. He
was in uniform. They were sitting drinking tea and
eating *küchen*. A lovely picture.

1 September. Went into the market and saw many
curious mushrooms, fungi, etc. arranged on the stalls.
Bought *Times* and *Express*. Studied Polish history all
afternoon. Tea at 6.10! Went for a walk and saw
Polish prostitutes and thieves being taken away in
a horse-drawn van. The street lamps shining on dark
wet pavements gave me a momentary *Sehnsucht* for
England.

2 September. Shopping in Vikki Olafsson [her *alter
ego* at that time] macintosh and battered Austrian
hat. Went to Czestochova by car with Mrs A. Long
ride, cold wet day. Forests and barefooted peasants. Saw

a wonderful church – turquoise marble, pink, grey, dark grey, white fawn, green crochet work around the pulpit and altars in green and puce. Virgin Mary picture with gold door sliding over it. And music.

3 September. At about five o'clock went to a dark romantic forest (belonging to the Prince of Pless). Had tea at the completely deserted Beergarden – great *Stimmung*. Walked in the forest and visited Golf Club. Very nice clubhouse, all the notices written in English.

4 September. Went on long excursion to the mountains beyond Bielska (used to be Austria). Walked up the mountain where we had lunch. Wonderful scenery with dark romantic forests.

6 September. Worked hard all day. In the evening went to see Zarah Leander in *Heimat*. In one part I was trembling with emotion and tears.[3]

Although the Albergs were kind and friendly, she felt very lonely and greatly missed English conversation. Quite soon, though, she found an interesting young man to chat to.

7 September. Went to the Vice-Consulate to meet Mr Thwaites – a sinister place! But he was very young and easy, intelligent and amusing. We lunched at Patria.

. *8 September.* At 4.30 I met the Vice-Consul and we walked in the woods. Talked all the time of Modern Art, poetry, America and Spain. I couldn't believe I was in Poland. It felt just like Oxford.

9 September. Went in the car with Mrs A. She went to the doctor. Talked to the chauffeur, a nice man and intelligent. He thought it must be *'Kolossal Langweilig'* for me here.

10 September. In the evening Vikki [B.P.] was temperamental – but after cigarettes, some Mozart and a

Brandenburg concerto felt better and went for a walk with the dog Bianco.

11 September. Went to tell Mr Thwaites we weren't going to Crackow and stayed two hours at his flat looking at modern pictures and hearing music. Then we had lunch together in a German restaurant and went for a long walk until 4.30 when we came back to the Albergs' for tea. I was the hostess – oh the delight of English conversation and pleasant company.[4]

She liked Katowice and the surrounding countryside and summed it up in a telegraphic fashion:

. . . the smuts on one's face, the bright pink soup, the barefooted peasants, the artistic pattern of the factories on a wet Sunday afternoon, the impossible but beautiful language . . . [5]

As the political situation in Europe became more serious and the tension between England and Germany increased, Dr Alberg felt that Barbara should return to England. Not understanding what it was like to live in a politically unstable country, whose very existence was sometimes in danger, Barbara felt it was all rather melodramatic. She saw that 'everyone was so terrified' in Poland, but she never really appreciated the seriousness of the situation – for the Albergs (who were Jewish) as well as for herself.

My departure was in many ways quite dramatic. I left with Dr Alberg and the chauffeur at 8 o'clock in the morning. Mrs Alberg took a bunch of gladioli out of a vase and handed them to me as a last gesture and I was given enough food to feed myself and numerous Germans all through Germany and still have a lot to bring home here. So the fine Polish sausage was much enjoyed by our gardener. Dr Alberg was so nervous all the way to Beuthen – the German frontier station from which I was to catch my train – he told me not to speak at all at the frontier but just to show

my passport and money, and not to speak to a soul
in Germany.[6]

But, having no experience of such things, she simply couldn't
believe in the dangers and obviously thought the Albergs were
making a great fuss about nothing. So, with fine English
insouciance – or obtuseness – she simply behaved in her
usual casually friendly manner.

> I had an eight hour journey from Beuthen to Berlin
> – and then the night journey from Berlin to Aachen
> – about another ten hours. And by the time I'd got
> out of Poland I wasn't nervous any more, because of
> course Germany seemed just as usual. Naturally they
> knew very little about the crisis and I talked to many
> people and everyone was very kind to me. I had time
> in Berlin to see Unter den Linden and to walk in
> the Wilhelmstrasse, and to feel rather disappointed
> that it didn't show signs of feverish activity. It was
> so dark and silent. I suppose everyone was having
> dinner.[7]

It was, however, not a comfortable or straightforward journey
back.

> I had a splitting headache, having to deal with half
> my luggage being lost and some to be registered to
> England, all alone. But no, I was not quite in tears
> on the Friedrichstrasse station. I just sat smoking a
> gold-tipped Polish cigarette, feeling as I used to feel when
> I came back from Oxford and sat waiting at Snow Hill
> station in Birmingham, that my whole life seems to be
> spent sitting on stations all over Europe leaving behind
> people I love.[8]

It is a fine cinematic scene – not for nothing did Barbara
go to the movies twice a week. Not surprisingly, when she
got back to Oswestry, she was unwell and had to stay in
bed for several days. She was thankful to be home and quite
willing to assure her parents (by now very worried about the
whole affair) that she had no intention of returning to Poland,

even if it should become possible 'now that Mr Chamberlain is safely back in England and thanks to him there isn't going to be any war'.

As soon as she had recovered from her adventure she decided she must 'get Something to Do'. Hilary had been in Greece (another country with an uncertain future) in the early part of 1938. Now, encouraged by her mother, she was taking a secretarial course in London with a view to joining the BBC as a secretary, the usual way for a woman to get into the Corporation in those days. Barbara decided to go to London with her.

They lived in lodgings where, for £1. 5s. 2d. a week (paid for out of the small allowance her parents made her), Barbara had a tiny room at the top of the house – 27 Upper Berkeley Street – 'in quite a good district of London – conveniently near all the shops and art galleries'. It would be the perfect arrangement: Hilary would do her secretarial course and Barbara would start a new novel.

> It is such a pleasant life – I don't think I've been so happy since I was a young girl of eighteen in my first year at Oxford! I work very hard and have done about a quarter of this new novel. . . . I honestly don't believe I can be happy unless I am writing. It seems to be the only thing I really want to do.
>
> I am very happy and don't need comforting which is something new! The only thing is to work at something you like and that you feel is worth doing, even if it's only a novel that doesn't get published. I suppose it is all good experience, anyway, and while I'm doing it I'm perfectly happy.[9]

She was also inspired to go on writing by the fact that Jock's novel, *The Almond Tree*, had been accepted by Jonathan Cape. He had written to tell her about it in their usual Compton-Burnett style:

> So I am in Bedford Square, and I am wearing my black hat which is rather too big for me which I bought when I was going to Paris and it was meant to look both half-mourning and respectable and Quartier Latin all at

the same time. But now I am thinking it looks more Bloomsbury . . .

Well I am shown up to Mr Cape, and he is a square grey man, and he is very kind but rather bleak, and, oh, I think, this is and is not Cressid [Barbara had referred to him as 'falser than false Cressid' when he rejected *Some Tame Gazelle*]. And he says 'Sit down' and 'I like your book'. . . . But he is going to bring out my book, he says, in June or July. . . . And he is saying it is so nice and restful, and it might be of any time, and I am not so-o-o pleased because do you think Mr Leavis, editor of that high-up rag *Scrutiny*, will think I am . . . 'an adult sensitive modern in a cultured drawing room'?[10]

A few months later he describes his first venture into the literary world.

'I am glad you have come,' said Jonathan Cape in a tone drained of all feeling. 'Have something to drink. I always think that makes things go better.'

'Passion fruit?' asks the barman in an interested tone.

'If you please,' said Jock in a high nervous voice.

'They are quite harmless, mostly fruit juice. People seem to like them,' said Mr Cape in a reassuring voice. 'I will introduce you to Miss Something.'

'How do you do?' says Miss Something. . . .

Presently Mr Cape was walking round the room, his arm round Miss Stevie Smith, a small dark long-toothed young woman of about 35, in a terracotta dress.

'It is a fine day,' said Jock.

'But we need rain,' said Miss Something in the tone of one repeating a lesson.

'The Square is looking nice,' said Jock.

'I suppose there are famous people here,' said Miss Something. 'But I do not know them.'

'Nor do I,' said Jock.

'You here!' said Spencer Curtis Brown. 'I hope you are beginning another book. Authors should have no spare time. Meet my wife.'

'I will ask for your book at Harrods' library,' said Mrs Spencer Curtis Brown.[11]

Jock had been fortunate enough to have been taken on
by the literary agent Curtis Brown, as he went on to describe
after the manner of Stevie Smith.

> Have you a literary agent, Jock? Yes, I've got a literary
> agent and he lives in a literary agency and is agent for
> my literary property. Well, I went to see Mr Curtis Brown,
> did I tell you that was his name? And he said . . . 'God
> willing you may sell a thousand copies, and God very
> willing fifteen hundred.' And then 'Of course I didn't
> read your book but our Miss Burton did. Would you like
> to see her?' Well, I saw their Miss Burton and she was
> very nice that one. And she is saying to me everything
> that I should like people to say, and a few things that I
> hadn't thought of.[12]

Barbara had actually approached Jonathan Cape about
getting a job in publishing, feeling, as young writers do, that
it would be a congenial way of making a living while she was
writing. There was no job, but Jonathan Cape remembered her
novels and encouraged her to go on writing.

In February 1939 she wrote in a letter to Elsie Harvey:

> I have been working hard at my novel [probably *The
> Lumber Room*]. It is nearly finished now, but I shall
> then have to go over it and make some improvements
> before I am really satisfied with it. When you start to
> write one you always wonder if you will be able to make
> it long enough, but by the time you get to the end it is
> always too long – I love cutting out bits and crossing out
> whole pages.[13]

She had been in fairly regular correspondence with both
Henry and Elsie since their marriage. In the beginning the
Compton-Burnett style was a great help as a disguise to her
feelings. Elsie became her 'dear sister' – part of the charmed
circle.

> And she is so *immensely* pleased with the photographs
> of her dear sister Elsie, who is so charming and who can
> speak Finnish, which is the most difficult language in the
> world.[14]

And later she wrote to the Harveys:

> I am imagining Jock coming back too and we can
> all be dear brothers and sisters together, except that
> some will be husbands and wives, which is an even more
> satisfactory relationship.[15]

Barbara also wrote letters to Jock and the Harveys in
the lively and eccentric style of Stevie Smith. Over fifty
years later Henry Harvey has fond and vivid memories of
them ('How beautifully, delightfully, cleverly, deliciously,
inventively dotty her letters to Finland were'[16]) – each one
reads like the brilliant *tour de force* it was intended to be. It
was as if she was asserting her own position in the group as
a writer, *that* was her status now. She wrote to Jock, who was
staying with the Harveys in Helsingfors, a letter obviously also
intended for the eyes of Henry and Elsie:

> And now you are saying, what is Miss Pym doing with
> herself . . . ? And I will tell you, she is writing, simply
> that. And she is writing a new novel, and Chapter One
> is nearly done, but it is not in rhymes, no sir, not even
> Miss Pym is as clever as that. And this novel it is oh-so
> sober and dull, and there are no parties of young people
> getting *beschwipst,* and there are no Finns or Swedes or
> Germans or Hungars and the *Magyar bor* is not flowing
> at all freely, and there is no farm on the *puszta* . . . no
> there is none of this. Well, there can be really nothing, you
> say. And you will be right – *die ganze Welt dreht sich um
> Liebe* you will be saying in a furry, *sentimentvolle Stimme*
> as you see darling Henry and more darling Elsie and how
> happy they are. And you will be coming back to England,
> and you will be meeting this so dull spinster which is
> like the old brown horse walking with a slow majestic
> dignity, and you will be saying Well-fer-goodness-sake,
> Miss Pym, like they say in the films. But this spinster,
> this Barbara Mary Crampton Pym, she will be smiling
> to herself – ha-ha she will be saying inside. *But I have
> that within which passeth show* – maybe she will be
> saying that, but she is a queer old horse, this old brown
> spinster, so I cannot forecast exactly what she will be
> saying.[17]

It says a great deal for Elsie's sense, good-humour and intelligence that she was not overwhelmed by this extraordinary
correspondence, but, instead, took her place in the group as
Barbara's 'dear sister', with all the surface jokiness that that
implied. Though, of course, she must have been thoroughly
conditioned to this sort of literary frivolity after having listened
for some time to Henry and Jock's conversation. Elsie, quite
simply, joined in.

> Well this is a lovely letter . . . and fancy, there is a
> page written by darling Elsie, and she shall have a
> separate letter all to herself from her loving sister.[18]

When the Harveys were in Oxford in the summer of
1938, staying at the flat in Banbury Road ('Have you got
Mrs Townsend looking after you? I hope you don't find her
as frightening as I do'), Barbara finally met Elsie and they
got on remarkably well together and conducted quite a cosy
correspondence.

> I hope that you are feeling much better. But please
> take care of yourself [Elsie had not been well] and don't
> try to do too much. You must let Mrs Townsend give you
> a charwoman's love – sometimes a mother's, a husband's
> and a sister's are not enough.

> Darling sister Elsie,
>   Thank you so much for your nice letter – it comforted
> me a lot. The only thing that didn't comfort me was to
> think that you are so far away and we couldn't be talking
> to each other as we used to in Oxford.[19]

A correspondence that had begun in bravado had, over the
months, settled into a friendly exchange of news. Barbara had
accepted Henry's marriage. There had been a certain amount
of self-dramatisation and self-mockery.

> 'I think Miss Pym is not quite herself today,' said
> Mr Liddell, in a nervous, hurrying tone. 'This talk of
> pressed flowers and sentimental tokens, it is not good. I
> understand that she was perfectly content at Oswestry.

That there were no regrets, no . . . ' he stood holding a beef in his hand, making vague nervous gestures with it.

'Oh, fancy if all passion should not be spent!' said the Fru Lektor in a high, agitated tone.

'Oh, do not speak of it. It is more than I can bear,' said her husband sinking down on to the couch, and taking a glass of schnapps.

'It is more than I can bear,' said Mr Liddell, casting the beef away, and sinking down beside the Herr Lektor.

'Well, well,' said Miss Pym, coming into the room. 'Two old men bearing an imaginary burden, that is what I see. It must be the more heavy because it is not real.'

'So there is no burden?' said Mr Liddell, rising to his feet.

'I will not say that,' said Miss Pym, in a quiet thoughtful tone, 'but you do not have to bear it.'[20]

But there had been other young men to divert her and she had, in a way, written Henry out of her system in *Some Tame Gazelle* and in *Adam and Cassandra*. Now she was getting on with her own life. London was a strange place in the early months of 1939. However much most people believed – or, rather, hoped against hope – that Chamberlain had really brought back Peace in Our Time from Munich, it was becoming increasingly obvious that this was not so. The London parks were scarred with trenches dug as shelters against air raids, every household had been allocated its gas masks, cinema newsreels showed disquieting pictures of refugees trundling through Europe with their pitiful possessions on handcarts, and there was an uncertain, unreal feeling of marking time. In March Barbara had noted in her diary that she

sat on a peach-coloured sofa in Grosvenor House and waited for Dr Alberg.[21]

British consular families had already been evacuated from Poland and Dr Alberg, who was desperately aware of his family's precarious future as Jews under a German occupation of Poland, was trying to make arrangements to bring them to safety in England.

In May there was conscription for men aged twenty to twenty-one and Barbara wrote to Elsie:

> If there is going to be a war – and we can't be sure that there won't be one – we may as well be prepared for it. . . . I am going to get a First Aid certificate . . . I am going to classes every week. Fancy me learning how to make splints and bandages! I rather look forward to it. . . . I made some boxes for gas masks when I was at home – it is rather a pleasant sensation to fool oneself into thinking that one is doing useful work.[22]

She spent her birthday, 2 June, with Jock, lunching at the Queen's in Sloane Square and later walking in Belgravia. She was now twenty-six. On 4 July she records seeing Julian in Upper Berkeley Street – perhaps casually from her window, or perhaps she was tracking him, she does not say – at 8.30, wearing white tie, tails and a red carnation. Later that month she was able to report that all the Albergs were safe ('at the Montague Hotel'). In August she joined Hilary and her parents at Pwllheli for their usual holiday. Everything in the little Welsh town seemed poignantly normal after the tensions of London.

> In the evening a drive to the little church of Llandegwning. Old Welsh deaf woman: 'There has been no burying here for twenty years.' One might write a poem. Walked to the harbour and saw six sleeping swans.[23]

Now war was seen to be inevitable. Hilary was going with the BBC to their emergency quarters in Evesham, and so the London lodgings were given up. Barbara put off making any decision about her own war work by simply going back home to Oswestry to help her mother, becoming part of what came to be called the Home Front.

Chapter Eight

When the family arrived back in Oswestry it was obvious that Barbara would be needed at home. Morda Lodge was a large house and very difficult to run without domestic help. When the war began, girls who had previously been in domestic service joyfully made their escape into the women's services and into the factories. The Pyms were lucky to keep Dilys, but even she was unsettled by the prospect of five evacuees. Billeting was compulsory and the size of the house decided the number of evacuees to be taken in. The children were to come from the shipyard area of Birkenhead, just across the river from Liverpool, a major target for German bombers.

There was so much to be done. The first priority was to fix up some kind of blackout for the windows, which, at Morda Lodge, were large and numerous. Heavy material was difficult to find in the shops and Barbara spent days sewing improvised linings into their existing curtains – some made of an intractible material she called 'Polish wolf'. On 1 September she was sewing some for the long windows of the dining room when she heard on the radio that Hitler had taken over Danzig and invaded Poland, bombing many towns, including Katowice, and 2 September was a 'long, busy day, moving beds, blacking out windows etc.'.[1] Barbara and her parents did not go to morning service on 3 September. They were still busy preparing the house for the evacuees who were expected hourly – though no one seemed to know quite when. But the Pyms, like millions of others, were tuned to the BBC Home Service waiting for the Prime Minister to speak at 11.15.

Mr Chamberlain spoke to the nation and told us that we were now at war with Germany. After his speech, darkly tragic when one thinks of all his efforts for peace, came

the National Anthem. Into my mind came irrelevant
past happinesses. About six o'clock the five evacuees
arrived.[2]

In a small country town domestic upsets seemed, in a
way, almost more important than national ones. The evacuees
were mostly from poor homes, and conversation now centred
around hitherto unmentionable topics like bed-wetting and
head lice. The Pyms were luckier than most, though they
obviously found the presence of noisy children and their
'desperately unhappy' mother very difficult to adjust to. After
only four days the mother decided that she couldn't bear being
away any longer and took the children back to Birkenhead,
feeling, like many other evacuees, that they would rather face
the bombs in their own familiar surroundings than be safe in
an alien one. Three more children came to take their place –
'They look very sweet but are reputed to be naughty.'[3]
    It was still difficult to accept the fact of being at war
('One wakes with a sinking feeling inside and then realises
why'[4]). The days were very full and very tiring. There were,
of course, virtually no domestic appliances – only, really, the
vacuum cleaner. Washing for the entire household was done
by hand (any sort of laundry service vanished practically
overnight along with petrol) and irons were heated on the
gas stove. Barbara's pocket diary (the only sort she kept at
this time) became full of references to washing, ironing,
bed making, washing up, mending, 'cleaning paint, mirrors
und so weiter and sewing sheets sides to middle'.[5] Things
wore out and couldn't be replaced so a lot of time had to
be spent in mending and refurbishing household articles and
clothes.
    Although Irena continued to do the cooking for the
now enlarged household, the shopping, which was mostly
Barbara's job, became more difficult and time-consuming.
Although food rationing was not introduced until January
1940, there were sudden shortages of such everyday necessi-
ties as matches, hairgrips, elastic and torch batteries (not
to mention cigarettes and drink of any kind), which meant
standing in queues in the damp cold weather. These endless,

boring physical tasks made life seem very dull ('I shall be lucky if the worst this war can make me feel is boredom'[6]). However, cinemas, which had been closed at the outbreak of war, now gradually began to re-open and were felt to be a great comfort.

> Went to the pictures for the first time since war started. Took gas masks but felt rather silly! Constance Bennett and Alice Faye in *Tail Spin*.[7]

Jock had gone back to Helsingfors with the Harveys and now, with the prospect of a Russian invasion of Finland, Barbara was worried about them all. She heard from Jock's brother Don that they were trying to leave Finland ('Flight from the Bolsheviks in an open boat!'[8]). When the bombing started they all went to an aunt of Elsie's outside Helsingfors, Elsie and Henry driving back to the flat at night to clear up. Henry very much regrets burning all his correspondence 'suitcase after suitcase . . . because I thought Stalin might get it'[9] including scores of Barbara's letters since 1934. Only a few stray letters from Barbara survived. Jock, Henry, Elsie and Elsie's mother reached Sweden eventually by driving round the Gulf of Bothnia. Early in March Jock returned to England and Henry went back to work in Finland. Later he was posted to Upsala in Sweden, where he worked for the British Council.

Dangerous and disagreeable as these adventures may have been, they and the news that Julian was now, rather dashingly, in Egypt, made Barbara feel left behind by events. In April 1940 Hilary had been transferred with the BBC to Bristol and soon after that the heavy air raids started. Irena Pym was very worried and had bought Hilary a little car so that she could live more safely outside the city. In spite of all these hazards, Barbara, for the first time, envied Hilary, who had a proper career, financial independence and freedom of movement. She felt frustrated and isolated in a small provincial town, since travel by train was uncomfortable and not encouraged by the government, who demanded on posters Is Your Journey Really Necessary?

30 September. Put in bulbs – hyacinths. Reading a
biography of Caroline of Brunswick. *Band Waggon* [on
the radio]. This is a war diary but this is or seems to
be our life.[10]

One thing, however, did make it all bearable for her. In
between the housework and the shopping and the mending
and knitting balaclava helmets for the forces and making
table mats and tray-cloths from green checked American
cloth to save the laundry, she was writing. Indeed, she was
writing more than ever, having several novels in progress at
the same time.

9 October 1939. Wrote quite a lot more of my Home
Front novel.

22 December 1939. Determined to finish my North
Oxford novel and send it on the rounds.

20 January 1940. Writing notes for my spy novel.[11]

The Home Front novel was unusual for her, in that she was
writing about events as they happened and in the place where
they were happening. This time there was no 'recollection in
tranquillity'. She was simply reporting what life was like in
Oswestry from 1 September onward – blackout, evacuees,
shortages, young men going off to war, the way people's lives
and attitudes changed under totally unusual circumstances.
It was exactly the sort of novel that was being written at that
time by other writers – E. M. Delafield's *The Provincial Lady
in Wartime* and Angela Thirkell's *Cheerfulness Breaks In*. They
all regarded the war from the same viewpoint: comfortable,
middle-class ladies living in villages or small towns and
regarding the startling changes around them with a calm,
ironic eye. It was a genre which, with its acute observation and
careful understatement, Barbara was particularly attracted to
and which had its logical development in *Excellent Women*.
Indeed, the excellence of the women of wartime Britain, with
their stoicism and humour, their courage in adversity and,
above all, their ability to find comfort and pleasure in little
things was something that she appreciated more and more, as

only people who have lived through that period and in those circumstances, will fully understand. It was a quality that an American reviewer recognised many years later, in Barbara's last novel, *A Few Green Leaves*.

It reminds us with some ladylike determination that there'll always be an England of wise spinsters and country retreats, part of the backbone of a bulldog nation known for its inability to admit defeat.[12]

Crampton Hodnet was set in pre-war North Oxford, a territory that had always fascinated Barbara, with its gloomy Gothic houses, elderly eccentrics and Sunday tea parties. It was meant primarily to be a *funny* novel. There was a promising (and familiar) cast of characters: the formidable Miss Doggett (the Miss Moberley figure[13]) and her apparently submissive Companion, who harboured romantic and rebellious thoughts; the rigidly conventional curate; the naïve girl in love with the dashing upper-class undergraduate with political ambitions; the beautiful heroine who wanted Romantic Love (embellished with suitable literary quotations) and there was the difficult and egocentric Man who Only Wanted One Thing and his wife who Understood him only too well, along with a joyful assortment of undergraduates, librarians and clergy. It was a rich mix and one that she obviously enjoyed working with. Henry and Julian appear, but as their surface, comic selves, rather than in darker vein. Just occasionally a more painful, personal note is struck:

Oh no, it wouldn't do at all! Even Miss Morrow's standards were higher than that, so high, indeed, that she feared she would never marry now. . . . For, after all, respect and esteem were cold lifeless things – dry bones picked clean of flesh. There was nothing springlike about dry bones, nothing warm and romantic about respect and esteem.[14]

By the beginning of April 1940 she had made a second version of *Crampton Hodnet* to send to Jock, now back in Oxford. He acknowledged its arrival, on 4 May, with pleasure and with a typical comment.

> I think *Crampton Hodnet* can be a very nice book. Is
> Hodnet named from Hodnet in Shropshire, the seat at
> one time of the Percy family?[15]

Later that month Barbara went to Oxford for a short
visit to see Jock. He gave her a copy of his new novel
The Gantillons which she read travelling uncomfortably home
in the blacked-out train and sitting over a cup of tea in
the refreshment room at Snow Hill station in Birmingham
('stained glass windows in a tree design') where she had to
change trains. Inspired by Jock's success, she got out the
manuscript of *Some Tame Gazelle*, which she now found 'crude
and too full of obscure literary allusions'. This version was, like
so many first novels, crammed with too many things that she
'wanted to get in'. As well as all the Oxford people living in
an English village, she had also introduced a Finnish girl and
many German references. It was, in fact, too full of 'in' jokes.
She sent it to Jock who saw the essential strength of the book
and gave her much encouragement together with some very
practical advice.

> I love *Some Tame Gazelle* and beg you to send it
> to Curtis Brown. Surely it is 'a clear and vital thing'
> as well as being an anthology in itself. I think you
> could remove quotations that are not sufficiently self-
> explanatory and perhaps some of the more local Bodleian
> references. . . . The plot doesn't seem too thin to me. But
> the Finnish girl could go – unless you like to graft more
> Finnish local colour on. And the German part is better
> away.[16]

He added the information that '86b Banbury Road is let to
Violet Powell and then to three young ladies, friends of Lord
Derby.'[17]

She did send it to Curtis Brown, in May 1940, but with no
success, and so she put it to one side again and, in between
knitting stockings for the soldiers manning the barrage
balloons, she resolutely got on with something else. Her spy
novel, tentatively entitled *So Very Secret* was, like the Home
Front novel, set in wartime Oswestry, with brief excursions
to Oxford and London. It had considerable potential. The

heroine, Cassandra Swan, is a gentlewoman, the daughter of a canon, in her middle forties, whose friend Harriet (Barbara was always economical with the names of her characters) was involved in secret work for the Foreign Office. When Harriet mysteriously disappears, Cassandra sets out to find her, able to move unobtrusively through North Oxford tea parties, First Aid classes and ARP posts in quest of her friend, and managing to hang on to The Papers although pursued by a formidable spy network. There was a typical Pym cast of characters – excellent women, umbrage-taking dressmakers, female dons, formidable elderly gentlewomen, eccentric clergymen and a dashing young Balliol man. Only the spies don't ring true, being the only two-dimensional characters, for she had never actually met a spy.

> It is getting rather involved and I don't quite know what I'm driving at – that's the worst of a plot.[18]

This literary activity had to be squeezed into a life very much dominated by domestic chores. Admittedly all the evacuees had gone by Christmas 1939, but soon the pace of the war accelerated and there was much to be done, even in a 'safe area' like Oswestry. Barbara's diary records a terrible, cumulative list of disasters, counterpointed by her comments on everyday events.

> *21 May 1940.* Grave news from France. The Germans have got Arras and Amiens, but a heartening talk from Mr Duff Cooper cheered us. Four kittens.

> *29 May.* Desperate fighting on Western Front. Dor went to LDV [Local Defence Volunteers] meeting.

> *31 May.* A good part of BEF is safely evacuated from Flanders.

> *3 June.* Paris bombed. Mr Duff Cooper gave a good talk from there – so calm and splendid.

> *10 June.* It rained and thundered after tea and at 6 we knew that Mussolini had declared war on us. Poor Italy!

14 June. Fine strawberries from the garden. The Germans are in Paris. A Brandenburg Concerto from Wien.

17 June. Today at 1 p.m. we heard that France had given up. But honestly the news didn't make me afraid.

20 June. Still no news of the [French] peace terms. The country is lovely, honeysuckle in the hedges. *How dare* the Nazis think they could invade it![19]

In her diary Barbara was echoing the general sense of resolution and determination felt throughout the country for, although the situation might have been thought to be desperate, there was an air of calm practicality as people got on with doing what they could, in however small a way, to repel a possible invasion. Rationing became more stringent and everyone was issued with an identity card. Frederic Pym joined the LDV [later to become the Home Guard] an auxiliary force of those too old, too young or too unfit to join the regular services. Barbara joined the ARP and helped to man a First Aid post set up to deal with casualties from the air raids that everyone knew would start very soon. Oswestry was unlikely to be the target of the German bombers, but they passed over on their way to Liverpool or Wales (and sometimes jettisoned a stray bomb on the surrounding countryside on their way home) and so on most nights the sirens went and Barbara had to go on duty.

I was sitting by the fire writing a little Edwardian bit in my [spy] novel when the siren went about 6.20. I got my things and rushed to the hospital where a great crowd of ARP workers turned up and we had a jolly night with cups of tea and some sleep on the floor. The All Clear went about 4.30. The next night the siren went soon after 8 and the All Clear at 5 a.m. It seemed as if we had never left this place – the Surrealists have nothing on us for odd situations! Listening to aeroplanes and later looking for them among the stars. And later still sitting on the stairs hearing the thud of bombs falling in Wrexham direction. Slept a little. Tired on Friday but had a good night's rest though they were over again.[20]

As well as working with the ARP, Barbara helped out at the Food Office ('I stamped 700 ration cards three times each. Aching in every limb!') and at the children's clinic at the hospital.

Went to the Clinic. I am gradually learning to pick up a baby with a nonchalant air. Was shown a suspected grown-together fracture in a baby's leg and a swollen ankle.[21]

She was also asked to help at the canteen at the Army Camp which had been set up on the outskirts of the town. So she made herself a checked gingham overall and bicycled up to Parkhall to serve food, wash up and ruin her Pink Clover nail varnish working a recalcitrant cash register. The canteen was really quite hard work, on top of everything else.

The cakes came late and there was a great scrum .... Busy poaching eggs in little machines.... Very busy at Parkhall and nearly losing my reason. Still no chocolates or cigarettes.[22]

And there were plenty of Pym situations:

General air of *umbrage* among the staff.[23]

But it was fun as well – she had many admirers among the soldiers. ('A Scotsman called me "a wee smasher" but what he meant is rather obscure') and, susceptible as ever, she found many attractive new faces.

There is a beautiful Pre-Raphaelite L/Bdr [Lance-Bombardier]! I was smiling to myself all morning as I thought of this.

At the camp Desmond, all violet brilliantine, rode my bicycle round the field. He took my magenta chiffon scarf and put his identity disc in its place. And now I wear it. Very busy evening and they were all singing 'When I grow too old to dream'.[24]

More seriously, there was a young Scottish gunner called
Stewart for whose sake, typically, she tried to learn Gaelic.

> I was able to get back for a walk with Stewart.
> We had tea at the Coach and Dogs then went to the
> pictures and afterwards learnt some more Gaelic. *Mo
> run feal dileas*. . . . At about 6 Stewart came and we went
> to the pictures. I thoroughly enjoyed it, holding hands,
> eating ice cream and being generally childish. . . . Went
> out to tea with Stewart. We had from 5–6 together, which
> was nice if rather melancholy. I think I really will miss
> him. . . . A beautiful sunny day at Parkhall with so many
> gone. The Flowers of the Forest are a' wede away.[25]

Little flirtations like this helped to lighten a drab existence
and wartime life went on – learning about poison gas ('Went
into the tear-gas van – the snouted figures. Got my badge'),
practising wearing her gas mask while making the beds, the
endless task of renewing blackout curtains, queuing for small
luxuries and helping with National Savings and War Weapons
Weeks. In June 1941 clothes were rationed, so more time had
to be spent on refurbishing and adapting clothes for herself and
her mother ('altering dresses of 1937–1938'). Always interested
in food ('Links managed to get a 7lb jar of marmalade – such
are the joys of going without. Not even love is so passionately
longed for'[26]), she lovingly recorded many meals:

> Had a fine supper – eggs, beans, cheese and new mar-
> malade. . . . Curried eggs for supper which are luxuries
> in times like these. . . . Had a marvellous supper of fried
> eggs and potatoes and felt really *full*. . . . Went to tea at
> Garth Derwen [her aunt's house just outside Oswestry].
> Lovely food – tomato sandwiches, blackberry jam – scones
> and bread – swiss roll and chocolate cake.[27]

The food situation was, of course, much easier in a small
town like Oswestry, where it was possible to find a little extra
meat and a few more eggs in the surrounding countryside,
and, like everywhere else, the lawns and herbaceous borders
of Morda Lodge had been dug up to provide vegetables and
soft fruit to eke out and enliven the rations.

There is Plenty of Everything Here. It is always better
in the country anyway. Mrs Pym says she will take her
sugar ration with her when she goes out to tea or evening
bridge, but Mr Pym ridicules the idea. 'One should be able
to get a special container for it,' she says.[28]

Life in wartime Oswestry could be tiring and boring,
but, unlike life in the cities, it was not actually dangerous:

A lovely letter from Rosemary [Topping] telling me
how she was buried in the ruins of her flat. Now one
has heroes and heroines for friends who before were
just ordinary people.[29]

Barbara was now twenty-eight and beginning to be restless.

Busy in the house and wondering (as I sometimes do)
whether I ought not to be doing other things – leading
a fuller life as one might say. But that passes.[30]

Hilary, now working for the BBC Schools Department,
came home occasionally for weekends.

Poopa arrived about 7.30 in her car. She does have
fun. I was frankly envious of her life this evening.[31]

Morda Lodge had become too large, too inconvenient
and too expensive and so Frederic Pym bought Blytheswood,
a smaller house nearer to the centre of the town. With some
of the domestic strain removed from her mother, Barbara's
thoughts turned again to a job away from Oswestry.

I was altogether in a restless and unenviable state
today wondering whether I ought not to be in some
job or one of the services for my own sake as well as for
patriotic reasons. It's awful to think I've only been here
and Pwllheli [the family had taken a few weeks' holiday
there in July] for over a year now.[32]

But at the end of 1941 matters were taken out of her
hands. All unmarried women and childless widows aged

nineteen to thirty were required to register for war work. The Ministry of Labour sent her details of a job in the Censorship Department (German Division) which she thought might suit her very well. When the application forms arrived she started brushing up her German by reading through her old letters from Friedbert.

> After tea translating a letter from F., one of the last I had and painful to me. One feels one ought to be ashamed of ever having been fond of a German.[33]

She went up to London for an interview and returned to Oswestry to help with the move to Blytheswood:

> A most exhausting but enjoyable day, moving still and putting up blackout. In the middle of it all came a wire from the Censorship offering me a job in Bristol starting *Monday next*. I accepted – it will be lovely to be with Poopa.[34]

These years in Oswestry were important to Barbara, since they formed a bridge between the lively frivolity of her Oxford days and the more varied experiences of her life in the later years of the war. She had come through her obsession with Henry:

> Found myself looking at old letter from Henry. Respect and esteem – perhaps the same for me now.[35]

and Julian was a sentimental memory enshrined among 'relics' in an old walnut box with a black and yellow inlay:

> People who are not sentimental, who never keep relics, brood on anniversaries, kiss photographs goodnight and good morning, must miss a good deal. Of course it is all rather self-conscious and cultivated, but it comes so easily that at least a little of it must spring from the heart.[36]

She had written them out of her system and although she would use both of them again in later novels, she was free of them and ready to pass on to the next experience.

She had completed 195 pages of the Home Front novel as well as finishing *Crampton Hodnet* and the first draft of her spy story – quite an achievement considering the distractions all around her – and it had proved to her that writing was the most important thing in her life.

> After supper I did some more writing which quells my restlessness – that is how I must succeed!
> Women are different from men in that they have so many small domestic things with which to occupy themselves. . . . I think I could spend my whole day doing such things, with just a little time for reading, and be quite happy. But it isn't *really* enough, soon I shall be discontented with myself, out will come the novel and after I've written a few pages I shall feel on top of the world again.[37]

This return to the scenes of her childhood gave her the opportunity, however unconsciously, to consolidate her attitudes and to immerse herself once more in the sort of life that provided a background for many of her heroines, even if they, like their creator, left it to pass out into the wider world. 'I seem to have decided already,' she wrote in 1940, 'the sort of novels I want to write.'[38] In Oswestry, in her late twenties, in the uncertain days of war, she acquired a grasp of the fundamentals of an ethos – practical, moral, almost stoical, yet with a kind of cheerful irony – that would sustain her (and most of her heroines) through many vicissitudes.

Chapter Nine

Barbara joined Hilary in Bristol at The Coppice, a large house in Leigh Woods on the hill above Clifton Suspension Bridge.

> We share with two families, who work with Hilary, and there are altogether six children so we know all about communal living, though the house is big enough for us to have our own sitting room and to keep ourselves to ourselves if we want to.[1]

The two families consisted of Dick and Mary Palmer, with their three children, and Honor Wyatt (she retained her maiden name professionally) and her two children, Julian and Prue. Honor had separated from her husband, the writer and broadcaster C. Gordon Glover, when she got her job with the BBC Schools Department and moved to Bristol. He was based in London and worked on the *Radio Times*, though he was actually living in Arkesden in Essex. It was a reasonably amicable separation. They had both found other attachments – Gordon with Anna Instone, who also worked at the BBC, and Honor with the writer George Ellidge, who was at that time abroad in the Army. Gordon used to visit Bristol to see the children and in her diary entry for Christmas Eve 1941 Barbara simply notes, 'Gordon Glover came.' He was there for Christmas and they all went to the BBC Club for drinks, walking back over the suspension bridge, 'lovely in the moonlight'.

Barbara found him very attractive and they shared many tastes and interests and silly jokes. In October 1942 she began a letter to Henry and wrote:

I have a great friend . . . who reminds me very much
of you in many ways. He is a journalist, very amusing,
a great philanderer, but very sweet and kind, and as I
haven't fallen in love with him I see only his best side.
So strange being reminded of you – I didn't think anyone
could ever do that. (He wouldn't say 'Otway is remarkably
fine' though.)[2]

But by the time she came to finish off the letter in November,
things had become much more serious – for her, at least.

I seem to be embarked on a kind of love affair, not
exactly of my choosing, it just seemed to happen very
unexpectedly and well, it is all very nice so far.[3]

Gordon was a delightful companion, rather like Henry in
looks – one can see why Barbara was immediately attracted
to him – though softer, less sardonic and more conventionally
good looking. He had a beautiful speaking voice (Barbara was
always very susceptible to voices) and great charm. He and
Honor had known each other since their very early youth and
she was still attached to him, in spite of his many infidelities,
and, indeed, remained so until his death some years later. He
had a splendid way with words and quotations that matched
Barbara's own and he wore his knowledge of literature and
music lightly, as Jock and Henry had done. After the years
in Oswestry, where there had been no one who could cap
a quotation or make an esoteric joke, he must have seemed
entrancing.

Secure in the knowledge that Honor was now deeply in
love with George, Barbara felt free to fall in love with Gordon
without feeling in any way disloyal to Honor, with whom
she had, almost from the start, formed a loving friendship.
She was particularly glad to have these new people in her
life at this time because in August 1942 Hilary had married.
Her husband, Sandy Walton, was three years older than she
was and had read architecture at Cambridge. He had done an
architectural survey in Greece several years before and shared
Hilary's passion for that country. They planned to live there
after the war, to which end they corresponded with each
other in modern Greek. Barbara wrote of him to Henry:

> Strangely enough he reminds me in some ways of
> Jock – he is fair and tallish and very musical – he
> has set some of Betjeman's *Continual Dew* poems to
> music![4]

Barbara was the only bridesmaid, wearing a crushed-
strawberry pink crepe dress and a black halo hat (Hilary
was in a blue crepe dress and coat). Hilary remained with the
BBC in Bristol, because Sandy was in the Air Force, but, since
he was still stationed in England, near Oxford, she naturally
spent all her free time with him and they acquired a cottage
at Compton in Berkshire.

Honor was slightly older than Barbara and certainly very
much more mature. She must have known that Gordon's
infatuation with Barbara would last no longer than other
such love affairs had done and that Barbara would be very
hurt indeed. When the inevitable break came she was there
to pick up the pieces. Surprisingly Barbara's other confidant
was Henry.

> Did I tell you that I was in love and that it was
> all hopeless? We parted at Christmas and haven't seen
> or written to each other since then – a really dramatic
> Victorian renunciation – the sort of thing I adore in
> novels, but find extremely painful in real life. Of course
> we may come together again in the future . . . but in the
> meantime he thought it better I should try and find
> somebody else who can marry me, which he won't be
> able to for at least a year – we neither of us wanted
> any other kind of relationship so a complete break was
> the only thing.[5]

She obviously realised how empty and pathetic that sounded
and went on stoutly:

> Luckily we both are rather comic people so it isn't as bad
> as it sounds. It has been hell being away from him, as he
> understands so well and we had all the same ridiculous
> jokes and things together. I haven't told Jock – I don't
> know if you did and I'd rather not if you haven't as he
> wouldn't sympathise – probably you won't either – but

I believe you do know something of these things, even if you have never been in a similar situation. My parents didn't know either – though everyone here did of course. I am quite resigned to it now and can even visualise the possibility of marrying a dashing naval officer – what – at nearly thirty, with lisle stockings and patched underwear?[6]

When the Glovers' divorce was heard in October:

My first feeling was one of elation. . . . But now of course I'm sobered down. There is really no cause for rejoicing as far as I'm concerned. . . .
I've really faced up to the fact that Gordon doesn't really love me as I love him and will never ask me to marry him when he's free. He told Honor a week or two back that he didn't intend to make any more 'experiments' . . . and that, according to Pen Lloyd James, he regarded it as a pleasant sentimental episode which was now closed. He must have said that as long ago as the winter. So now what becomes of my illusion that this was a great renunciation and that he had ever for a moment wanted the same things as I do? Well, the illusion is dead or dying. . . . I still love him of course and in the months (or years!) that follow I shall no doubt ache for him sometimes – sweet, hopeless person, the most delightful companion.[7]

Once again she had made the mistake of expecting more than the other person was prepared to give, of building a great romantic castle on shifting sand. What she did retain from it was a certain stoicism and a sentence from Logan Pearsall Smith's *Trivia*:

So I never lose a sense of the whimsical and perilous charm of daily life, with its meetings and words and accidents.

This thought, more broadly applied, was to remain with her for the rest of her life, giving her pleasure and interest in the minutiae of daily life, its opportunities, eccentricities and its small comforts.

Since she had been in Bristol she had done no more writing. In a letter to Henry she says:

> I'm afraid I haven't written anything for ages, though I fully intend to when I have time. And I expect it will be better than any of my early work. How pretentious that sounds![8]

She did, however, throughout 1943, fill two notebooks which she entitled 'After Christmas I' and 'After Christmas II', since they dealt with the time after she and Gordon parted (on 28 December) in 1942. The two volumes are diaries, but very consciously written, as if for a reader. The style is more complex than the exuberant (or desolate) outpourings of her Oxford journals, not a spontaneous overflow of powerful emotions, but, mostly, carefully considered descriptions of places and incidents and analyses of feelings. The tone is usually one of settled melancholy – often self-indulgent, like weeping at the Mendelssohn Violin Concerto or 'the old B Minor Tchaikovsky'.

> A bad day. Beware of complacency, and you must fight all the time and have the same struggles. Tears on top of the bus going to Avonmouth, up into Sea Mills . . . and Johnny Doughboy in the park. And at lunchtime when I was alone, I *howled*.
> I went into the Public Library. It is open till seven and was now full of ruins of humanity, come into the reading room for learning. And on my blotting paper I write 'A Testing Time' in Red Pencil – to remind me.
> I thought, the greatest luxury now would be to be allowed to write a great, long, silly letter to Gordon. As it is I suppose I must go on drearily in this book. My clever book. I seem to write in it only when I'm depressed, like praying only when one is really in despair.[9]

By now she was watching herself being miserable and that was some comfort. She dwelt also upon Romantic and Gothic things, for which she had always had a predilection – a neglected churchyard, a beautiful Pre-Raphaelite tomb.

I often pass the Pre-Raphaelite tomb, or rather the path leading to it, but I have never been there again. But I will go one day. You (reader) may say, Why do you make such a thing of it all? To which I will snap (like *Trivia*) Well, what about your own life? Is it so full of large, big wonderful things that you don't need tombs and daffodils and your own special intolerable bird, with an old armchair or two, and occasional readings from Matthew Arnold and Coventry Patmore?[10]

As well as tombs and Coventry Patmore she had Honor, who was deeply sorry for Barbara and sometimes indulged her passionate wish to talk endlessly about Gordon ('Really we have discussed Gordon so much that one would hardly think that there was anything left to love'[11]) and was sometimes more bracing ('She thinks I ought to have a really good affaire. I quite agree, but OH DEAR.'[12]). They spent a lot of their spare time together, cooking, shopping, taking Honor's children to the seaside for the day, listening to music, laughing together as they Baldwinned [defuzzed] their legs or did the 'Up In The Morning Early' exercises with which the BBC endeavoured to improve the health, fitness and morale of the nation. In June

Honor told me about a communication in which Gordon has apparently demanded the big armchair in the sitting room.... Oh, my darling – can my love stand this.... Could it be because of an armchair that I first began to fall out of love with you! But of course one doesn't fall – it's a slow wrenching away, painful at once, afterwards just sad and dreary.[13]

The memory remained with her and there is quite a lot of Gordon in Rocky [*EW*] – the charm and the casualness. Years later, in one of her notebooks, Barbara equated him with Fabian [*J&P*]:

A Gordonish character. His wife, to whom he has been consistently unfaithful, died – his outraged surprise and confusion of sentimental symbols.[14]

'

and:

> The disillusion of finding out that something else (say
> *Trivia*) has been his thing with someone else.[15]

But Gordon had none of the vulgarity which Robert Liddell
so rightly finds in Fabian and was intellectually far above him
– though perhaps Gordon's was a slightly showy, dilettante
kind of culture. When she was able to look back on the
affair, Barbara described him in a short poem as 'Successful,
Byronic, rather second rate'.

Their affair only lasted for two months, but it had a very deep
effect on Barbara – not just the dwelling on unhappiness for
a time, but, in the long run, a diminishing of her confidence.
Even before she became involved with Gordon, she had noted
in herself 'a little less joyousness and hope', and she quoted
some lines from Matthew Arnold, always one of her favourite
poets:

> The foot less prompt to meet the morning dew,
> The heart less bounding at emotion new,
> And hope, once crush'd, less quick to spring again.

And now, here was another failure. A disastrous love affair
is always difficult to cope with, but for a woman of thirty
it is particularly painful. Before the war, most women of her
age and class would have been either married, with children,
or resigned (or resentful) spinsters living with ageing parents
at home or settled in a career. Even in wartime, women's
expectations were not greatly changed. Barbara felt, in some
way, that it was the end of her youth – never, in fact, 'glad
confident morning again'. Perhaps it would not be too fanciful
to say that she had at last grown from her Marianne phase
(flinging herself into emotional situations that ended in floods
of tears) into that of the more thoughtful and ironic Elinor. The
Barbara who took Yeastvite as a cure for love would certainly
have come to appreciate the healing effects of Mr Jennings'
fine Constantia wine.

Still, to set against all this, was the fact that she was
leading an entirely new kind of life, with all the interest

that novelty can bring. For the very first time she was living out in the world, away from the intellectual cocoon of Oxford or the comfort and security of her home. Simply to be earning her own living at last was quite exhilarating. Fortunately Bristol was having a lull in the terrible bombing that it had faced and would face again. There was a great deal of damage, getting about was often difficult and life was full of small austerities. Like the others, she found it tiring to do a full day's work, often with little sleep at night when she was firewatching ('sitting in this uncosy high-roofed room with no sound but the ticking of my common little alarm clock and the click of my companion's knitting needles'[16]), and to be faced with domestic chores in the evening – really no time for proper writing, only the indulgence of a diary. Though, influenced (as she always was by her latest love) by a couple of plays that Gordon Glover had had produced on radio, she did start to plot out a play of her own. It never actually got written, but it occupied her mind and kept her creative spirit in trim.

Barbara took to office life with great pleasure, finding it, as she always would, a marvellously rich mix of incidents, comic or pathetic, of eccentricities and incongruities, and, of course, umbrage. As an Examiner, as they were called, she did not, as it happened, need her German, since the Bristol censorship office mostly dealt with letters to and from the Republic of Ireland, a neutral country, a great many of whose citizens were living in Great Britain.

The Censorship for which, very fortunately, no high qualifications appeared to be necessary, apart from patience, discretion and a slight tendency towards eccentricity.[17]

Elderly women are flocking into Government offices and becoming 'Temporary Civil Servants'. Our new recruits get older and older. And more and more peculiar. The other day one of them came into the room wearing a turban and carrying an umbrella. Well Miss Pym and what about yourself? Were you not seen only yesterday, wearing fur-lined boots in May wrapped in a rug and your head tied up in a scarf?[18]

There were still conventions about dress and an English gentlewoman would have felt uneasy wearing trousers, for example, or going without stockings.

> When I got back to the Academy [where the censorship office was housed] the first thing I saw was a new examiner sitting at a table, wearing earrings, gaiters and a hat. By teatime she had removed the hat, as if (somebody said) she had really decided to stay.
> I am afraid one of our elderly censors will think me not such a beautiful natured girl after all. This afternoon I was washing, or waiting to wash my hands when I said, 'I wish people wouldn't clutter up this basin with flowers.' And of course they were hers and, worse, she was taking them to an *invalid*.[19]

This and other incidents were stored away until she was ready, years later, to use them in her novels.

She found the work interesting 'though the secrecy is rather annoying as I can't talk about it or share jokes with any except my colleagues'.[20] Sharing jokes about her work was always important to Barbara. Fortunately she did find a sympathetic colleague in the censorship. Her name was Margaret Bryan and she was also a university graduate. She was a tall, rather formidable woman, slightly older than Barbara, brisk and cheerful, with a lively and sarcastic turn of phrase. Years later Barbara would work with her again, in very different circumstances, and give her a kind of immortality.

As well as her work there were small pleasures: buying material to make a new nightdress, reading (Charlotte M. Yonge – 'so well-written, very Compton-Burnett' – Robert Graves, Saroyan, Chekhov – 'so very like the Coppice' – and a life of Cardinal Newman), listening to the radio (music, a play by Louis MacNeice, a programme by Stephen Potter, *ITMA*, and *The Armchair Detective*) and occasionally visiting friends.

She went up to London to stay with Rupert Gleadow (Barbara nearly always kept in touch with her old loves) and his second wife, Helen, in Chelsea.

> I rang a likely bell and in a minute the door was opened – 'Are you Helen?' – 'You must be Barbara.' I've

done this before, in the summer of 1938 when I met Elsie for the first time in 86 Banbury Road.[21]

As with Elsie (and of course with Honor) Barbara liked Helen and got on well with her. It was a pleasant little interlude out of time and away from the war.

> I really feel it did me good going away and being with Rupert and Helen, who are so blissfully happy together they hardly seem to be real. Oh but it *can* be done![22]

But her true solace was Honor. Not only was she prepared to listen patiently to Barbara endlessly analysing her relationship with Gordon (which must sometimes have been painful, even though she was no longer in love with him), to 'discuss the technique of misery' and even to make them both bowls of nice comforting groats (easier to come by in wartime than the classic hot, milky drink). She was also a splendid companion in her own right. She had a similar sense of humour and (even more important) a sense of fun, she was intelligent and well-read and had the added advantage of being a writer herself – a journalist and writer of radio programmes – and a friend of other, very distinguished writers, such as Robert Graves. Barbara realised that she was very fortunate to have her as a friend. She became deeply devoted to Honor, agonising over her separation from George Ellidge almost as vehemently as she agonised for herself.

> It is the one thing I want at the moment – that she should have a letter [from George]! It's so awful not being able to comfort a person you love – all I could do was vain words, half a bottle of Drene [shampoo] and a large sheet of blotting paper I got from the office. . . . After tea I did some washing for Honor – this dreary spinster pounced on it joyously – here at last was something![23]

Life at The Coppice proceeded on its Chekhovian way. Barbara felt that she needed to break away from its ups and downs and the constant reminders of her unhappiness, and so she decided to join the WRNS. She was also influenced by the fact that censorship examiners under forty-one years of age would soon be liable for call-up.

She would not necessarily have been conscripted into one of the women's services. Certainly the WRNS always had enough volunteers and the ATS and WAAF only needed to call up women from nineteen to twenty-five to keep up to strength. Had Barbara waited to be called up, she would probably have been directed to work in a factory and she felt that service life would be infinitely preferable. It was a big step, though, and she realised this ('I've never before felt so conscious of "making a life for myself" – I suppose the continuous effort is good for me'[24]). Again, like many other women of her age and class, she had reached the age of thirty without ever having had to organise her life or make important decisions that would affect it.

Having made her application and had her first interview and medical, she was impatient to hear if the WRNS would take her – it was the one thing she longed to do ('Oh I do hope I get it now. My heart is set on it!'). On 31 May she had her Selection Board at WRNS Headquarters in London and then another more hopeful interview in June, when it seemed that her experience in the Bristol censorship office would stand her in good stead, and she might be able to join the WRNS as a censor.

> Apparently I must serve three months in the ranks and after that I am pretty sure of my commission.
>   Well it came this morning. And when it does come, it's like Love – make no mistake about it, you *know*. A long envelope with a railway warrant, Bristol to Rochester (Single, this time there is No Return).[25]

She said goodbye to her colleagues at the censorship office, who gave her an expensive box of talcum powder as a going-away present ('Well at least I have got on with people and made friends – that's something'), had a few days at home in Oswestry and a sentimental Final Day at The Coppice. On 7 July she gave into Honor's keeping the first volume of her 'After Christmas' diary and Gordon's letters and rode down to the station with her.

Honor held my hand tight in the taxi and she was
crying too. She and Prue and Julian came with me
some of the way. As she said, she and I were the worst
possible people to be left together at the end![26]

Just before four o'clock Barbara arrived at the Nore Training
Depot at Rochester and began her life as a pro-Wren.

Chapter Ten

The Nore Training Depot was quartered in a large house that looked like a North Oxford Victorian Gothic theological college, which Barbara found somehow cheering. Also comforting was the fact that she was to share a room (or 'cabin', because naval terminology prevailed throughout) with

> a girl of 19, my own class and quite nice. She has a long rather melancholy face and I can see her when she is older as an English gentlewoman – one of her names is Mildred.[1]

Barbara was part of a new intake of about fifty pro-Wrens, so-called because they were literally on probation to see if they were suitable for the service. The WRNS was the most fashionable of the women's services – partly because of the aura of glamour which always seems to attach to the Navy, and partly, it was said, because the uniform was the most becoming. Certainly it attracted the most volunteers.

Barbara was much older than most of the new recruits, who were in their late teens and early twenties, and she didn't have much hope of finding any really congenial companions among them.

> I don't think there are really any of our kind of people, though there are one or two pleasant ones.[2]

By 'our kind of people' she meant intellectually and culturally (on the same wavelength, as she used to say), since this, rather than any social difference, was what was really important to her. For the first time in her life, like so many women at that time, she had to live with a real cross-section of people – out in the world with a vengeance. Fortunately she was used to other kinds of communal living. Boarding school was no bad preparation for service life in wartime. Not only were you used to living in close proximity to a lot of other people, but you were also used to discipline and petty and apparently meaningless restrictions, as well as to minor physical discomforts. The food on that first evening was reassuringly like school food – toad-in-the-hole and bread and jam.

Barbara's trade at the Nore was a 'writer' (i.e. a clerk) and she was a 'white paper entry', which meant that she was considered to be officer material. Writers were given various lists of ranks and commands and naval abbreviations to learn and there were lectures on pay and allowances, hygiene ('everything but everything!') and fire fighting. They had a test ('I got the rates of pay right purely by luck') and had to write an essay on Life in the Nore Command – just like being back at school again. There was also squad drill.

> We learnt how to stand at attention and ease etc. and also saluting which is more difficult than it looks. . . . I had a slight feeling of desolation . . . thinking but what am *I* doing here and why on earth am I standing out on the grass drilling with this curious crowd of women?[3]

There were also four-mile route marches, enlivened for Barbara by passing 'a remarkably fine cemetery on a hill' or 'a very nice eighteenth-century church'. Her spare time was spent either lying on her bunk (bed) reading (Graham Greene and a life of Cardinal Newman) or in the fo'c'sle (the communal recreation room) where the radio was usually tuned to the forces programme – *Happidrome*, Sandy Macpherson at the Organ or *Memories of Musical Comedy* and no hope of being able to switch over to hear Marlowe's *Edward II*. Sometimes she was lucky enough to find the fo'c'sle empty and then

> I have heard the whole of Liszt's Piano Concerto . . . and am halfway through *Hary Janos*, though a group of stewards have come in and suggested we should have Jack Leon [a dance band].

> I feel apologetic for Kodaly when he makes a specially peculiar noise! And one eyes anyone who comes near the wireless with suspicion.[4]

Off duty, she went out with some of the other WRNS – to the forces canteen at the YMCA (where she found it amusing to be on the other side of the counter) and to the cinema. More often she wandered about by herself, to the museum, to a bookshop (where she bought a copy of *Tristram Shandy*) and to the Cathedral and the Close, discovering

> a nice little old teashop (perhaps run by a widow of one of the Canons – or sister of the late Dean) – Also a nice set of tombstones and a well-kept churchyard belonging to the Cathedral. . . . And for about half an hour I was my old gothick self.[5]

Church services were another point of contact with her old life. There were Divisions each morning (like school prayers) and once she went to the Cathedral to hear the Archbishop of Canterbury preach – and spent most of the service admiring the wall urns – including one to a favourite poet, Henry King. One Sunday she had a Day of Religions, starting off with the usual Sunday service in the Mess ('I got nothing from it'), then Evensong in the Cathedral with a dry theological sermon about original sin.

> What can one get from this but peace and the pleasure of music and the loftiness of the Cathedral? You couldn't expect anyone to come in and be inspired or even very much comforted – at the best soothed a little. Or even damped down and saddened as I was. Age and dry bones.[6]

But finally, in the recreation room at the YMCA canteen, two young clergymen held an impromptu service with people choosing hymns:

> I could only think of 'Lead Kindly Light' [Cardinal Newman again] and the one about keep our loved ones now far distant 'neath thy care. Anyway it was all very nice.[7]

She had plunged into the WRNS, in a way, as she had plunged into other things, not really knowing what it was going to be like, and at first her life was too busy for much thought of any kind, gloomy or otherwise. Only gradually did she begin to realise what she had let herself in for. In a letter to Honor she told her:

> How one feels – first of all not oneself at all, then gradually more oneself, until one day you wonder what on earth you are doing here – *you*.[8]

'But,' she goes on, 'it's not too bad', and on 19 July she was enrolled and became a proper Wren. Up till then they had worn their civilian clothes so there was the excitement of being kitted out.

> My hat is lovely, every bit as fetching as I'd hoped, but my suit rather large, though it's easier to alter that way.[9]

She was drafted to a holding depot at Westcliff-on-Sea, on the coast near Southend, where she shared a room with another girl, Beatrice Pizzey, in what had been a boarding house on the sea front.

Westcliff was much more Proper Navy. There were no clocks; instead, the day was divided into watches by various bugles, bells and bosun's pipes, from first bugle at 6.30 a.m. to Pipe Down (lights out) at 10 p.m. The work was harder too and much more menial. Barbara scrubbed out a lot of rooms, cleaned windows and bathrooms and dusted and swept.

> It amuses me to pay exaggerated respect to very young sub-lieutenants and even midshipmen, flattening myself and my broom against the wall as they pass, less than the dust indeed.[10]

After about ten days it was discovered that she was a 'white paper entry' and so she was given a job in the Regulating Office, which meant taking on a lot more responsibility. Sometimes she managed quite well:

Had to march a squad of pro-Wrens back – managed quite successfully. What will I turn into at this rate?[11]

Sometimes it wasn't so good. At roll-call and drill

I couldn't swing my arms properly so Third Officer Honey had to move me. Gradually people will begin to discover what a fake I am – how phoney is my Wrennish façade. . . . I am going to try hard to be really efficient – it doesn't come naturally to me, no use pretending it does, but it will be good for me to learn to be.[12]

Wrens were sometimes taken out to do clerical jobs actually on board some of the ships lying off Southend, which was interesting but involved climbing up precarious rope ladders. Life at Westcliff was very busy. Since it was a holding depot there was a constant coming and going of naval personnel, with all the checking in and out and revictualling that that involved.

Busy and weary in the evenings. Not busy with doing things entirely, but with wondering if I've forgotten things and coping with people. And yet it doesn't really worry me – and I'm not frightened of anyone. It has given me confidence – and I feel I can do something I thought I couldn't before.[13]

She was gaining confidence in other ways. She went to a Wardroom dance and found it enjoyable – it would have been even better, she decided, if she had had 'someone nice (and tall) to dance with'. She and other Wrens went out in groups with some of the sailors and marines who were stationed at HMS Westcliff and occasionally she went out to dinner and to the cinema with a nice Petty Officer.

Sometimes, when she was really gloomy, she felt that she was living in a cultural desert.

It occurred to me why the Army is more cultured than the Navy. The former is composed of conscripts as well as volunteers, the latter of volunteers only. And what person of culture and refinement would choose to enter the services of their own free will?! Only a broken heart or the desire for an *Erlebnis* could make one do such a thing![14]

Nevertheless, she was finding more kindred spirits among her fellow Wrens and went to concerts with them and was able to talk once more about books and music. She pinned postcards above her bunk: Braque, two Turners and Renoir's 'Boulevard in Fruhling'. She read Virginia Woolf's *The Common Reader* and *A Room of One's Own* and wondered what *she* would have made of the WRNS. She also started a course of evening classes in German at Southend Municipal College.

A crowd of spinsters, spectacled young men, nondescripts, Forces men and women. . . . It was all like an early H. G. Wells novel – *Kipps* or *Love and Mr Lewisham*. Surely there ought to have been a beautiful young woman teaching wood-carving?[15]

Occasionally she went up to London for the day and once she had dinner at the Berkeley Buttery, with some friends from the Bristol censorship office ('cocktails and baby chicken – and *oh* I enjoyed it all so'). One time she went up for a concert and then, as so many of the characters in her novels have done, went into a Lyons' Corner House for tea. She got into conversation with a young man ('dark and very good looking, reminded me of Friedbert') who said that one needn't ever feel lonely in a Lyons'

which was a new aspect of it to me, as I've always thought of it as the sort of place where one was essentially lonely, especially with all the crowds and music . . . [16]

Honor wrote frequently, as did Hilary and her mother, who sent her a drawing from the *Tatler* of Captain Julian Amery, which made her heart turn over.

She spent her leaves either in Oswestry, where she wallowed in the luxury of hot baths and soft beds and civilian clothes ('changed into a red dress with unwrenlike red bows in my hair'), or at The Coppice. There she let the warm, loving atmosphere wash over her and wallowed, in a different kind of way, in memories of Gordon and their time together. She tore up his letters, but kept her 'After Christmas Diary'.

Sometimes she wrote a poem or thought about her possible radio play or a story.

> Thought of a story about Southend – meetings in Wien, Bristol, Oxford, the Balkans and anywhere else – you see the idea.[17]

It wasn't that she had no time for her writing; indeed, she often found time lying heavy on her hands, but rather that there was so little privacy. Anything other than letter writing would have been looked upon by her fellow Wrens as 'odd' – even writing up her diary must have been difficult in the early days. When she finally achieved a room of her own, she was much busier and the whole atmosphere and tempo of life was not conducive to the sort of concentration that she needed to start a new novel. In the services there was no difference between working life and leisure as there is in civilian life. One was with the same people all the time and there seemed to be no natural break, no period when one could be a different person – a writer rather than a Wren.

The pain of her relationship with Gordon was gradually fading though she still indulged in the occasional outburst of misery, but it was all much more conscious. One day she cycled to Leigh-on-Sea and sat on a seat looking at the rolls of barbed wire that bordered the muddy sea with 'great tears plopping down my cheeks', and once when she heard on the radio (alone for once in a room at the Services Club) some of 'their' music – Mozart and Tchaikovsky – she

> felt dramatic, standing alone in that room, too lazy to do the blackout. It's better to be dramatic than just a lonely spinster, though it comes to that in the end.[18]

In a letter Honor had advised her to forget Gordon, telling her, with some perception, that it was really a person she wanted, not specially him.

He's let me down pretty badly – Waly, Waly indeed –
and now it's the loneliness I feel more than any special
need for him. . . . In time I shall get to feel it in my heart
as well as know it in my mind.[19]

After the war she met Gordon again – it says something
about her personality and her relationships, that her old loves
nearly always kept in touch with her. By then he was married
to Modwena Sedgwick, whom he had known before his affair
with Barbara. She had lunch with him several times. 'Pagani's',
she noted briefly in her diary, 'Lobster'. But the episode had
left a scar. She never talked about him, as she often did about
Henry, because the pain was of a different, deeper kind. In
February 1976, her two loves coming together as it were, she
wrote in her notebook:

Henry came to tea with a bad cold and bringing
crumpets. Destroyed (in the fire, it being a cold day)
some pages of a 1943 diary. The person who inspired the
main reason for it [Gordon] is now dead. Parts of it are
worth keeping.[20]

By September things were beginning to look hopeful about
her commission – there were forms to be filled in and interviews.

I shall be quite the phoniest thing in the Navy. A
grown up person playing a fantastic game – the most
unlikely person to be in the Wrens – but there's
no reason why I shouldn't do it as well as other
people.[21]

Nevertheless, she was, perhaps unconsciously, beginning to
feel part of things at last. Her conversation was embellished
with Naval slang and one can detect a certain pride in the
service.

We went into the Star and Garter and had a pint,
and while I was there, hat adrift, face flushed, glass
in my hand and voice talking loud naval jargon, a

woman came up to me and asked how she could join
the WRNS![22]

She got her commission and, because of her experience
in Bristol, was assigned to the censorship section. In March
1944 Third Officer Pym was stationed in a large neo-Palladian
mansion near Southampton. Preparations were in train for the
invasion of France, which was to come in June, and England,
especially the South Coast, was one enormous staging post,
full of British, Canadian and American troops. Convoys of
tanks and armoured cars trundled through the streets of
quiet English country towns, camouflaged landing craft were
drawn up on the beaches, and there were army camps everywhere. Barbara found that there was a great deal of social life
('whether you like it or not'). As in her Oxford days, there were
far more men than women and the Wrens were inundated with
invitations.

Although her officer's uniform – made to measure with
gold buttons – and her becoming tricorne hat gave her great
pleasure, she was glad that Wrens were allowed to wear
civilian clothes at the dances 'as a stiff collar and tie isn't
very comfortable'. There seems to have been no shortage,
here, of nice (tall) partners, one of whom had been up at
Magdalen ('I couldn't remember anyone I knew who'd been
up at Magdalen', she wrote to Henry, 'except Oscar Wilde
and your tutor [C. S.] Lewis'[23]). He was younger than she
was, as were many of the young officers there. Writing to
Henry again in May she protests:

> Don't think that because I mention all this social life
> that I have changed in the least. I don't really like
> meeting and making conversation with all these people
> but it has to be done and naturally I manage to see the
> funny side of it.[24]

She says that she has 'a fine idea for a novel about this place
and all the queer people in it', including, perhaps, the Captain
(RN) who appealed to her taste for the flamboyant – 'a great
personality with a silver-headed stick and a Great Dane'.[25]
The strain of waiting for D-Day in that hothouse atmosphere

affected them all, even those who, like Barbara, would remain
behind in safety.

> I am vaguely depressed, waiting for things to happen,
> as we all are now. I wish it could be over and done with
> – we shall know so many people in it and I suppose a
> good many of them won't come back. Still, I wouldn't be
> anywhere else now . . . [26]

> I remember once – oh it was so depressing – there was
> just a dim bulb [in the ladies' cloakroom] that made every-
> thing look ghastly and I was never going to see him any
> more . . . you know the kind of thing, tears and whisky
> and then going out into that dreadful darkness.[27]

She remained in the south of England until September
1944, when she was posted overseas, to Naples. The Allied
forces had taken Sicily in the summer of 1943 and landed on
the mainland, at Salerno, at the beginning of September. Italy
had surrendered, but fighting against the Germans, who had
taken control, was very bitter. However by September 1944
the Allies had broken through the Gothic Line in the north
and had taken Rimini. A lot of the time Barbara was in Naples,
fighting was going on in the north of the country, as well as
naval activity in the Mediterranean. Although the Naples base
was never in any danger, this, and the fact that the war had
been going on for five years, explained the hectic quality of
the social life in Naples. People were constantly coming and
going and there was an atmosphere of impermanence, casual
affairs and a general determination to have a good time.

By now Barbara was totally assimilated into Naval life.
She was still in the Censorship Division and had become
confident and efficient. Indeed, when she was demobilised
her testimonial from the Director of WRNS described her as
'an intelligent and adaptable censor officer' – a far cry from
the days of the false Wrennish façade.

Her trips abroad before the war had all been to Northern or
Central European countries, like Germany, Hungary or Poland,
and the warm southern charms of Naples, especially after the
rigours and shortages of wartime Britain, were delightful. Even
in these romantic surroundings and 'with the exhilaration of

being in a foreign land', however, she found the work dull and the social life unsatisfying, so once again she began a formal diary.

> Now I start [the diary] because I have a faint feeling of dissatisfaction with life here, the dull day's work and empty social round and the fear that I shall never, never write that novel or do anything at all worth doing.[28]

She begins with a description of a day in Capri, with careful observations, especially of churchyards, and a view of Naples from the sea:

> From the ship layers of orange and pink and biscuit-coloured buildings and in the evening a mass of twinkling lights[29]

and the smells – of incense or 'perfume, passing a barber's shop', and the girls 'nicely dressed, nearly all wearing shoes with high wedge heels'.

In spite of her gloomy remarks about never writing another novel, it was, obviously, all being noted down as potential 'material'.

> There are still a lot of things to work in – social life, the view from the window – Wren life – *Stimmung* – how one feels inside – a lot more.[30]

As before, there were far more men than women and there was a very rich social life for those who wished to take advantage of the situation. There were dances almost every evening, often on board the ships in the Bay – all very romantic, with dancing on the quarterdeck in the moonlight to the music of a Royal Marines band,

> Then a lovely trip back by motor boat. Wind and spray and stars and the dark shape of ships and the lights of Naples![31]

Sometimes she dined in the various officers' messes or at local restaurants or at the Fleet Club. There was always a party somewhere every night and drink and cigarettes were plentiful here (unlike England) and all at duty-free prices. She delighted in the baroque decoration of the Opera House and some of the villas that the Navy had taken over – though the white and gold of the British Officers' Club reminded her (nostalgically) of a Lyons' Corner House.

At first she had no special escort, often going out with a group, but soon she met a young pay-lieutenant, secretary to the Chief of Staff, whom she called Starky (which was not his name) or Iain (which was). It was probably the only relationship she ever had which was based solely on physical attraction. He was tall, dark and good looking, 'with nice short-sighted brown eyes', but, she decided, common – with an accent, which 'gets on my nerves'. Nevertheless he had a striking personality and was, unlike most of the officers she met, highly articulate.

> The first person in Naples with whom I've had any conversation. About sex! on the balcony overlooking the bay. He has a cynical attitude to life and the technique of outrageous rudeness. He told me I would make a good mistress because I would be able to hold a man's attention by my intelligence.[32]

He was due to return to England at any moment and she was suddenly 'in agony' wondering whether she would hear from him.

> Oh let him be gone and no more hankering for this, second-rate as it is. . . .
>   Morag [a fellow Wren] says I enjoy wallowing in emotion – perhaps I do, but I still mind.[33]

As usual she rushed to write him a note, which he replied to by phone, 'chiding me for letting sentimentality get the better of cynicism'.[34] For the remaining few weeks that he was in Naples they saw a lot of each other, dancing, driving about the countryside and walking together up to the crater of Vesuvius.

> Our relationship is physical and intellectual, but not, repeat *not*, cultural. He has awful manners.[35]

She told Jock (then in Egypt) a little of what was happening and he replied cautiously:

> I do not think you would be very long happy with your handsome beast, irresistible as the appeal of handsome beasts is to intelligent and educated people. I hope you will not throw yourself away.[36]

Starky was not very popular with his fellow officers, who found his cynicism and brashness difficult to cope with, and this made Barbara feel 'fiercely protective'. So must Ianthe have felt about John in her own unsuitable attachment.[37]

Their final evening was a mixture of comedy and misery, but ended with a show of common sense on both sides.

> ... without much hope or wish for any future. It isn't, as we said, that one's cynical, it's just that one *knows* from experience how these things peter out.[38]

When he had gone she did miss him, but tried not to fling herself too fiercely back into things, knowing how easy it would be in that place to embark on a series of casual affairs.

> Parties and drink are a bad thing when one has a little misery lurking somewhere. Better to bear it with dignity. If I'm not careful I'll begin hating myself again. Not that it really matters, but I must keep myself in hand.[39]

So she went decorously to dances with a variety of uninteresting young men, to the concerts, and to cocktail parties on the terrace of the Admiral Morse's villa, where she observed with amusement young Wren officers in their ill-fitting white uniforms trying to catch the eye of Rob Long, the Admiral's 'handsome, conceited flag-officer'.

October had been quite a month. She kept a table of events, which gives a little flavour of her life at this time – and puts the Starky affair into perspective:

October

1st. Night in.
2nd. Out with Starky, Andrew, Jack, Cynthia and
   Dotty to the Orange Grove.
3rd. Censors' Dance. Met Jimmy.
5th. Out with Flash and Force V.
6th. Out with Jimmy (should have been S[tarky]).
7th. Lt. Cdr. Paul's farewell party at CHQ Mess.
8th. Went to Sorento with Force V.
9th. Out with Flash.
10th. Starky crisis! [She thought he was leaving Naples.]
11th. Starky crisis!
12th. Ditto.
13th. Excelsior Dance (didn't go!).
14th. Our [Censors'] cocktail party. Dinner with COS,
   I/O Parks and Starky at Fleet Club.
15th. Bathing at 22 Club with Jimmy. Concert.
18th. Evening with Starky at the Orange Grove.
19th. CHQ Dance.
21st. Lunch with Starky – Vesuvius – drinks at Wrennery
   – Italian party. In at 3.
22nd. Out with Jimmy.
23rd. Said goodbye to Starky for the last time.
25th. Out with Jimmy, Bruce and Morag.
26th. U.S. Naval Do.
27th. Starky went. Out with Jimmy, Bruce and Morag.
   Dance at 22 Club.
28th. Dinner at Jimmy's Mess. Early night.
29th. Concert at Opera House. Tchaikovsky.
30th. RAF Dance.
31st. Night in.[40]

As time went on she was able to travel about more
in Italy and went to Ischia, Positano, Ravello and Amalfi,
driven about in jeeps or large American cars by some of the
Army officers who were now posted in Naples. And going to
the Opera and more parties and more drinks with 'too many
drunken majors'.[41]

A description of *me* – somebody said to Jimmy –
'that very blasé Wren officer with a perpetually bored
expression'. . . . I told Cynthia and she gave me another

description – 'the girl with the fascinating eyes'.

CHQ dance. Cyclamen chiffon, agonising stiff neck
and the magic of 'Long Ago and Far Away' sung by
dear Edward Astley-Jones while he danced with me, oh
so cheek-to-cheek. . . . [42]

In March 1945 she had a few days' leave in Rome where
she was intoxicated by the architecture and the flowers and
the fountains, and where she peered into the Vatican City 'in
the hopes of seeing the carpet slippers slopping up and down
the backstairs'.

At the end of her diary there are half a dozen ideas
for Naples stories.

The Opera House on an April evening, during one
of the intervals. The dusty plants where we stub out
our cigarettes, show young green leaves and even buds
of flowers. If this can happen anything can.[43]

Barbara was still in Naples when the war in Europe ended
in May 1945, but, in April, she had learnt that her mother had
abdominal cancer and was very ill. She immediately applied
for compassionate leave and left for home on 31 May.

Chapter Eleven

Irena had had an operation at the beginning of April and was home again in Oswestry by the beginning of June when Barbara arrived back in England. Hilary had joined the BBC Gramophone Department in 1944 and was now working at Broadcasting House in London and living in lodgings at 41 York Street while her husband was still abroad with the RAF.

Barbara was assigned to WRNS Headquarters in Queen Anne's Mansions, Queen's Gate, 'hanging around', as she put it, waiting to be demobilised. She was allowed to live out, so Hilary managed to get her a room in the house in York Street as well. Although she describes it as 'a sordid furnished room – rather Katherine Mansfield' it was marvellous for her to escape from the communal living of the WRNS.

In June Barbara paid a visit to Honor in Bristol and in July she joined Hilary for a few days at the cottage at Compton. But by August their mother's condition had worsened and they both spent all the time they could get away from their work in Oswestry. Irena died on 10 September, leaving a gap in their lives that could never be filled. But they had been living away from home for several years and the daily contact had been broken. They kept her memory green, as she would have wished, by continuing her jokes and phrases and by remembering her humour and her liveliness – and Barbara drew a loving portrait of her in *Jane and Prudence*. Jock, whose dearly loved brother had quite recently died, wrote to her:

> How dreadfully you must feel your mother's death – church is indeed an ordeal. That part of it gets better, but other things don't. I am so glad your father is so cheerful – what a comfort Hilary must be to you. I hope writing will be a comfort to you too.

> Small trials are the best thing to take one's mind
> temporarily off – one can be sure you have them, for
> who hasn't?[1]

After Irena's death Blytheswood was sold and Frederic
moved into the Wynnstay, a large, old-fashioned hotel in
the centre of Oswestry, opposite St Oswald's Church, where
Irena used to play the organ. The following year he married
a widow, Alice Pearce, with two grown-up children. Neither
Barbara nor Hilary had much in common with her ('What
is the use of reading English at Oxford,' she once asked
Barbara '– what does it *lead* to?'), but they were relieved
that Frederic would have company and someone to look
after him which she did until his death in 1966. They
visited their father and stepmother from time to time but
the ties with Oswestry were broken. They were both glad
to escape from the confines of a small town to London,
which they found a more exciting and agreeable place
to live.

When Sandy returned to England, he and Hilary agreed
to separate. Jock wrote:

> So you have lost a brother-in-law and gained a step-
> mother, a step-brother and a step-sister. It is rather
> like the end of *A Family and a Fortune*. . . . As I see it,
> it sets you and Hilary free now from other ties to spend
> your old age together – I hope you will start doing so at
> once.[2]

Thirty-two and twenty-eight could hardly be considered
old age, but Barbara and Hilary did decide to take a flat
together. It was at 108 Cambridge Street, in Pimlico – 'so
very much the "wrong" side of Victoria Station, so definitely
not Belgravia'.[3] Jock wrote:

> Pimlico used not to be *quite nice* – one called it S.
> Belgravia in polite circles.[4]

Barbara agreed, in a letter to Henry:

Not a very good district, but perhaps we shall raise the tone. It is on the corner of Warwick Square and really quite nice. Anyway we are so lucky to get anywhere at all, as it is practically impossible to get flats and you really can't choose at all.[5]

People were coming back from the war to a London where accommodation was very short indeed, since so many houses and flats had been destroyed by the blitz. They were very lucky that Hilary was able to find them a flat, through the BBC Housing Officer, that they could afford – £150 a year – and without having to pay the 'key money' that many unscrupulous landlords were demanding. The flat was on the second floor of a house belonging to a Mrs Monckton, whose husband was a colonel, still away in the army, and it was not self-contained. They each had a good-sized room, Barbara's was on a corner and had windows on both sides, making it seem light and airy and giving her a good view of Warwick Square and St Gabriel's Church. Next to her room was a small kitchen and, along the landing, Hilary's room, overlooking Sussex Street, and the bathroom, which they had to share with the occupants of the flat above.

'I have to share a bathroom,' I often murmured, almost with shame, as if I personally had been found unworthy of a bathroom of my own.[6]

They furnished it with pieces they had brought with them from Blytheswood so it was both comfortable and comfortingly familiar. Again, they were fortunate to have such things, since one required 'dockets' for new furniture, which was mostly poorly made anyway. As it was, they had to do a great deal of adapting and converting – tablecloths dyed to make bedspreads – because everything was in such short supply.

The people in the flat above were a retired Brigadier and his wife, Bill and Siddie Palmer, together with their large Alsatian named Belinda. The Palmers played a great deal of bridge and he actually had a job in a bridge club in Park Lane. She was very undomesticated and often used to run downstairs to ask their advice when overtaken by some culinary crisis. This rather unusual household was completed by Mrs Monckton's tabby cat, whom Barbara and Hilary called Perfidia, because she would visit them very affectionately and then, as is the way of cats, ignore them if they met her elsewhere in the house.

To get to work they would walk to Victoria Station and take a bus from there, often calling on the way home at the grocer's in Warwick Way, where they were registered. Rationing was still in force – more severely for some things than during the war itself. Clothes were rationed until 1949, petrol until 1950 and food rationing didn't finally end until 1954.

Jock, who had, by then, written about Ivy Compton-Burnett and had actually made her acquaintance, sent Barbara a splendid account of a visit he paid to Cornwall Gardens at this time.

'Marge?' said Miss Compton-Burnett in a frank open tone. 'This cream cheese is not bad with it.'

'We buy sour milk, and hang it up in bags,' said Miss Jourdain.

'One really needs something solid,' said Miss C-B. 'Though here in London one can go out to meals, and it is possible to have enough to eat. Have some gherkin?'

Tea still goes through all its stages.

'Home made plum jam? Not too sweet,' said Miss C-B.

Miss C-B has grown more solid in these years and is one of the few people who like the Peace better than the War.

'Oh, it is so nice to have no bombs,' she said. 'I could not bear them.'

Dame Una Pope-Hennessey and Elizabeth Bowen had lunched with them, so they had a day full of great literary interest.

'It's nice to be home,' said Miss C-B. 'I hated Lyme: She did not mind it.'

'We are going for a fortnight to Kelmscott,' said Miss Jourdain. 'It is a guest house for "literary and artistic people". I do not think we shall like them, but our servant must have a holiday.'[7]

Few people had servants and life in London was still very spartan. Those buildings that had escaped the blitz were very shabby, there were still many shortages – bread was rationed for the first time – and, because of the fuel shortages, public transport was crowded and unreliable.

On the whole Barbara and Hilary led fairly separate lives. Hilary had many friends in the BBC and she was also involved, in her spare time in archaeological work in Berkshire, working on Romano-British finds, and she and the archaeologist Sinclair Hood were publishing the results. Barbara kept up with most of her WRNS friends, especially Frances Kendrick, who was with her at WRNS Headquarters. But both Barbara and Hilary were socially inclined and, for the first time, they had somewhere to entertain their friends – the bedsitters in Upper Berkeley Street and York Street had been very small and had no kitchen and life at The Coppice was too communal for entertaining as such.

> We do quite a lot of entertaining in a mild way – hardly any drink and mostly foreign dishes like moussaka and ravioli, owing to the scarcity of meat! I have become quite an efficient and resourceful cook and enjoy the domestic side of it very much.[8]

Drink was mostly a virulent Algerian red wine at about 5/– a bottle and Hilary remembers Barbara spending a whole afternoon trying to make ravioli ('the consistency of the finest chamois leather'[9]).

People ate out quite a lot because there was still a five shilling limit on restaurant meals, so that it was possible to eat (though usually not very well) at rather grand places. It was a wonderful time for theatregoers – and they both went often – Olivier and Richardson at the New Theatre, Gielgud and Peggy Ashcroft at the Haymarket, and marvellous revues with Hermione Gingold, Henry Kendall, Max Adrian, Joyce Grenfell and Elisabeth Welch. They also went quite frequently to the opera and Barbara particularly records a visit to the first production of *Peter Grimes* at Covent Garden.

So Barbara and Hilary set up house together – Harriet and Belinda – in their thirties still and not their fifties as Barbara had foretold ten years before. They had always got on well. When they were children Barbara was very protective of her younger sister, but as they grew up the roles were reversed and it was Hilary who, more and more, took the lead. Best of all they were very easy together; not only did they share memories of a happy childhood, with family jokes and names for things (boiled eggs were 'bolies'), but they also had the same sense of humour (on the same wavelength), the same frivolity and the same eye for eccentricities of remark or behaviour.

'It is marvellous being with Hilary,' Barbara had written to Elsie in 1938, 'we have the most wonderful jokes about everything.'[10] They went on having wonderful jokes together for the rest of their lives.

Barbara's work at WRNS Headquarters was dull and undemanding, but the pay was quite good. She was beginning to look around for something to do when she was demobilised.

> If I can get a nice little job to earn me a bit of money I shall then settle down to writing again and see if I can get a nice novel published.[11]

There was never any question of her having 'a career', like Hilary. Any job she took would have to leave at least part of her mind free to get on with her real work, which was writing. All she required was something that would provide enough money to support her while she wrote her novels. She was sensible enough to realise that she would not be able to live on her literary earnings (if any) and she also knew that she needed the discipline of a job to give a shape to her day and the common currency of everyday life to provide the characters and situations for her novels.

> I feel I must also have a job, not only because of earning money but because I find routine work soothing (as long as it isn't too boring) and the best way of keeping out that *Angst*, from which we all suffer in some degree nowadays. Though creative work is better still.[12]

Her friend Frances Kendrick had an aunt who was the Secretary of the International African Institute. It was one of those strange coincidences that seemed to be woven into Barbara's life, that her name should have been Beatrice Wyatt – the name Barbara had given to the heroine of her unfinished novel, *The Lumber Room*, which she had written before the war. Beatrice Wyatt was at that time actually married to her second husband, the theologian Professor Sam Hooke, but she retained her previous married name at work. She suggested that Barbara might like to help her with the Institute's publications and so, after she was demobilised, Barbara joined the staff of the Institute on 28 February 1946.

The International African Institute was founded by Lord Lugard in 1929 for the 'study of African languages and culture'. Although its headquarters were in London, it was an international organisation, having on its Executive Council representatives of France, Belgium, Italy, Germany, Sweden and the United States. Its first Director was the charismatic Sir Hanns Vischer, who had a lot in common with Sir Felix Mainwaring[13] – including the use of the country-house party to choose research fellows. With Lord Lugard and the eminent colonial administrator Lord Hailey, he had built up the Institute's reputation before the war, and had organised the great task of writing down the many African languages that had never previously been recorded.

As an international organisation the Institute's work had naturally been curtailed during the war, but now it was to be revived and the man appointed to do this was Daryll Forde, Professor of Anthropology at University College, London. He was in many ways a most remarkable man, having been appointed Professor of Geography at the University of Aberystwyth when he was only twenty-eight, very unusual in pre-war days. He was now in his forties and an outstanding figure in the world of anthropology. He was tall, broad-shouldered and good-looking, with a shock of grey hair. He looked like a successful businessman – only his heavy spectacles gave him the air of an academic. His father had been a clergyman (he seemed a most unlikely son of the rectory) with a living in Tottenham, and Daryll had been brought up in the area and retained a slight London accent, which, with his vitality and brash manner often made people think he was an Australian. He was, in some ways, to be a central figure in Barbara's life for the next twenty-five years.

He had immense energy and that rare thing, a truly clear and incisive mind, that could cut straight through to the heart of any problem, administrative or academic. Unfortunately his temper was short and his patience limited; he did not suffer fools, gladly or otherwise. But it was his intelligent assessment of the situation and his forcefulness and drive that re-established the Institute after the war. There were many problems, including the reintegration of German and Italian scholars into the scheme of things. Most important of all, he was a brilliant fund raiser. The Institute had no central source of funding – there were basic contributions from various governments, but it was Daryll Forde who could always manage to coax just one more grant from UNESCO or the Ford Foundation for a new project – and this provided the Institute's real income. Although the Institute was registered as a charity, money was always short and one of the main savings was on staff salaries. Apart from the typists and the bookkeeper, nearly all the members of staff either had independent means or were married women, supported by their husbands. Barbara's salary, when she first joined the Institute was £5 a week and she was only earning £1,500 a year when she left in 1974. Barbara was fortunate to be able to live with Hilary, who had a good salary from the BBC, and share expenses with her, Hilary providing the little luxuries for them both.

The Institute's journal, *Africa*, was edited by Professor Forde. As its Assistant Editor, Beatrice Wyatt was also responsible for seeing through the press the various books – monographs resulting from research studies in the field, or collections of papers given at the Institute's international seminars – and Barbara was to help her with this editorial work. As a sort of crash course, Barbara went to a series of Professor Forde's lectures at University College and this was her only training in anthropology.

On Monday I spend the day at University College or the London School of Economics, attending lectures on anthropology. Would you believe I could sink so low? But it helps me with my work, which is quite interesting though I work for a maddening professor.[14]

After this, she was considered capable of working on the Institute's formidable new project, the Ethnographic and Linguistic Survey of Africa, which was nothing less than an attempt to cover anthropologically and linguistically every group of tribes and languages in Africa, each group being documented in a separate volume to be written by an expert in that area. Barbara was to do the administrative work, keeping in touch with all the authors, editing their work, proof correcting and indexing.

The Institute was at that time housed in two floors of an office building rather grandly situated in Lower Regent Street. The offices, though, were decidedly cramped, and at the top of the building – though this did give access to the roof, with a wonderful view of royal processions passing down the Mall. The main room on the top floor was devoted to the Institute's fine specialist library, under the care of their formidable Librarian, Ruth Jones. She and her assistant worked at desks in the library and next door there was a large room for the bookkeeper, Freda Cooper, and the membership secretary, an Excellent Woman called Hilary Alpin. Next to that was the general office where the typists (constantly changing because of the poor pay) lived. The Director's room and that of the Secretary were intercommunicating, which meant that they could carry on their continual loud, usually irascible, conversations without leaving their desks. Mrs Wyatt was older than Professor Forde and equally forceful so that a great deal of their time was spent in fierce argument. He used to say, 'Bea is so domineering' and she said, 'Daryll is not a gentleman and has no manners', but each respected the other's hard work and dedication to the Institute.

On the floor below was a large room, divided into two by a partition. In the smaller cubbyhole was Miss Hirschler, an eccentric German refugee who was a library assistant, and the large, remaining area was occupied by editorial and research workers on the Surveys. The researchers came and went, some

English, some American, but an actual member of staff on the Linguistic Survey was Margaret Bryan who Barbara had last worked with in the Censorship office in Bristol. Barbara was delighted to have a kindred spirit with whom to share the inevitably esoteric jokes about her work and she also found the other members of staff congenial. She was a little nervous of Professor Forde and shrank from his hectoring manner, occasionally returning to her office in tears.

> I work for dear Professor Daryll Forde, who is brilliant, has great charm but no manners, and is altogether the sort of person I ought to work for.[15]

He was essentially a kind man, but insensitive, and obviously had no idea of the effect he had on those of a more retiring nature. But, as Barbara said, he did have great charm and got the maximum out of every member of his staff who, either from fear, or inspired by his enthusiasm, always gave him that little extra effort. He never appeared in any of Barbara's novels. The economist Arthur Grampian, Director of the 'vague cultural organisation' where Prudence worked, and the object of her affections, is too grey and nebulous a creature to bear any resemblance to him, and there is nothing of him in Crispin Maynard,[16] though in Aylwin Forbes[17] there is a hint – a certain turn of phrase or a lack of perception at some delicate moment. Only his memorial service – he died in 1973 – at the University Church in Gordon Square inspired Barbara to record it – as the memorial service of Esther Clovis in *A Few Green Leaves* and *An Academic Question*.

He was, really, too much larger than life, too vehement to fit comfortably into the more delicate confines of her novels, but she found him a fascinating character, inhabiting as he did a narrow world totally circumscribed by his work, for he had no other interest. The only thing he ever wished to know about a new acquaintance, always an anthropologist, was if he was 'able' in his field. He lived in some splendour in a house in The Boltons in Kensington, with his second wife who was a doctor (of medicine not anthropology). He spent part of his time at University College, often coming in to the Institute late in the afternoon – the loud voice in the corridor making everyone bend over their desks a little more industriously – expecting staff to stay on late in the evenings and looking bewildered and hurt if they indicated that they had lives of their own outside the Institute.

Although the Institute, under its new Director, was becoming an important international influence in the world of African studies, in the London office at least, there was still a pleasing atmosphere of accomplished amateurism. This was, perhaps, because it was run by academics and excellent women and there were still missionaries and District Officers in the field as well as anthropologists. Even as late as the 1960s it remained very much the kind of Learned Society that Barbara depicted in *Excellent Women*. This atmosphere suited Barbara very well and she enjoyed being with academics again after her years in the WRNS, even though anthropology in London was worlds away from English literature in Oxford.

While she was in Oswestry in 1945, to take her mind off her mother's illness, Barbara had started to look through the manuscript of *Some Tame Gazelle* to see how she might 'improve' it. Jock wrote sympathetically:

> I am glad you are working at *Some Tame Gazelle* – if you can it will help and one can even in very bad times. Like me, your writing self is solidly rooted in the past and lives largely on memories. This is one of the reasons why Henry will never do us justice, I fear.[18]

That summer, when he came back from Egypt for a few months, Jock happened to meet Jonathan Cape and wrote to Barbara:

> 'Once you introduced two very attractive young women to me,' said Mr Cape.
> 'That would be the Miss Pyms,' said Robert in the reserved tone of one recollecting Miss Manning's experience.

'One of them wrote a book,' said Mr Cape. 'I did not publish it, but yet it remains in my mind. Why should I remember it?'

'Because it is such a good book,' said Robert in a full salesmanlike tone. 'What other reason could there be? I should not expect you to forget it.'

'Yes, there must be something about it,' said Mr Cape. 'Do you still see the author? What does she do?'

'She will always write,' said Robert. 'I think she is a natural writer.'

'I think I should see that book,' said Mr Cape.

'I will give you Third Officer Pym's address,' said Robert quickly.

'No, no,' said Mr Cape. 'Will you not write to her. Be vague. I do not know that I wish to see the book exactly as it was before.'

'I do not think that Third Officer Pym would let you see it without revision,' said Robert firmly.

'Let her make it more malicious,' said Mr Cape in the tone of one desiring to make a book strong enough for the Cape list.

'What was it like?' said Mr Wren Howard.

'It was very funny,' said Robert, 'with much, perhaps too much, apt quotation.'

'Oh, I should not like that,' said Mr Wren Howard.

Is this not interesting news? Let us hope that it is great news.[19]

The following week he wrote again:

Take Mr Cape's wish for malice quite seriously. Proust, you know, went round all his characters making them worse. . . . Tidy up points of style and matter that now seems to you to be lacking in maturity.[20]

With this encouragement and other kind words from Jock ('I have always thought you (after Miss C-B) the finest comic writer of the century'), Barbara revised and rewrote *Some Tame Gazelle*, and by February 1946 she was writing to Henry:

I have done a lot of alterations to *Some Tame Gazelle*
and may try it again, after an interval of eight years
it may be more acceptable. There is so much I want to
write now, that I hardly know where to begin.[21]

The new version was more tightly constructed, with all
the extraneous Germans and Finns pared away, as Jock had
suggested. The observation was more acute and the tone more
steadily ironic – Belinda's view of the Archdeacon, though still
loving was more clear-sighted and amused. Barbara was fortunate that *Some Tame Gazelle* had not dated too much. Although
the war had changed the English social scene pretty radically,
enough remained of pre-war life, especially in the provinces
and countryside, to make a novel set in the late 1930s perfectly
acceptable. She sent the revised novel to Cape in February 1949
and this time it was accepted. Jock rejoiced with her at being
published at last.

I know the burden that is lifted off one, when at
last the reproach of one's barrenness is done away.[22]

Inspired by this she sent her radio play *Something to Remember*
to the BBC and it was broadcast the following year with the
well-known radio actress Grizelda Hervey as Edith Gossett,
an archetypal Pym heroine.

At this time there was a great blossoming of women's maga-
zines, after years of austerity and wartime paper shortages –
the older ones were revamped and there were many new titles.
Barbara began to write short stories for them, hoping to make
some money from this new market for fiction. Her Institute
salary had scarcely risen (no automatic pay rises in those
days) and her bank balance in July 1949 stood at £35. 12s. 1d.
One of these stories, 'The Jumble Sale', was accepted by
the magazine *Woman and Beauty* and published that year.
But although Barbara, professional as always, attempted to
conform to the magazine fiction formula, her stories were
too delicate and too allusive to be successful and none of
the others found a market.

Her own personal life was busy but uneventful. She had
the knack of remaining on friendly terms with her old loves

and her diaries record that she had lunch occasionally with Gordon Glover and once with Starky. Whenever Henry was in England (he was still working in Sweden) they would meet as old friends and she still corresponded with him:

> Do let me know when you come to London and we will meet and do cultured things and perhaps you will even take me out to lunch and we will certainly ask you to the flat and give you the kind of meal one gives people in post-war England. We have *enough* to eat but it is so deadly dull most of the time; do bring me a grapefruit or an orange from Sweden [both these fruits had been unobtainable in England for some years] if there are any. But at least we have some Camembert cheese at the moment, so life has its little glories.

> How lovely that you are in England – most unexpected . . . . Have you really brought a grapefruit? I shouldn't have thought you would remember. . . . I have had my hair cut short like a poodle or sheep so maybe you won't recognise me.

> I suppose you have either died of pneumonia or gone back to Sweden. Or can it be that you have perhaps taken what I should have had the first refusal of – umbrage? Maybe I did refuse it and so you took it over. I expected you to ring last week – we had lots of food, even a chicken, and should have been glad to ask you to a meal. But the days went on and you didn't and now I'm afraid I can't be bothered with letters and you have no telephone. But if you would like to come to a meal or take me out to one (ha-ha) ring up some time this week. I was *terribly* busy when you rang before, also rather annoyed.[23]

It is noteworthy that, now, it is the question of food (a chicken was a rare and splendid treat) that seems to be uppermost in her mind rather than actually seeing Henry.

In 1952 Henry and Elsie were divorced and Henry married a German girl called Susi, Jock wrote to Barbara:

> Elsie is divorcing Henry. . . . what a relief it is to write irreverently of Henry and how angry he'd be! like people

making fun of the Devil. I'm jealous enough for Elsie not
to want her [Susi] to be a 'dear sister' to us. I'd like
her to make Henry very happy and take him RIGHT
OUT OF OUR LIVES. This must confirm you in your
state of single blessedness – and such a blessed state it
is! . . . Surely you will not feel fluttered now that poor
H is (or soon will be) for a short time free? I feel sure
you will not. 'She's far too sweet for him, sir,' said Mrs
Townsend. . . . 'Miss Pym is a very sweet young lady.'[24]

Barbara did not feel fluttered. Just before Henry's marriage
to Susi, she wrote him a note in which the elegiac and the
acerbic were nicely mingled.

We were both young and stupid in those [Oxford]
days and I can see that I must have been just as
trying in my way as you were. Goodness knows what
I expected! Anyway, you can be quite sure that I don't
bear you any ill-will about anything. I even look back
on those days with a certain amount of pleasure – or
do I mean emotion recollected in tranquillity, *Samson
Agonistes* and Langbaine and Jock being there and our
quarrelsome excursions into the country.
   Now we can have the satisfaction of being mean
to each other – I by not giving you a copy of my new
novel and you by not buying it. I wonder if you'd like it
anyway? I suppose every man I've ever known will see
himself as Rocky (the rather shallow character). Doesn't
the British Council buy books?[25]

The new novel was *Excellent Women* which gives an ambivalent view – to say the least of it – of the single blessedness
that Jock had always so wholeheartedly recommended for
Barbara.

'But my dear Mildred, *you* mustn't marry,' he was
saying indignantly. . . . 'I always think of you as being
so very balanced and sensible, such an excellent woman
. . . . We, my dear Mildred, are the observers of life. Let
other people get married by all means, the more the
merrier. . . . Let Dora marry if she likes. She hasn't
your talent for observation.'[26]

After her love affair with Gordon she wrote to Henry:

> So it looks as if you and Jock may get your way
> and have me as Miss Pym all my life.[27]

And later, after Hilary's divorce:

> Hilary is happier without her husband. . . . They were
> not really madly in love when they married but it seemed
> a good thing, and of course lots of marriages of that kind
> turn out very well. But personally I would prefer the other
> thing, even if it wore off, as I am told it does. Maybe I shall
> be able to keep my illusions as it doesn't look as if I shall
> ever get married.[28]

As far back as 1938 she had been playfully referring to herself
in her Stevie Smith letters to Jock and Henry as an 'old brown
spinster' and inventing with relish Compton-Burnett remarks
such as: 'It is known that every woman wants the love of a
husband, but it is also known that other women have to be
content with other kinds of love.'[29] She also wrote in her
diary after a visit to her friend Rosemary in 1943: 'We both
want the same kind of things. And fancy people not getting
married and having children when they are able to.'[30] It was
still the accepted convention that all women wanted to be
married and that to be a spinster (the word was still in use)
was to be, in some way, a failure. Mildred sums it up with
rueful clarity:

> That was really it. It was the ring on the left hand that
> people at the Old Girls' Reunion looked for. Often, in fact
> nearly always, it was an uninteresting ring, sometimes
> no more than the plain gold band or the very smallest
> and dimmest of diamonds. Perhaps the husband was also
> of this variety, but as he was not seen at this female
> gathering he could only be imagined, and somehow I do
> not think we ever imagined the husbands to be quite so
> uninteresting as they probably were.[31]

But increasingly she was thinking of marriage as 'mild,
kindly looks and spectacles' (a phrase she had used several

P

PROGRAMME

The

MAGIC DIAMOND

will be presented by

by

MORDA LODGE OPERATIC SOCIETY.

on the evening of ...., April .... 1922.
at . o'clock..

The audience are requested not
to insist on more than the usual
number of encores as the vitality
of the actors will be strained to breaking
point!

Thank You!

KING ANTONIO (of PARROT-AREA)	.... ANTHONY A.B. SELWAY.
QUEEN MAYFLOWE ( )	.... DIANA SELWAY.
PRINCESS ROSEBUD (daughter of Antonio)	.... BARBARA PYM.
PRINCE GEORGE (various friend of Florian)	.... N.C. SELWAY.
PRINCE FLORIAN. (son of Antonio)	.... JOHN. B. SELWAY.
VIOLET (a flower-girl)	.... HILARY PYM.
WIZARD	.... ANTHONY SELWAY.

AUTHORESS .... BARBARA PYM.

PRODUCER ...... N.C.SELWAY.   STAGE MANAGER . A.O. SELWAY.

The Profits (if any) will be given to an Waifs & Strays.

ADMISSION,
STALLS..... 6ᵈ   Standing . 2ᵈ

ACT.I. ..... KINGS GARDEN,
ACT I ..... SAME.

PTO.

The programme for Barbara's production of *The Magic Diamond* in 1922.

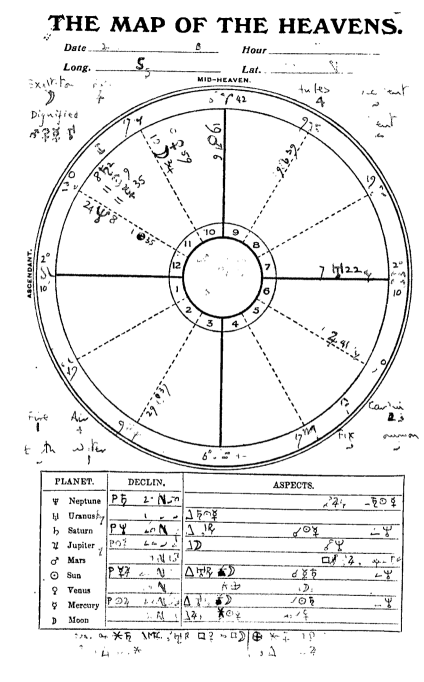

The horoscope Rupert Gleadow drew for Barbara in 1933.

Irena Pym and her motorcycle in Oswestry.

Frederic Pym with his two daughters at Tenby.

Elsie in the 1930s.

Barbara with Bob Smith in Barnes, 1959.

Robert Liddell.

Skipper.

Harry Harker in India.

Barbara and Henry.

Rupert Gleadow (on the right) and Miles Macadam at Oxford.

Barbara and her mother at Morda Lodge.

Barbara in the WRNS.

Barbara at her desk at the International African Institute.

Barbara in 1964.

Barbara and Hilary in Greece, 1966.

Barbara with Philip Larkin at Finstock.

Barbara at Barn Cottage.

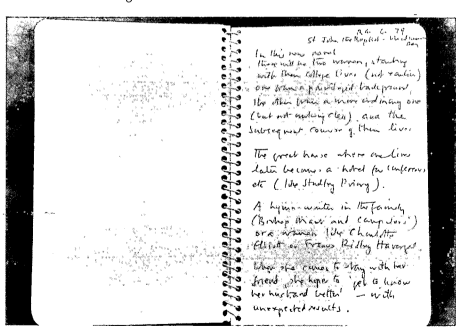

A page from Barbara's final notebook.

times over the years), and in her notebook in 1949 she notes, perhaps half-seriously:

> It is the only occasion when one really wants a husband – in a pub with uncongenial company and the feeling of not belonging.

It was not really marriage that she wanted – in a way, she never had, certainly not marriage for its own sake, since she had rejected two possible husbands when she was younger. She was not very fond of children, was, indeed, uneasy with them, as Julian Glover remembers, so that she certainly did not regret the lack of a family. What she really enjoyed – like Prudence, the heroine whom she often said that she resembled – was being in love. She would go on being attracted ('attached') to men (often 'unsuitable') until the end.

> [Deirdre] was as yet too young to have learned that women of her aunt's age could still be interested in a man; she would have many years to go before the rather dreadful suspicion came to her that one probably never does cease to be interested.[32]

Now Barbara was poised to begin the novels to which her maturity would give an added depth, a new Pym dimension. She had always been acutely observant, had seen the world from a unique viewpoint, and, in her early novels, these qualities had been enriched by a felicitous style. Now her experience could add feeling and understanding. The periods of unhappiness and intense emotions (real enough in spite of the self-indulgent wallowing) were all there waiting to be transmuted into something valuable for her writing. Her favourite quotations about 'all passion spent' and 'emotion recollected in tranquillity' were true and valid about her own work. Her post-war novels are characterised by a delicate, ironic detachment, but, as we have seen, it was a detachment hardly won. The 'emotion' and the 'passion' had to be experienced in the first place.

Chapter Twelve

So many parts of London have a peculiarly village or parochial atmosphere that perhaps it is only a question of choosing one's parish and fitting into it. Pimlico was certainly very village-like in the late 1940s, and Barbara chose as her parish that of St Gabriel's, Warwick Square.

> We pray for streets. 'Warwick Square', says the vicar, his tone seeming to gain in fullness.
>   In the vestry I look round with frank interest – two rows of chairs, a grand piano. An assortment of vases and bowls, a small brass crucifix in need of cleaning, rolls of Mission posters. . . .
>   Worshipping in a Victorian church (St Gabriel's) – no nice monuments round the walls, but the brass tablets and the atmosphere of Victorian piety is in its way just as comforting.[1]

On her return to civilian life Barbara had resumed her churchgoing with a renewed, and slightly different, interest. She had always had a strong personal faith and going to church had been a regular and natural part of her life at school and in Oswestry. At Oxford she had enjoyed a good University sermon and had many lively discussions with Jock (who was a Roman Catholic convert) about religion in general and 'the vagaries of clergy of all denominations in a way that, I am sure, was disrespectful, though I hope it was not irreverent'.[2] Working erratic hours in Bristol she had not been to church so much, but she found the familiar form and pattern of the church service a comfort when she was in the WRNS.

Apart from her fundamental faith, her attitude to things religious had been predominantly literary – pleasure in the language of the litany and of the Authorised Version, a penchant for Metaphysical religious poetry and eighteenth-century sermons, and a 'Gothick' delight in churchyards and in tombs and urns and monuments. Now she became interested in the ceremony and ceremonies of the Church itself.

St Oswald's in Oswestry had been fairly High Church, but St Gabriel's was definitely 'spikier' and Barbara found pleasure in the increased ritual and all that that implied. The outward manifestations of this ritual – the fascinating names of the various kinds of incense, the celibate clergy with their cloaks and birettas, the days of obligation, 'all those Sundays after Trinity' – provided richness indeed to someone with an observant and ironic eye.

St Oswald's had featured in *Civil to Strangers*, where the rector preached his splendid sermon about Jacobean embroidery. It was also the Archdeacon's church, where Harriet and Belinda worshipped, and there is a great deal in the novel about parish affairs and events – the fête, the visiting Bishop, a general atmosphere of rivalry and gossip. The Archdeacon, however, remains Henry Harvey made into a clergyman – the outward flourishes are clerical, but the important facts about the man are not – and Mr Donne is really an extension of Barbara's jokes about Hilary's youthful passion for curates. Mr Latimer in *Crampton Hodnet* and Mr Paladin in *Civil to Strangers* are both archetypal curates, included for the amusement they generate. Only Michael Randolph in the Home Front novel has the potential to become a more complex character had the book been completed.

Although Barbara revised *Some Tame Gazelle* after the war (adding extra 'parish' details as well as a few jokes about her newly acquired discipline of anthropology), its atmosphere remains very much that of 1930s rural churchgoing, something taken for granted, even-tenored, definitely middle of the road. She was soon to explore the theme more deeply.

After she had finished revising *Some Tame Gazelle* Barbara felt that the scope and style of her novels was set, she knew 'the sort of novels' that she wanted to write, and one of the themes that attracted her was the Church. It was the Church,

though, and not Religion that intrigued her. As her friend
Bob Smith has said:

> Religion, for Miss Pym's characters, involves no anguish
> of conscience ('social' or 'personal') no dark night of the
> soul, but decisions about what vestments should be worn
> on Mid-Lent Sunday, what shall be served for luncheon
> on Friday in the clergy-house, who is to query that enig-
> matic entry in the church accounts, and (in *Some Tame
> Gazelle*) 'that rather delicate affair of the altar brasses
> and the unpleasantness between Miss Jenner and Miss
> Beard'.[3]

'Unpleasantness' – the very stuff of domestic comedy –
certainly flourished in the Church. Later, when she and
Hilary were living in Queen's Park, she wrote delightedly
to Bob Smith:

> Hilary set to work the other evening compiling a list
> of all the people who had 'worshipped' at St Laurence's
> since we came here that we could remember. We then
> analysed the circumstances of them leaving – if they had
> left – and came to the conclusion that they had been
> removed by *Rome, Death and Umbrage*. A good title for
> a book, don't you think? Umbrage of course removed the
> greatest number.[4]

She was, on a different level, fascinated by certain aspects of
past struggles in the Church and several times records reading
various lives of Cardinal Newman. This interest also led to her
devotion to the works of Charlotte M. Yonge, who, with her
brilliant gift for narrative, used her novels to explain and pro-
mote the thoughts and aims of the Oxford Movement. Another
of Barbara's favourite Victorian novels was Mrs Humphrey
Ward's *Robert Ellesmere,* which dealt with religious 'doubts'.
   Barbara set her new novel *Excellent Women* in the little
village of Pimlico and St Gabriel's, Warwick Square became
St Mary's and in Julian Malory she created the first of her truly
'churchy' characters, using all the richness and complexity
she found in her newly aroused interest in things clerical. She
combined this with two other strands in her life. The first was

her past love affair with Gordon and her 'social' time in Naples
– this resulted in Rocky Napier, the first of her 'charmers',
whom in this novel she balances against the more austere,
less apparently attractive Everard Bone – again using the
technique of writing something painful out of her system.

The other new theme that she introduces is that of
the anthropologist working on 'the dustier fringes of the
academic world' that she herself was now inhabiting. She
borrowed the actual premises of the Royal Anthropological
Institute in Bedford Square for her Learned Society and in
this novel she celebrates the final days of the old school
of anthropology, that of missionaries and district officers.
About this time she wrote a radio play, that was, in fact,
never performed. Its title, *Parrot's Eggs*, referred to the custom
of sending five parrot's eggs to a Nigerian chief when his
suicide was required, so it was probably written when she
was working on one of the early, Nigerian sections of the
Ethnographic Survey. In this play she makes a reference to
the dichotomy she found so interesting, between the old and
the new in African studies, when she contrasts the missionary
hero's publication *With Cassock and Surplice in Lyamboolooland*
with the anthropologist heroine's *The Fission and Accretion of
Certain Fragmentary Patrilineal Kin Groups in Lyambooloo Social
Structure*. She also introduces Dr Apfelbaum (later to feature
in *Less Than Angels*) and Miss Jellink ('Now, Herbert, no milk
for Miss Jellink, remember!'). *Excellent Women* is full of people,
incidents, settings and situations that she found in her own
life. For the first time she was actually making notes (in the
little spiral-backed notebooks that she was to keep for the rest
of her life) of all the trivia that she enjoyed so much – the odd
overheard remark, an 'atmosphere' at work or at church, any
small incongruity or eccentricity of behaviour – notes taken
'in the field' that were to enrich her work and give it its own
special quality. Thus Esther Clovis (who was to appear and
reappear throughout her books) was a combination of Beatrice
Wyatt and Ruth Jones (with slight overtones of the formidable
Miss Brackett who had ruled the Institute with a rod of iron in
the days of Sir Hanns Vischer) and Everard Bone had at least
the physical characteristics of one of the Institute's linguists,
Wilfred Whiteley. Her heroine, Mildred, has a hasty lunch at

the self-service cafeteria in the Coventry Street Corner House, where members of the Institute staff were often to be found.

> Our trays rattled along on a moving belt at a terrifying speed, so that at the end of it all I found myself, bewildered and resentful, holding a tray full of things I would never have chosen had I had time to think about it, and without a saucer for my coffee.[5]

Mildred later visits Buckfast Abbey, as Barbara did that year, and notes, as Barbara did, that 'the walls looked bright and clean, there was a glittering of much gold and the lingering smell of incense was almost hygienic.' Like Mildred, Barbara too had found herself going out to dinner unexpectedly, carrying a life of Cardinal Newman in a string bag.

The novel is set very precisely in its period, with references to husbands coming back from the war, whale meat, and the lunchtime Lenten services held in the still partially ruined church of St Ermin's (St James's, Piccadilly) where Barbara herself had come upon a little grey woman heating a saucepan of coffee on a primus stove.

She worked at her novel at weekends and sometimes in the early morning before she left for work, and it grew slowly but steadily.

> *7 January 1950.* Writing – $8\frac{1}{2}$ pages of new novel typed .... *14 January.* $2\frac{1}{2}$ pages typed.[6]

In the July she and Frances Kendrick went on one of those holidays on Exmoor that she imposed upon several of her characters. They stayed at Malmsmead, the 'Lorna Doone' farm, and it poured with rain nearly the whole time. But this was fortunate since it enabled her to write a great deal of *Excellent Women*, sitting in the parlour at the round table with its chenille cloth, while outside the coach parties came for their cream teas. The novel was finished and sent to Cape in February 1951.

Some Tame Gazelle had been published in May 1950 and was very well received. Pamela Hansford Johnson in the *Daily Telegraph* said:

Miss Pym's sharp fresh fun is all her own. There is also an amiable air of scholarship about this novel which I find most pleasing.

Antonia White in the *New Statesman* noted that,

working in *petit point* [she] makes each stitch with perfect precision. She keeps her design so perfectly to scale, and places one mild tint in such happy juxtaposition to another that this reader . . . derived considerable pleasure from it.

Lionel Hale in *The Observer* wrote:

She creates a small well-bred Eden, but contrives to insert a little old Adam as well.

While *The Manchester Guardian* called it

an enchanting book about village life, but no more to be described than a delicious taste or smell.

'The wonderful thing,' Jock wrote to her, 'is that you haven't spoiled it – it is still the book we knew and loved – and yet it is tidy and shapely, and every tiny blot removed.'[7]

It was an impressive début, with such approving and substantial reviews, and for almost the only time in her life Barbara moved, just a little, in literary society. She went to publishers' cocktail parties and on 27 November she went to tea with Philip Hope-Wallace to meet Elizabeth Bowen and Veronica (C. V.) Wedgwood.

Elizabeth Bowen is in black with grey and black pearls and pretty ear-rings (little diamond balls). The young author in her nervousness talks rather too much about herself! E.B. discusses methods of working – better at a typewriter than curled up in an armchair. She is very kind and obviously feels she ought to know more about me than she can possibly know! Her stammer is not really as bad as I had expected. Veronica tells me that both Daniel George and William Plomer [at Jonathan Cape] were in

agreement over *Some Tame Gazelle* (apparently unusual)
and think it very amusing.[8]

And the following January she had tea in Fortnum's with
the novelist Elizabeth Taylor, who was also a friend of Jock
Liddell. There were publishers' lunches with Daniel George at
the White Tower, and she was even asked to open a church
bazaar in East Croydon. At last she could consider herself a
published author.

Back in July 1949 Barbara and Hilary had decided to move to
a larger flat. They found one in Nassau Road, Barnes, 'which,
while it was undoubtedly a suburb, was highly desirable' and
'took the overflow from Kensington'. 'And Harrods *do* deliver
as . . . Mrs Beltane so often repeated.' [9]

The flat, though self-contained this time, was the converted
upper floor of a house and the owner, a very 'refined' lady,
whose main preoccupation was with her appearance (like Mrs
Beltane, 'scented and jingling with bracelets'), lived on the
ground floor. Still, Barbara and Hilary each had a bedroom
and there was a good-sized sitting room, a kitchen and bathroom and a loft, which housed a rather temperamental water
tank. Their journey to work (on the elusive number 9 bus) took
longer, but, once they had got used to the idea of living in
the suburbs rather than in central London, they found many
compensations. The river was just at the top of the road and it
was pleasant to walk along the towpath on summer evenings.
Barbara also found a highly congenial church, St Michael's,
Barnes Bridge, where, in the fullness of time, she became a
member of the Parochial Church Council.

There were changes, too, at the Institute. The offices and
Library were moved to St Dunstan's Chambers in Fetter Lane,
just off Fleet Street. In September 1950 I had joined the staff of
the Institute as an assistant librarian. It was my first job (I was
straight from Cambridge) and I had no library qualifications, so
was rather nervous. I was set to work on the first day, just like
Caroline Grimstone[10], sticking labels on to books. Fortunately
Professor Forde was lecturing in the United States for a few
months, so I was spared that particular baptism of fire. As I
was an English graduate the fact that there was a novelist on
the staff was naturally expected to be of interest to me, but

the title of the book, *Some Tame Gazelle*, together with the name
of the Institute, somehow gave me the idea that the book was
about big game-hunting in Africa, which was very much *not*
my cup of tea, and it was only when someone actually lent me
a copy that I nerved myself to read it. And then, of course, I
was enchanted. I didn't have much to do with Barbara at that
time but I looked with considerable interest at the tall, quiet,
reserved woman who had written this perfect book. When the
Institute moved to Fetter Lane there was a great rearrangement
of staff. I was put to work on the Institute's new journal *African
Abstracts* and, to my great satisfaction, I found myself sharing a
room, which carried the noncommittal legend 'Editorial', with
Barbara.

Neither of the rooms we shared at the Institute, for over
twenty years, can have been more than eighteen feet square.
Taking up most of the space in this one were two large wooden
desks, set facing each other. Their cigarette-scarred surfaces
were obscured by stacks of wire trays which held slipping
piles of galley proofs, dog-eared folders of yellowing manuscripts and dangerously leaning towers of books, endlessly
awaiting review. In a small clearing on each desk was an old-
fashioned typewriter, since we typed not only our own letters
but also long passages of revised manuscripts, bibliographies
and indexes. We both typed with two fingers. Around the walls
stood a collection of olive green metal filing cabinets, since
we also did our own filing – eccentrically, but efficiently.
Next to these, in a wooden cabinet of some antiquity, was
kept a quantity of papers, handed down to the Institute by
some long-vanished department of the (then) Colonial Office.
They were a source of great interest – and some mystification
– to anthropologists, who found the nuggets of sociological
information difficult to disinter from the splendid day-to-day
administrative chat ('The key to the jail at — is kept under
the *mat*; I think that you will have no difficulty in finding
it'), which was, of course, what we found most fascinating.
Barbara had arranged them in the most general way:

> I met John Ballard once and I think he was rather
> shocked when I showed him a rather chaotic collection
> of Intelligence reports we have at the IAI, and when he

suggested mildly that it might be nice to have a list of
them, I said roughly that there was certainly no hope
of *that*. It might be a nice job to do on those long, dusty
August afternoons . . . [11]

Beside these cabinets was the map cupboard, mostly used
to store maps used in the Ethnographic Survey, which is why
they were under Barbara's nominal control. The cupboard was
only waist-high and profoundly inconvenient, and, since their
arrangement was haphazard to say the least, she had to spend
some time crouching (to use one of her favourite words) on
the cold linoleum in search of an elusive map. She quite
enjoyed the mystique attached to them, though, and used to
have little technical talks with Daryll Forde about scales and
so forth. Inadequately covering the linoleum was a square of
carpet ('I am to have a new carpet – speckled black and
white that won't show the cigarette ash'[12]) which we chose
at Gamage's, the wonderful, old-fashioned store that was just
up the road in High Holborn, where, in common with half
the population of the City, we spent many happy lunch hours
wandering mindlessly around.

The walls and paintwork of our office were a dingy cream
colour. Cleaning at the Institute was rather sketchy and we
kept dusters in our desk drawers. Once, in a fit of exasperation
at the grit and grime in the curtains (London was still being
rebuilt around us after the devastation of the blitz), Barbara
took them home and washed them herself.

Behind her desk was a bookcase which held, in addition to all
the file copies of *Africa*, the Ethnographic Survey and other
Institute publications, a motley collection of novels and poetry
of the kind that find their way on to bookshelves for no apparent
reason: *David Blaize* by E. F. Benson, *The Cathedral* by Hugh
Walpole, Palgrave's *Golden Treasury, Metaphysical Poetry from
Donne to Butler*, and a Gilbert Murray translation of *The Trojan
Women*.

Hanging beside this bookcase was the Juju. This was constructed from various 'magical' objects: a wooden bull-roarer
(brought back from Nigeria by one of our anthropologists), a
Salvation Army badge, a feather, a lock of my hair (Barbara
had trimmed it for me one afternoon in the office when we

were feeling bored) and the signature of the Father of Anthropology, Professor Malinowski, cut from a letter in the files. Occasionally 'offerings' – a pressed flower or a paper clip – were made to the Juju if we needed a new reviewer or if our proofs were late – only partly in jest.

When Beatrice Wyatt retired, Barbara became the Assistant Editor of *Africa*, which was at that time the leading journal in its field, and took over responsibility (under Daryll Forde) for all the Institute's publications. Each year the Institute would publish, funds permitting, two or three full-length monographs, three volumes of the Ethnographic Survey and one of the Linguistic Survey (linguists being notoriously more difficult to urge into print) and one or two volumes of seminar papers, as well as the four quarterly issues of *Africa*. Barbara saw them all through the press, from the initial copy editing to the final proof reading. To my great delight, I was promoted to be her assistant. Barbara had no formal title at the Institute, being simply 'in charge of publications'. She was, of course, Assistant Editor of *Africa*, a position that gave her considerable satisfaction. It was a source of pride to her that, even during various printers' strikes and disputes, *Africa* always appeared on time. Daryll Forde, naturally, chose the articles, but it was Barbara who was responsible for editing them (often rewriting them if they were written by anthropologists whose first language was not English). She also had the task of finding reviewers for the ever-increasing stream of books that landed on the editorial desk.

> Are you beginning to experience 'some problems of a review editor'? It makes one almost *hate* people when they don't send in reviews, I find, and I have my own private black list on which it is very terrible to be.[13]

Then there was the compilation of the Notes and News section and the frustrated novelist complained that 'D.F. won't let me keep in that bit about "the beautiful lakeside campus".' Since *Africa* was bilingual, she had to organise French or English summaries for each article and annually she compiled the subject and tribal indexes.

She was also in charge of the *Africa* advertisements. This was another bit of mystique that gave her pleasure. When she was

dealing with the agency that handled the more important advertisements, for banks, airlines and so forth, she would assume a
slightly dashing air, the faintest hint of Madison Avenue.

Excellent Women was published in March 1952, with, gratifyingly, a Book Society Recommendation, and was the most
generally popular of all her novels. 'I don't think I've ever
before recommended a novel as one that everybody will
enjoy,' wrote Marghanita Laski in *The Observer*, 'and yet – even
with a certain assurance – I'm prepared to vouch for *Excellent
Women*.' Even now, it is the novel that one recommends new
Pym readers to begin with.

The *Church Times* made the first flattering comparison with
Jane Austen: 'This book reveals flashes of insight into female
characters worthy of Jane Austen' and the *News Chronicle*
followed it up with: 'We needn't bring Jane Austen into it,
but Miss Pym is writing in a great tradition and knows it.'

Perhaps the review that pleased her most was the one in the
Daily Telegraph from John Betjeman – one of her favourite poets
and a writer who, in some ways, influenced her more than any
novelist – who recognised the fact that she had added a new
phrase to the English language: 'Barbara Pym is a splendidly
humorous writer. She knows her limitations and stays within
them. *Excellent Women* is England, and, thank goodness, it is
full of them.'

Most of the reviewers (and readers) at that time took
the novel at its face value as a perceptive and entertaining
comedy (though *The Irish Times* noted that 'under a varnish
of superb comedy . . . there lurks a most poignant tragedy');
later they were to look below the surface and find a darker
side to it. When the book was first published Jock Liddell,
perceptive as always, had written to her:

> The tone is beautifully and faultlessly managed – one
> feels Mildred genuinely expects so little for herself that
> it is almost sad. This is quite original: other narrators of
> similar chronicles always have their archness or vanity.[14]

and recently he wrote:

Excellent Women, a novel of the very lean years, shows the Pym woman at the lowest ebb of her experience and expectations.[15]

while Philip Larkin, writing to Barbara in 1964, described the book as

full of a harsh kind of suffering very far from the others [novels]: it's a study of the pain of being single, the unconscious hurt the world regards as this state's natural clothing – oh dear, this sounds rather extravagant, but time and again one senses not only that Mildred is suffering, but that nobody can see why she shouldn't suffer, like a Victorian cabhorse.[16]

When Barbara gave a copy of the book to her friend Richard Roberts he found it terribly witty, but sad. 'Why is it,' she asked, 'that *men* find my books so sad? Women don't particularly. Perhaps they (men) have a slight guilt feeling that this is what they do to us, and yet really it isn't as bad as all that.'[17]

The fact that women's expectations are (or, perhaps, were) so different from men's, lies beneath all her novels. Women 'could always wash stockings or something' Rocky suggested when he and Mildred were discussing rejection[18] and, indeed, they do, being able to overlay their loneliness and grief with a multitude of little tasks – the trivial round, the common task – that sees them through many of life's crises. Barbara knew from experience that this was so and *Excellent Women* is a triumphant affirmation of the fact.

Chapter Thirteen

In 1952 Jock Liddell sent Barbara a new friend. His name was Bob Smith.

> Poor Robert is very sweet and cosy and I am glad you found him so. He hates being transferred to London [from Egypt] and the only thing he looked forward to was meeting the authoress of *Some Tame Gazelle*.[1]

They quickly discovered that they had much in common – the Church and books – and the same sort of sense of humour. He was six years younger than Barbara, but with a formal manner and an old-fashioned courtesy, which together with a deep, rather clerical voice, made him seem older than his years.

Soon after they met, she had felt a brief surge of attraction towards him and wrote in her diary:

> The agony of wondering if he will send a Christmas card! And he, wandering in his provincial town on Christmas Eve, as we used to do in Oswestry.[2]

But very soon she decided that he was to be a good friend and they often had lunch or went on 'church-crawls' together:

> Bob to lunch. Induction of new vicar. . . . 6.30 Wine Lodge Baker St. Bob. Induction at St Cyprian's. . . . St Cuthbert's Philbeach Gardens High Mass. Bob to lunch . . . Bob, Holy Redeemer, Clerkenwell 10.50. . . . Bob, All Saints Notting Hill, High Mass.[3]

Their points of view were not always the same.

Even at this moment something dreadful may be happening . . . somebody dying, languishing with hopeless
love or quarrelling about the Church of South India
in the Edgware Road as I nearly did with Bob on
Sunday.[4]

Bob Smith was at this time a civil servant, but he had
been in Poland with the Foreign Office and had written
a novel set in that country. He hadn't been able to get it
published and so he asked Barbara to read it and give her
opinion. This was difficult for her since she never trusted
her critical judgement about other people's novels. She
could spot the technical weaknesses – years of editing
made that fairly simple – but, in a way, she didn't feel
she knew what really made a piece of fiction work. She
knew what she liked and what she didn't like, but she
was unwilling, or unable, to criticise in depth. In some
ways this applied to her own current novel – she was
always eager to get another opinion, to have an outside,
critical eye.

Do I really seem to be so unfeeling about your novel?
I think perhaps that I must, because I can never think
of anything comforting to say or never say it if I do.
Perhaps I should do better if I had not been through it
myself and had my friends say that I wrote deliciously,
which is *no* consolation really if a publisher doesn't think
so. So you see . . . if I say that you write better than I
do (which is true in some ways), what then? I can see
now what was wrong with my early attempts, but I can
see nothing wrong with *The Winter World* and can only
think that 'they' don't like the subject of it . . . or they
think it won't sell, which is another powerful reason
and nothing at all to do with whether one can write
or not.[5]

She did try to place the novel for him at Cape, but
with no success.

He [Daniel George] said that he had liked it himself
but William Plomer had not *because of the subject*. Then
apparently Jonathan himself had read it (he does not
seem to have opinions of his own) and was persuaded
by William, but the thing they all asked themselves was
'Will it sell?' and they decided that it would probably not.
He then asked how old you were and I said: 'Oh, quite
young, about thirty-six', then the talk passed to other
things less interesting.[6]

Barbara's third novel *Jane and Prudence* appeared in September 1953. It, too, was a Book Society Recommendation
and was well received, though some critics were uncertain
about the more flexible structure. *The Observer* found the
book 'too loose and rambling not to disappoint after *Excellent Women*'. She did, in fact, have several hostile reviews.
Paul Bloomfield in *The Manchester Guardian* observed sternly,
if obscurely:

It is a horrid disappointment after *Excellent Women*.
God and the Devil would never make over even the
smallest English village, let alone suburb, to a set
of miseducated nincompoops like the people in this
tale.

and the anonymous critic of the *Times Literary Supplement*
wrote, more in sorrow than in anger:

Some incidents occur; they are not easy to recall after
one has closed the book. A former English don, Jane
is highly literate, as indeed her creator evidently is.
For Miss Pym writes well, and this chronicle of her
heroine's doings is really very small beer indeed to
have come from a brewery in which Oxford, a taste for
Jane Austen, and an observant eye have all played their
parts.

But other critics were kind. Jock found it 'so witty and
kind and sharp' and Frederick Laws in the *News Chronicle*
called it 'a brilliant and charming novel, which you will not
easily forget', while Lady Cynthia Asquith wrote:

Miss Barbara Pym has a wonderfully perceptive eye, and the delicate derision with which she describes what she sees could scarcely be bettered. Her dialogue, too, is very deft; at times almost as delectably dry as Miss Compton-Burnett's, it is yet always differentiated. You can hear the voice of each speaker.

The book also brought her a delightful fan letter from Lord David Cecil, who is mentioned briefly in the novel as Flora's tutor at Oxford ('imagine doing *Paradise Lost* with Lord Edgar!'):

Forgive a total stranger writing to tell you how very much he enjoys your books. I have read *Excellent Women* before with great pleasure and admiration. You have so much sense of reality and sense of comedy, and the people in your books are living and credible and likeable. I find this rare in modern fiction. Thank you very much.[7]

Jane Cleveland is a loving celebration of Irena Pym (with academic overtones) and Prudence, with her predilection for unsatisfactory love affairs is only a slightly distorted mirror image of Barbara herself.

Jane Cleveland and her daughter Flora are transferred unchanged from the Home Front novel, as is Miss Doggett (triumphantly herself) from *Crampton Hodnet*. Jessie Morrow, from the same book, however, has undergone a change and has become harder and more scheming, more determined to marry. The woman who refused Mr Latimer would never have bothered to entrap Fabian Driver. She is one of Barbara's few 'dark' characters, and we can sometimes hear in her conversations echoes of Ivy Compton-Burnett.

'Yes, some things must be known,' said Miss Morrow. 'It is no use nodding and pursing lips and saying dark things.'[8]

Barbara wove two strands of her life into the book. There was the church side, with the parochial church council meetings and umbrage taken over the parish magazine cover, and there was the minutiae of office life – the making of tea or coffee (at the Institute the typists made the tea – tea money 6d a week – but one made one's own coffee) and the various interpersonal tensions and 'atmospheres'.

> 'I wonder if we might have one bar of the fire on?' asked Miss Clothier at last.
> 'Oh, it isn't cold,' said Miss Trapnell. 'Do you find it cold, Miss Bates?' . . .
> 'Well, of course I have been sitting here since quarter to ten,' said Miss Clothier. 'So perhaps I have got cold sitting.'
> 'Ah yes; you may have got cold sitting,' agreed Miss Trapnell. 'I have only been here since *five* to ten.'
> Prudence, who had arrived at ten past ten, made no comment.[9]

Fabian, of course, owed something to Gordon Glover, though he had none of Gordon's wit and intelligence, only his egotism, and even that Barbara was now able to view objectively. When he rejects Prudence,

> Jane felt that he would write from the depths of a wretchedness that would not necessarily be insincere because its outward signs were so theatrical. Presumably attractive men and probably women too must always be suffering in this way; they must so often have to reject and cast aside love, and perhaps even practice did not always make them ruthless and cold-blooded enough to do it without feeling any qualms.[10]

Although *Jane and Prudence* was generally well received it didn't make very much money. In April 1954 Barbara wrote to Bob Smith:

> I had a letter from Jock recently. He liked *Jane and Prudence* very much. But the Americans and the Continentals most definitely *don't* and now I am feeling a little bruised! In answer to my enquiries Cape tells me that 8 American and 10 Continental publishers saw and 'declined' (that seems to be the word) *Excellent*

Women and they are still plodding on with *J & P*. So humble yourself, Miss Pym, and do not give yourself airs.[11]

But life was agreeable, she was busy at the Institute, having lunch with Bob, invited to the occasional publisher's cocktail party, and in August she went to Portugal for a holiday with Frances Kendrick. Her interest in clothes remained as great as ever and, even on her meagre Institute salary, she was able to buy or make enough to look reasonably elegant. A note in her diary gives some idea of her wardrobe:

Clothes: Spring–Summer 1954

	£	s	d
Peacock blue poplin dress	4	14	6
Charcoal grey suit	13	2	6
White blouse		16	11
Yellow hat		14	9
Tan gloves		7	11
Black court shoes	3	5	9
Black bag	2	2	6
Lime and black cotton [to make a dress]	2	0	7
Black gloves		7	6
	£27	12	11[12]

By now she was absorbed in her next novel which was to be wholly devoted to anthropologists and the Institute. It opens in one of Barbara's favourite places, the Kardomah café in Fleet Street. Perhaps one day someone will write a learned paper about the place of Kardomah cafés in English literature. William Cooper has drawn an affectionate portrait of the one in Leicester in his novel *Scenes from Provincial Life* and, indeed, many young provincials will retain happy memories of their own particular Kardomah. In the 1950s there were three main branches in central London: one in Knightsbridge, one (rather grand) in Piccadilly, near Hatchards, and the one in Fleet Street. They were all decorated in an extravagant art nouveau manner (at a time when that particular movement was considered bizarre and old-fashioned), with mosaic-covered walls – featuring peacocks with spreading tails on a sea-blue background, stained glass borders to the windows, rather rickety tile-topped tables and a great deal of hand-beaten copperwork.

It was a self-service café and the food can only be described as 'dainty': poached eggs on toast, fishcake with potato croquette, small dishes of stewed apple and chocolate biscuits. The ability of whoever was in charge of the catering to make everything seem 'refined' made us wonder if one day we would find on the menu 'Whole roast ox on toast, with croquette'.

We usually tried to sit upstairs – the ground floor was devoted to a shop selling tea and coffee and the basement café was a favourite place for clandestine, lunchtime meetings, usually of rather pathetic, greyish men and women, whom it was difficult to imagine feeling any sort of passion. Sitting at a table by the window upstairs you could see fascinating things in the street below.

> I look out of the window of the Kardomah and see a pale, moony youth, though with a rather sullen expression, selling a newspaper – *Individual Action* – Anarchist Publication – in huge letters on a poster.[13]

Another lunch place was Hill's in Fleet Street, much favoured by male office workers because it served large plates of unexciting but filling food quite cheaply. It was here that Mark and Digby once memorably took Miss Clovis and Miss Lydgate to lunch:

> They all finished their first course and ordered the next. Miss Clovis and Miss Lydgate had Apple Pie with Ice Cream (1×6); Mark and Digby declared that they were passionately fond of Jelly (6d).[14]

In the blurb for *Less Than Angels* Barbara wrote: 'It is surely appropriate that anthropologists, who spend their time studying life and behaviour in various societies should be studied in their turn.' She had certainly done her field work thoroughly.

Some of the techniques of anthropology she had, in fact, been employing herself for years: observation, notation and deduction. 'Not even the slightest expression of amusement or disapproval should ever be displayed at the description of ridiculous, impossible or disgusting features in custom, cult or legend.' This quotation from the anthropologist's handbook *Notes and Queries in Anthropology* always gave Barbara particular pleasure and that kind of dispassionate quality of examination and evaluation is certainly present in her work, though there is amusement in abundance. Which is one of the reasons why she was a novelist and not an anthropologist.

The Institute provided fellowships for anthropological work in the field, the results to be written up in monographs which Barbara edited. She had, therefore, her 'own' anthropologists, whose progress she would follow and whose lives she examined minutely. Some became friends – John Middleton, Peter Lloyd, David Gamble, Ioan Lewis, Clare Hopen – and the longueurs of office afternoons (that interminable time between 2.30 and tea at four o'clock) would be enlivened by visits from the prototypes of Tom Mallow, Mark and Digby. The inhabitants of this world slipped – 'with a little polishing' – quite easily into her fictional world: Margaret Bryan became Gertrude Lydgate, a French anthropologist, Jean Rouch, was Jean-Pierre le Rossignol, and a Belgian linguist, Father Van Bulck (notable for having taken a plastic portable altar into the field) was Father Gemini.

This time she used the Institute's own building in Fetter Lane as the setting for her anthropologists, even down to the little room (in actual fact the inviolate kingdom of the bookkeeper Freda Cooper) where Tom and Deirdre were discovered in deep, non-anthropological conversation.

The anthropological world, with only a few exceptions, however, saw Barbara's name in print only on the cover of *Africa* and in formal acknowledgements: 'I am also grateful to Miss Barbara Pym for the considerable work involved in preparing the final version of the text for the printer.' She noted: 'I looked at the author's acknowledgements, the first thing I always do with books of African interest.'[15] Only a few, more perceptive Africanists realised that the beady eye of the novelist was upon them. After her death and

the publication of her letters and diaries, John Middleton
wrote:

> It is at times heartbreaking to read her words, to realise
> that I was such a dimwit that I never got to know her, by
> which I mean that I never tried to do so. She terrified me
> often, as I scented something there far deeper and more
> subtle than I could deal with, and I recall her humour
> and dry chuckle at so many oddities that were around
> all the time.[16]

Although Barbara had six novels published while she
was at the Institute, not every member of the staff seemed
particularly impressed. Daryll Forde read one, found it, I sus-
pect, largely incomprehensible, and read no more. But, then,
he was more or less impervious to literature of any kind. He
once borrowed a copy of *Lucky Jim* from Barbara 'to see what
all the fuss was about' and once he told us that he had, many
years before, been taken by his friend Raymond Mortimer to
a Bloomsbury party given by Virginia Woolf. At that time the
history of Bloomsbury had not yet been extensively examined
and we were all agog to hear what this fabulous literary circle
had been like. But, alas, all he could remember was that the
refreshment had consisted only of buns and cocoa.

One person who did appreciate Barbara's novels was
the new Secretary of the Institute, Ailsa Currie, who had
taken over when Beatrice Wyatt retired. She was about
Barbara's age and had also been in the WRNS so that they
had a common fund of knowledge and reminiscence. She
also had a pleasantly frivolous attitude to anthropology and
quickly became a friend.

Part of *Less Than Angels* dealt with life in a London
suburb – Barnes, where Deirdre and Bernard could sit and
watch Mr Dulke exercising his dog by the river – a suburb
where everything in the least out of the ordinary (and Alaric
Lydgate and his African masks were certainly that) was the
subject of intense scrutiny.

> What was the point of living in a suburb if one couldn't
> show a healthy curiosity about one's neighbours. . . . The
> sisters [Rhoda and Mabel] had been sitting in Rhoda's

bed-sitting-room, which commanded an excellent view
of the next door back garden. They often did this on
the lengthening spring evenings.[17]

Less Than Angels was published in October 1955. It received
less critical attention than any of her previous books, though
some reviews referred to her 'gentle and unerring wit' and
her 'truth and insight' and David Holloway noted that: 'Miss
Barbara Pym has a very keen eye for the tribal customs of the
English middle class and a great ability for reporting them in
a cool detached way.'
It was the only one of her earlier novels to be published in
America during her lifetime, but, alas, it had no great success,
was hardly noticed, in fact. There was at the time, however,
some thought that Twentieth Century Fox might be interested
in taking an option on it and a copy was sent to their London
agent Bill O'Hanlon. He and Barbara met several times and he
seemed to be attracted by her, but nothing came of it, perhaps
because of a ludicrous incident that Barbara recorded with
great relish.

Evening out with Bill O'H., pub visiting. Standing with
feet hurting a little at bars, one all mirrors and mahogany
and happy little queer couples – another semi-Moorish in
decor in Leicester Square wedged between two cinemas.
  It was to have been an evening of seduction (?) in
the office over the Rialto cinema, the room lit by the
pinky glow from the neon sign outside. A balcony with
an interesting view – packed humanity round Lyons' and
the Prince of Wales Theatre. But it didn't turn out quite
as he wished. How hungry I was eating ham sandwiches,
why don't men think of eating more? Then I wanted to go
to the lavatory but the cloakroom was on another floor
and had to be unlocked and we *couldn't* find the right
keys! Got the mortice key stuck in the lock. All the
time I was striking matches and feeling more and more
uncomfortable. But there was such a strong element of
farce that one couldn't help laughing! Eventually to a
pub in Rupert Street (the Blue Posts) where the landlord
preceded me up the stairs apologising for not very good
provision for a Ladies Toilet. It was a large room with a
big mirror over the mantelpiece and tables with chairs

piled on them. The kind of room that might be used
for a meeting. In a corner and up some steps the door
leading to 'the toilet', quite adequate! Why are people
always apologising to me for such things when all one
wants are the bare essentials?[18]

Not surprisingly, she doesn't seem to have seen him again.

While Barbara was on holiday in Portugal she had read *Maiden
Voyage* and had become 'besotted with Denton Welch – am
collecting and reading everything'. She passed her enthusiasm on to me and we both became obsessed by his books –
especially the Journals, so beautifully – though frustratingly
– edited by Jocelyn Brooke. We knew them almost by heart
and used to set each other test papers (as we did later with
Anthony Powell's novel sequence, *A Dance to the Music of Time*).
We longed to know more about him. Barbara went to Somerset
House to get a copy of his will, Hilary knew someone in the
BBC who had known him (he had died in 1948 at the age of
thirty-three) and provided tantalising scraps of information,
his friend Noel Adeney had written a *roman à clef*, *No Coward
Soul*, about him and his friend Eric Oliver. . . .
   One wet September day Barbara went on a bus to Greenwich
to look at the house where Denton had once lived. Her
description is a cross between a novelist's notes and a private
detective's report:

   34 Croom's Hill . . . stands back a little between 32 and
   36 – square and flat with a nice front door and fanlight.
   Three floors, white painted windows, dull red brick, net
   half-curtains. Green plant (azalea?) in upper window.
   Tiny patch of rather bald grass in front with dustbins.
   I sat down on the low stone wall opposite by the park
   with my umbrella up for it was raining and gazed for a
   few minutes, but I saw nobody.[19]

Later, staying with Ailsa Currie, who lived quite near
Middle Orchard in Kent, where Denton had lived for the
last two years of his life, she went on 'a Denton Pilgrimage'.
After a 'Denton picnic' with cheese, Ryvita, hard-boiled eggs

('the sad egg shells'), chocolate and coffee in a thermos, they drove

> through Plaxol to Crouch – noticed a pub, the Rose
> and Crown. . . . We . . . came to a board saying Middle
> Orchard on the right. There were two houses, one near
> the road. You go down a short grassy lane, bumpy, to get
> to Middle Orchard. It is a clapboard house, white (with
> grey and black) with a balcony on the side nearest the
> road. Two men were working in the garden or orchard
> between the houses. We didn't speak to anyone.[20]

Almost she might have been tracking down someone still alive, and, indeed, through his writings, he was alive to her in a way that very few authors ever were.

> Rereading all of Denton now, beginning with *Maiden
> Voyage.* 'Nothing could be gayer than a red lacquer
> coffin,' he says. Oh darling Denton. . . .[21]

She was intrigued by his moody, difficult personality, and fascinated (as she always had been by such relationships) by his life with Eric Oliver. She loved Denton for his acute, miniaturist observation and vibrant interest in everything he saw, focusing in on the smallest object or incident so that it became something brilliant and living. He could devote two months of his short life to refurbishing an eighteenth-century doll's house, and describe the process in such vivid and loving detail that it seemed like a journey into an unknown and enchanted land. Above all, he realised, as Barbara too had realised, the value of small comforts (of trivia) in an embattled life:

> How tedious [he wrote in his journal] the little details
> seem written down, yet it is always that littleness that
> seems to have, banked up behind it, great walls of fight
> and resistance.[22]

He showed, too, that this 'littleness' can build up into something moving and universal in the right hands. This was always Barbara's strength in her novels and also, quite

casually, in her notebook, where she produced many pieces
in which observation of the eccentric, humour and pathos
are all combined in a way that Denton himself would have
approved of.

> Cats Protection League Bazaar. . . . A few men, perhaps
> two or three, but the rest women and me as dotty as any
> of them. Tea in pink or blue plastic cups, not very hot. A
> woman sits by the door collecting money just 'for the cats'.
> She has a gentle face, wears slacks, voluminous coat and
> fine brown straw hat. Stuffed frog by her on the table, but
> of no significance (at first I thought it was a raffle). This
> simple collecting was something, perhaps the only thing
> she could do.[23]

Chapter Fourteen

To those who have never invented and maintained a 'saga' the whole thing must seem very strange indeed. The subject can be anyone at all – a famous person you don't actually know, a fictitious character, or even an animal – but it is most rewarding to weave a saga around someone you can actually observe. Irena Pym had greatly enjoyed inventing sagas and for Barbara and Hilary they had always been part of their lives. The great chronicler of the saga was one of Barbara's favourite authors, the late Rachel Ferguson, whose novel *The Brontës Went to Woolworths*, describes, stage by stage, the way a saga, built up around a remote person (in this case a high court judge seen from afar) can develop, with a little luck and perseverance, into a real-life friendship. She describes how he 'owned, occupied and paid taxes on our imagination'.[1] She (and her mother and sister) looked him up in *Who's Who* (the first obvious move), collected photographs, walked past his house (to note when the window boxes were changed), hunted for someone who knew him, and then gave invented characteristics to the people around him (his wife, his clerk in chambers), and conducted imaginary conversations between them.

In her autobiography Rachel Ferguson writes:

And so we lived amid a cloud of witnesses, using the voices of their owners. And if you begin to think we are certifiable, I can only refer ·you to the stacks of letters I received [when the novel was published] from readers with sagas of their own. . . . I don't doubt that Freud would have plenty to say about it, and all damaging! . . . So be it. All I do know is that the saga is one of the most dependably amusing games in life.[2]

The Fergusons had a splendid saga about their white wire-haired terrier Crellie, who was variously a Boer War veteran, the Pope and, finally, a Sloane Square dressmaker.

> So Crellie became Madam Dan (Mods and Robs), and wore a black satin Directoire gown, slashed to show one hurrying white leg. He once muffed a fitting for Mother, who, so real was the story by this time, became slightly but genuinely annoyed with the dog.[3]

Barbara's cats, too, had characters and backgrounds. The black and white Tom Boilkin (so called because of his loud purr) was President of The Young Neuters, a very exclusive club, where selected cats would drop in for a bird and a bottle (of milk), and where the other, female, cats, Kitty and Minerva, were allowed to attend on Ladies Nights. Kitty, who was fluffy and dainty, ran The Kittens' Training School, which provided perfect secretaries (a sort of feline Mrs Hoster's), who were much in demand for retyping illegible anthropological manuscripts at the Institute.

Since neither Barbara nor I were at all interested in anthropology (or, indeed, in Africa) we leavened the tedium of our work by invention and imagination. The anthropologists themselves provided rich grounds for mini-sagas, since we usually only had little scraps of information about their home lives. To one we gave a splendid Mother (always there with a hot milky drink and a ready typewriter), to another an elegant social life (going up to London especially to have his hair cut at Trumpers), while a Belgian Jesuit, living in Rome, was the centre of a splendid religio-political intrigue (carpet slippers treading stealthily at night up the backstairs at the Vatican). Barbara usually got the character right, though. Several years later, when she was in hospital she wrote to me: 'I had a card from dear John Beattie – how nice of him to write to me and so typical of the character we have invented for him.'

And then there was The Indigent Anthropologists' Food and Wine Fund (Rachel Ferguson's charity was The Browbeaten Barristers), which provided good, nourishing lunches for some of the younger, poorer anthropologists, whose woolly gloves Barbara found so pathetic.

The most extensive saga Barbara and Hilary ever invented, and one which, like Rachel Ferguson's, ended in a real friendship, was begun in Barnes in 1956. Barbara and Hilary, like Rhoda and Mabel (and Harriet and Belinda), liked to sit by the window – they sat in their upstairs sitting room at the front of the house – from which they could observe the comings and goings in the road beneath. A perfectly ordinary suburb could yield some surprising sights.

A station wagon draws up outside the home of the Siamese diplomats next door and out get two Buddhist priests in orange robes. We wait to see them leave – two of the servants come out and a basket, obviously containing food and drink is put in the car. Later the priests themselves come out and are driven away by the (English) chauffeur. I wonder if the appearance of two English clergymen would arouse such interest in the suburbs of Bangkok.[4]

But it was not the exotic that really intrigued Barbara and Hilary – or, perhaps, a different kind of exotic. Over a period of time they had become aware of a little household – two young men and their dog – living a few doors up the road. They began to look out for them and gave them names: the larger one, square and comfortable-looking, they called Bear, the small, slight one was Squirrel or Little Thing or Little Treasure (Little Tresh). The little dog, a poodle, they called Tweetie. Sometimes they met the young men, walking along beside the river ('Those two and their little dog against a hostile world') and once Hilary tried to stroke the dog and Squirrel said: 'He wouldn't come to *you*', and so they heard his voice.

Bear had a grey car (a Hillman Husky) and on most Sundays he drove off wearing a cassock. Since Barbara and Hilary didn't have a car it was all most frustrating, but one weekend, when they had hired one for a week's holiday, they were able, at last, to follow him and find out where he was going.

Hilary, feeling like something in a movie, drove behind the Husky, across London, from Barnes, all the way to Queen's

Park, near Kilburn, to the church of St Lawrence the Martyr, Chevening Road. They went inside, sitting near the back, and discovered, to their delight, that Bear was the organist. After the service they were swept up with the rest of the congregation, into the church hall for cups of tea, and found that they were being welcomed enthusiastically by the vicar's wife, holding a jar of sugar and a pink plastic apostle teaspoon. After that, they quite often made the difficult journey by public transport, to St Lawrence's.

Another young man (whom they called Paul) joined the household, then Little Thing went away, then Paul moved out and Little Thing moved back with someone else (Tony). It was all very interesting. By now Bob Smith and I were equally agog at the developments (Bob had actually been to St Lawrence's), and, in a way, it had, as all well-maintained sagas have, all the fascination of a soap opera. When I was away on holiday, Barbara kept me up to date, by letter, with a detailed report:

> *Well* – Little Thing is definitely here, but what an elusive little creature we are, like a moth coming out only at night. Hilary and I saw him coming from the bus stop about 10.30 last night (we had come from Hammersmith), he from the other stop (I think) as if he had been seeing a friend off. When he made to cross the road to his house he (knowing that there was someone behind him) flung out his arms in a ballet-like gesture and ran across the road! The 'friend' *might* have been Bear, for Bear was definitely there on Sunday. We saw him emerge about 5 o'clock, wearing a rather nice brown tweedy suit (milk chocolate bear, solid all through). Later he was at St Lawrence's in splendid form, playing very well. But no Paul. Is there being a sort of rapprochement? Tony is still in residence with masses of rather peculiar-looking friends. They had a car at the weekend and went out in it on Sunday, but not Little Thing. Presumably Bear came to lunch.
>
> STOP PRESS! Hilary saw Tony at lunchtime today going into the staff entrance at *Heal's*. What about going there for our office lampshades? I also need some curtain material! I do hope he is actually serving in a department – I suppose he might be a clerk or something.

It was a lovely saga, meticulously plotted, with timetables of 'sightings', and which involved us all in various investigations, taking us not only to St Lawrence's, where the vicar's wife was a mine of information, but also to a flower shop in Shepherds Bush, a cemetery (informative gravestones) and a private hotel in the West Country, so that, after a while, we knew a great deal about the main characters. It also, as it turned out, led Hilary to buy a house in Brooksville Avenue, Queen's Park, just around the corner from St Lawrence's, where she and Barbara became parishioners and, eventually, members of the parochial church council. And, of course, Bear (now settled with Paul) became a friend. Rachel Ferguson has described what it feels like to come face to face with a major character in one's saga.

> The main trouble lay in the fact that I came to [her] aware: primed with a thousand delicate, secret knowledges and intuitions, whereas to her I was, I suppose, merely so much cubic girl, so to speak. I felt at once at an everlasting disadvantage and as though I was taking her friendship under false pretences. A sort of Judas at the keyhole.[5]

Certainly certain conversations had to be edged round delicately ('and you mean, *you* actually used to live in Barnes, as well! How extraordinary!'). As Barbara would sometimes say: 'Are we supposed to *know* that?' or 'Is it true or did we make it up?'

This blurring of fact and fantasy was accentuated by the fact that Barbara was also using several of the saga characters in her new novel.

> What is my next novel to be? It can begin with the shrilling of the telephone in Freddie Hood's church and end with the flame springing up – the new fire on Easter Saturday in the dark church. Hope and a blaze of golden forsythia round the font.[6]

This novel, *A Glass of Blessings*, which she originally called *The Clergy House*, was, indeed, richly 'churchy'. She was, at that time, visiting a variety of churches with Bob Smith. All

Saints, Notting Hill was particularly rewarding ('splendidly Catholic – 3 priests') and the Vicar, Father Twisaday ('an elderly dried-up celibate, irritable and tetchy'), gave her a lot of material for Father Thames,

> The sermon, urging us to keep Ascension Day as a day of obligation, was quite good. Then he remembered a notice about a meeting in the Albert Hall and began talking about that, all mixed up.[7]

One of the other celebrants was Sean MacAteer, a friend of Bob Smith, who obviously provided the inspiration for Marius Ransome.

> He has charm, wrinkles his nose when he smiles. Such a display of charm is surprising, even a little shocking.[8]

Jock Liddell was delighted with it all.

> I adore Mr Bason and all the arrangements at the Clergy House. And (do tell me) do Anglo-Catholics now conform to R.C. fasting rules? I suppose they must, as Fr Thames has something after midnight mass and must have to celebrate again.[9]

But the two young men she had observed so closely in Barnes provided another, unexpected theme. Peter Greene, reviewing the book in the *Daily Telegraph*, writes of the shock he experienced when he suddenly came upon a homosexual relationship in what seemed at first to be simply another Barbara Pym comedy of manners.

> I don't normally raise much enthusiasm for spry little domestic novels sprayed with the incense of upper-middle-class Anglo-Catholicism. . . . But Barbara Pym's *A Glass of Blessings* caught me up short: her naïve heroine, all unawares, falls in love with an obvious homosexual (though this is never explicitly stated) and the queer goings-on of male housekeepers and so on are described with catty accuracy.

When *A Glass of Blessings* was published in April 1958, before the permissive sixties, it was still a fairly unusual theme to find in a novel, especially a novel written by a woman. What is interesting about Barbara's treatment is, first, Wilmet's innocence, which would hardly be possible today when the subject of homosexuality is discussed in schools and people look sideways at the most harmless relationship and secondly, given the period in which she was writing, the calmly matter-of-fact way she treats it. Once Wilmet has got over her own personal shock about Piers, then she, and indeed everyone else in the novel, accepts the situation as being quite natural, as, in fact, they have already accepted the very 'camp' Mr Bason.

Barbara had always been fascinated by this relationship, ever since her days at Oxford, and her portrait of Keith and Piers is sympathetic. Keith is, in appearance at least, Little Thing: neat-featured, rather appealing face, sombre brown eyes and the short-cropped hair that glistened like the wet fur of an animal, wearing the same clothes that she had observed from the window in Barnes – the tangerine-coloured shirt and black jeans. Wilmet's relationship with Keith (and eventually with Piers) became easy and *cosy*, which is, in effect, what Barbara found appealing about her relationships with her own homosexual friends, a feeling she expressed again in *An Academic Question* in the friendship between Caroline and Coco – though she dealt with the darker side of such friendships in *The Sweet Dove Died*.

Bear became Bill Coleman, driving a Husky (there had, also, actually been some 'unpleasantness' at St Lawrence's over a cassock) and Rowena's husband Harry was one of the dashing majors from Naples, now settled down into comfortable middle age ('strong and reliable, assuming that he would be the breadwinner and that his wife would of course vote the same way as he did'[10]). Poor selfish Wilmet (so unlike her namesake in Charlotte M. Yonge's *The Pillars of the House*) resembled her creator in her capacity to love, her capacity to be hurt and her capacity to come through it all, having learnt something about herself in the process.

The 'saga' also gave her the theme for her next novel, *No Fond Return of Love*, concerned with 'research into the lives of ordinary people', which is what a saga is really about. Her heroine, Dulcie (the heroine who is most like Barbara herself), follows almost the same course that Barbara and Hilary did in seeking out Neville Forbes's church. She also (as Barbara did) goes down to the West Country to investigate Aylwin's mother's private hotel and check the inscription on his father's gravestone. Like a good investigator, Dulcie cultivates Viola Dace because she knows Aylwin and she also has the good luck to find a jumble sale (in aid of the organ fund) going on when she goes to look at Mrs Williton's house, and is thus able to see inside and to meet Mrs Williton and Marjorie.

> [In the hall] she lingered for a moment hoping to see 'something interesting', as she put it to herself. But there was only the evening paper stuck through the letter box and a bill from the Electricity Board lying on the purple and ochre tiled floor. It was greedy of her to expect any more when she had already received so much.[11]

The visual detail of all Dulcie's observations is a tribute to the combined talents of the novelist and the natural 'investigator'.

The coincidences which push the plot of this novel along – Dulcie's good fortune over the jumble sale, her being able to overhear Marjorie and her mother 'having it out' with Aylwin at The Eagle House Private Hotel, the various chance meetings – which may seem strange and unlikely, were, in fact, far less extraordinary than some of the coincidences Barbara encountered in her own 'investigations'.

She wrote to Bob Smith:

> I'm so glad the book [N.F.R.L.] arrived safely and that you have enjoyed it. You are one of the few who know how *truly* B. Pym it is – but really Dulcie had an easy time of it compared with us searching for Bear's church, didn't she?[12]

Her heroine's occupation (freelance indexer, proof reader and bibliographer) gave Barbara the opportunity of describing this odd little world, where she herself was at home. She enjoyed making indexes and liked that feeling of inhabiting a quiet, enclosed space that indexing gives. One of her favourite 'getting to sleep' games at this time involved trying to think of as many African tribal names as possible, all beginning with the same letter (Yakö, Yaunde, Yoruba . . .).

She had wanted to call this novel *A Thankless Task*: ('dedicated to my wife, who had the thankless task of compiling the index . . . '), but her publishers felt that it was 'too negative' and asked her to find a title containing the word 'love'! So she went through the index of first lines in *The Oxford Book of English Verse* until she came upon an eighteenth-century poem by Fanny Greville which begins: 'I ask no kind return of love' and, altering 'kind' to 'fond', she used that.

> 'Of course,' [Dulcie] went on, 'those are the people from whom one asks no return of love, if you see what I mean. Just to be allowed to love them is enough.'[13]

It was a sentiment to which Barbara could wholeheartedly subscribe. Fanny Greville's poem was called 'Prayer for Indifference'. It asks for an end to hopeless loving and all the pain it causes – the last verse, especially, sounded echoes in her own mind.

> Far as distress the soul can wound,
> 'Tis pain in each degree:
> 'Tis bliss but to a certain bound,
> Beyond is agony.

No Fond Return of Love was not widely reviewed, though those who did review it were enthusiastic, especially Siriol Hugh-Jones in the *Tatler*:

> A delicious book, refreshing as mint tea, funny and sad, bitchy and tender-hearted, about what it is like to be a fading lady in her early thirties living in North London and trying to soothe the niggling pangs of disappointed love with hot milky drinks and sensible thinking . . . . I love and admire Miss Pym's pussycat wit and profoundly unsoppy kindliness, and we may leave the deeply peculiar, face-saving, gently tormented English middle classes safely in her hands.

Barbara also had a certain amount of ecclesiastical and other comment from Bob Smith:

> It's not, I think, your easiest book, but somehow the most purely Barbara Pym, her art at its quintessence (if you see my meaning). There is just one ecclesiastical error . . . it is on p.146; if anything one would light *extra* candles for the Magnificat, because in some economical churches the acolytes' candles are put out during the psalms and lit again for the office hymn and the Magnificat.[14]

and from Jock:

> I loved the private hotel and the search. But I do *not* like your heroine carrying on with a divorced man. One sees of course that it comes of not being a good churchwoman and of only going to church in the evenings (nor to Evening Mass either) – but do you think you have made that clear to every reader?[15]

No Fond Return of Love was published in early 1961. Shortly before, Barbara and Hilary had moved to Queen's Park. The area was decidedly unfashionable, part of North London that had not yet 'come up', bounded as it was on one side by the Harrow Road and on the other by Kilburn High Road. But Brooksville Avenue was in a quiet neighbourhood, and at the end of the road there was a little park, one of those oases that brighten the less attractive London suburbs, with grass, a few flower beds and a tiny bandstand.

Number 40 was part of a terrace of small Edwardian houses, substantially built and with fair-sized rooms. Because the downstairs front room was rather gloomy, they made their sitting room upstairs (with a good view of comings and goings in the road outside). This house also had a garden at the back, rather small and overshadowed, but with a fine grapevine growing against the wall of the house. They were pleased to have a garden because they now had a cat. Her name was Tatiana, and she was a tortoiseshell, very handsome with a golden streak across her face, which gave her the look of a fierce bird of prey. She was also very difficult and neurotic

and caused them much worry and heartbreak, finally being
run over when she was only a year old. She is lovingly
portrayed as Faustina in *An Unsuitable Attachment*. She was
followed by a brother and sister, Tom Boilkin and another
tortoiseshell, Minerva (also known as Nana), another eccentric
animal, though more placid, whose favourite diet was custard
and fried tomato skins. They were also adopted, for a time,
by a fluffy half-Persian tabby, called Kitty (a banal name to
match her rather banal nature). A house full of cats, with
happy memories of their childhood at Morda Lodge, made
Brooksville Avenue seem like a proper home to them both.

The Vicar of St Lawrence's, Father Parry Chivers, blessed
the house (Tom Boilkin drank some of the holy water, which
they decided was a good omen) and they settled down happily.
They took a very active part in church affairs, as Barbara wrote
to Bob Smith:

All goes well at St Lawrence's – we now have a thing
called the Parish Meeting which usually takes place in
the vicarage with much jollity and Mrs P. C. going round
with drinks. Last Sunday [Mothering Sunday] we had the
Parish Breakfast and I was asked to pour tea at one of the
tables![16]

And later:

[Easter] was very nice at St Lawrence's. Mrs P. C. as
usual with hot cross buns after the Liturgy on Good
Friday. We didn't go to the ceremonies and Midnight
Mass this year, remembering how exhausted we were
last year, but went on Sunday morning instead.[17]

From all this they formed happy friendships, not only with
the Vicar and his wife, but also with Bear and Paul, the latter
lasting until Bear's early death from cancer several years later.

Bob Smith was now a professor of history in Nigeria
and he and Barbara conducted a lively and continuing
correspondence, sometimes about his life in Africa –

I went for an amusing though strenuous expedition into
the bush last week with two students to find the Oke

'badan, a holy hill, seat of the huge-breasted goddess 'Atage. You would see all about it in Parrinder's excellent book on religion in Ibadan. We succeeded at last, after bribing nervous guides and wading a river, in getting to the place and even in struggling through a dense wood, impeded by magic, to the hill top. No white man . . . [18]

– though he still passed on to her church gossip from home.

News from All Saints. Fr T. has at last resigned .... There's also a rumour that poor Fr Finch is Romeward. I am upset by this, and also incredulous.[19]

Because the house in Brooksville Avenue was bigger than their flat had been, they were short of furniture and Bob suggested that they might like to use some of his furniture which was in store.

Your 'things' have settled down very well with us – we couldn't find the Chinese ginger jar lamp, though it may have been at the very bottom of one of the crates that we didn't take everything out of, so we have got the gilt candlestick one. The coffee table glass *was* rather badly broken, I fear. I forget how it happened – did John C put a hot jug down on it or something like that?[20]

A rather strange incident happened when Barbara and Hilary went to collect the 'things'. They found that some of them had already been taken by a Miss Wales. On investigation, this turned out to be another of Bob's friends, of whom they had never previously heard. It was a situation that Barbara was able to use to some effect in *The Sweet Dove Died*.

In April 1961 Barbara had an unexpected treat. Her friend Ailsa Currie, as Secretary of the Institute, decided that Barbara should go with her and Daryll Forde to the annual Executive Council meeting, which was to be held that year in Rome.

Barbara had very little to do with the actual meetings but greatly enjoyed renewing her acquaintance with Rome. She was also delighted to see one of her favourite anthropologists on his home ground. Professor Vinigi Grotanelli was a tremendous Anglophile and, since he was also a Papal Count, got his supply of whisky and cork-tipped Craven A cigarettes from the Irish College at the Vatican.

> At the party [at the Grotanellis' flat], as we were leaving, a nice glimpse of Vinigi in his study, handing out offprints of an article to admiring Africans.[21]

He had great charm and a wonderfully courtly manner – he was once heard to remark that one could not possibly take a *lady* to India. He was a splendid addition to her gallery of eccentrics and appears briefly in *An Unsuitable Attachment*.

After the Council meeting, Ailsa and Barbara went on (as Sophia and Ianthe did) for a little holiday in Amalfi and Ravello and had (as they did) 'the little bundles of dried lemon leaves which you unwrap to reveal a few delicious lemon-flavoured raisins in the middle'.[22]

Barbara loved Italy and enjoyed her stay in Rome, but perhaps only she would see the Eternal City primarily as a setting for a parish holiday for the vicar and congregation of a North London church.

Chapter Fifteen

At the end of 1962 Barbara wrote to Bob Smith:

> I thought, surging through Smith's in Fleet Street today, 'I'm just a tired-looking middle-aged woman to all those (mostly young) people; yet I have had quite a life and written (or rather published) six novels which have been praised in the highest circles.' Did I tell you (I think not?) that I had a charming letter from *Lady* David Cecil (Rachel, daughter of the late Desmond MacCarthy) saying how much she had enjoyed *No Fond Return*? . . .
> My next is getting on, quite flowing now. I am at the depressed stage when I begin to type out some of the early chapters and think that not much of it will do – I can only hope that I will get through this stage, but my first four chapters always seem so dragged out, even when I rewrite the beginning. It is nice of you to have wanted a new BP for Christmas.[1]

It was not only Bob Smith who asked for a new BP. In January 1961 she had had a letter from Philip Larkin, who wanted to write a review essay on her books. She was 'very pleased and flattered' and promised to let him know when her next novel would be ready. He responded enthusiastically and asked for a proof copy of it.

> If I then see an article clear and shining ahead of me I will propose to one or two literary editors that I do a leader on your novels. I enjoy them so much this would be pleasure for me. I've given away my first *No Fond Return* and lent my second so I can't refer to it closely, but I thought all the Devon part was splendid, and it was nice to meet Wilmet and Keith again. There is something

very special about these two, they are memorable not
only in themselves but in their relation, as if Wilmet's
reward for her 'sins' is this ridiculous unwanted incubus,
endlessly chattering of lovely homes and boiling things in
Tide. There is a dreadful kind of justice about it. One feels
she will never get rid of him. None the less, my feeling
is that Angela Thirkell, for instance, vitiated her later
books by mentioning everyone in every one, and I think
it's a device needing very sharp control if this danger is
to be avoided. I realise of course you are using a different
method – coincidence rather than Barchester – but it has
its pitfalls, to my mind, all the same. I hope this doesn't
sound too presumptuous.[2]

About the reintroduction of characters, Barbara replied:

It can be a tiresome affectation. With me it's sometimes
laziness – if I need a casual clergyman or anthropologist
I just take one from an earlier book. Perhaps one should
take such a very minor character that only the author
recognises it, like a kind of superstition or a charm.[3]

The fact was, that she had created such a complete world
that it was perfectly possible for a character from one book
to move about easily in another. And, of course, many of her
friends and readers simply wanted to know 'what happened
next' to their favourite characters after the book had ended.

Barbara worked hard at the novel that was to become *An
Unsuitable Attachment*, blending Queen's Park and Italy, the
clergy and the anthropologists, and drew on her reawakened
memories of Naples for a young man, like Starky, who would
be a sort of anti-hero. She was puzzling over the character of
Sophia, much more complex than anything she had attempted
before. In her notebook she considers:

Hymns with soppy words and Romish tunes – Mark
chooses these as being more suitable. Sophia agrees
– everything he does is so *right*. She is not really a
believer? Only goes because of him?[4]

but this theme was not developed and she makes a more
homely note:

The smell of fish cooking – but it is Faustina's coley, not Mark's Friday fish.[5]

Meanwhile Philip Larkin had been ill with what was first thought to be 'a cerebral attack [which] seems to be a superior kind of faint', but which turned out to be rather more serious.

I seem to have survived the polio, 'wich [sic] is good' as Nat Gubbins' sweep used to say, and, if not yet free from a sense of imminent seizure and death, am at least no worse as far as I can tell. . . . If anyone has written about your books I haven't seen it, and I do think they deserve 'art' recognition as well as 'commercial' recognition, and this it would be my earnest intention to give. I can't *bear* to look at *A Girl in Winter* [one of his early novels which she had mentioned in her letter]: it seems so knowing and smart. I did it when I was about 23 and hoped I was going to lead that wonderful 500-words a day on the Riviera life that beckons us all like an ignis fatuus from the age of 16 onwards, but alas I wasn't good enough. . . . I still get about £1 royalties every 6 months from it.[6]

Although they did not write to each other very often, it was obvious that they both enjoyed the correspondence and, as well as letters, occasional postcards would flash between Hull and London bearing messages such as:

Delighted to say that our holdings of *Africa* are solid: Vol I – (1928–). One problem of a librarian the less![7]

In January 1962 he wrote:

I have just begun reading your corpus in earnest, pen in hand . . . there are dozens of things I should like to ask, but it is probably better for me to put down what I think unprompted. I remember the tremendous trepidation and trembling with which I put my most cherished critical ideas to Mary MacCarthy: had she intended, etc.

She listened to the end and then said 'No', that was all.
Moments with the Mighty.
I have sought *Africa* in the stack and find that recent
volumes have been used a little. . . . Our books, as I may
have said, are published by O.U.P. and sink like stones
– the next we hope will be a big hit, 'The Geography of
Communications', by J. Appleton. Look out for it on your
station bookstall . . .
I hope we don't get a smallpox epidemic [there was
a current scare]. I'm afraid I always feel London is very
unhealthy – I can hear fat Caribbean germs pattering
after me in the Underground.[8]

They exchanged comments on the weather – a poet and
a novelist:

Isn't this time of year [February 1963] dreadful? It was
just the same last year, if you remember – frigid hostile
air that makes life a misery.[9]

and she replied:

Was there a time when we were not forever on our
knees filling paraffin stoves? I hope you are well (perhaps
centrally?) heated – poets should not have to worry about
how to keep pipes from freezing and all that dreariness –
but I suppose it should be part of every novelist's experience.[10]

He sent her little incidents that he knew would amuse
her (one of which did, indeed, find its way into a novel)

. . . the Warden in a Hall here who makes the conference
secretary's life a misery with 'several tea pots and hot
water jugs were left standing on a polished table last
night, instead of being replaced on the tray provided.
The table was marred in consequence . . . '[11]

He knew instinctively that she loved to hear about the
trivial details that made up his everyday life:

My carpet has come back from the cleaners and feels like an unmown lawn. . . .

I have celebrated it [the New Year] by ordering a new gas cooker and a new bedroom carpet. You may wonder what kind of life I lead to wear the existing ones out. In fact my gas cooker was a very small table model and my bedroom has been carpeted for nine years with odd scraps with newspaper underlay. The cooker, the new one, hasn't come yet (it is to be white, not cream, which upset the Gas Board a bit), nor has the carpet, which is a decided yet restful pattern of green leaves. Already the zestful glow which prompted their purchase is fading. With such gewgaws does one get oneself through the New Year.[12]

He too was publishing (or, rather, republishing) 'a juvenile novel called *Jill*'.

So one day in Spring 1964 the weeklies will have articles headed 'From Immaturity to Decadence', 'A Talent in Decline', 'Gentility's Victim', etc., etc. It's good of you to encourage me in this, but I rather dread it. I have a great shrinking from publicity – think of me as A. E. Houseman without the talent or the scholarship, or the soft job, or the curious private life – anyway, not as John Wain depicts me [in his autobiography].[13]

Barbara finished *An Unsuitable Attachment* and on 24 February she wrote to Philip Larkin:

I sent my novel to Cape last week but don't know yet what they think of it. I feel it can hardly come up to *Catch 22* or *The Passion Flower Hotel* for selling qualities, but I hope they will realise that it is necessary for a good publisher's list to have something milder.[14]

On 20 March she had a letter from Cape rejecting *An Unsuitable Attachment*. For all her premonitions, it was such an unexpected blow that at first it didn't really sink in. Only a few days later, when she had written about it in her notebook, did the full force of her personal loss strike her. Inevitably, she made the analogy with being rejected in love:

> To receive a bitter blow on an early Spring evening (such as that Cape don't want to publish *An Unsuitable Attachment* – but it might be that someone doesn't love you any more) – is it worse than on an Autumn or Winter evening? Smell of bonfire (the burning of rose prunings, etc.), a late hyacinth in the house, forsythia about to burst, a black and white cat on the sofa, a small fire burning in the grate, books and Sunday papers and the remains of tea.[15]

Her books had replaced her love affairs as the chief preoccupation of her life, and in this rejection she felt all the cumulative pain of her early unhappinesses. Pain was followed by anger and she wrote to Bob Smith that week:

> 1963 has been a bad year so far. Just after the two burglaries [at Brooksville Avenue] and losing my typewriter, I had a great blow from Cape, who said they didn't want to publish my novel.... And that after six novels and thirteen years and even a small amount of prestige to the house of Cape! This was not altogether a surprise to me because I had been warned by Jock of the dreadful things that were happening now that this Tom Maschler had joined the firm. Ronald Fraser, and I think also P. H. Newby, have been similarly off-loaded and their whole policy is obviously to publish only best sellers like Ian Fleming. Of course I wrote an indignant but very dignified letter of protest, and Wren Howard in his answer sounded genuinely sorry and distressed about it all (but they say he has no moral courage and in any case is getting old now). But now an even worse thing has happened – poor old Daniel George has had a stroke and lies in Hampstead hospital. According to Philip Hope-Wallace, whom Hilary saw, he has just been pensioned off with 3 months' salary. He was apparently very distressed at the way I'd been treated.[16]

It does not appear that Barbara's novels, although by no means best sellers, ever lost Cape money. A note in her diary of her sales to December 1958 reads:

A Glass of Blessings	3,071
Less Than Angels	3,569
Jane and Prudence	5,052
Excellent Women	6,577
Some Tame Gazelle	3,544[17]

It was unfortunate that this particular novel should have been submitted at this particular time. Barbara herself had never been really satisfied with it. She realised that there was a gaping hole where the hero should have been. John Challow had no real substance, he was something and nothing, not strong enough to be a hero, not bad enough to be a villain. In the 'swinging sixties' the attachment, too, would not be seen to be really unsuitable, since it was not the fact that John was younger than Ianthe that was the real bar to their happiness, but that he was of a lower social class. Ianthe, even in the context of the novel, was perceived to be old-fashioned – that was an essential part of the plot – but to many readers of that period she would have seemed unbelievable. We can accept her now because the sixties themselves have become history, and both the age and the characters in the novel can be seen in perspective. The fact that the Church formed the main background of the novel also did it a disservice, as did the gently ironic tone.

More practically, the closing of many of the circulating libraries did incalculable harm to books of this nature. A large market of middle-class, middle-brow readers – the backbone of the novel-reading public at that time – was gone and, although they took books from their public libraries, that did not greatly help sales, since they were, by and large, book borrowers and not book buyers. Many other writers of this period disappeared: Elaine Howis, P. H. Newby, Ronald Fraser and M. J. Farrell (later to reappear triumphantly as Mollie Keane). They too, like Barbara, cannot be dismissed as merely 'circulating library novelists'.

Today, when the real importance of Barbara's novels is

recognised and they are read and appreciated for what Philip
Larkin called her 'plangent qualities' as well as for her high
comedy, it seems extraordinary that she should have been
dismissed so casually and so cruelly.

She wrote to tell Philip Larkin of her disappointment,
ending with a typical understatement:

> It ought to be enough for anybody to be the Assistant
> Editor of *Africa*, especially when the Editor is away
> lecturing for six months at Harvard, but I find it isn't
> quite.[18]

He was '*astonished*' and deeply indignant on her behalf.

> I can't understand why the publishers are taking this
> line. I have introduced several people to your work and
> they all like it (my sister introduced *me*): not everyone
> yearns to read about S. Africa or Negro homosexuals
> or the woes of professional Rugby League players. Of
> course Cape's will have the sales figures, which I
> suppose cannot be gainsaid, but it seems a sad state
> of affairs if such tender, perceptive and intelligent
> work can't see the light, just because it won't 'go' in
> America, or some tasteless chump thinks it won't 'go' in
> paperback.[19]

In 1981, when Philip Larkin was writing an introduction to
the posthumous publication of *An Unsuitable Attachment*, he
wrote to the Chairman of Cape, who at the time of the rejection
had been their literary adviser and in his late twenties, and
asked for his view of the affair. The reply came:

> When *An Unsuitable Attachment* came in it received
> unfavourable reports. Indeed they must have been very
> unfavourable for us to decide to reject an author for
> whom we had published several books. At that time we
> had two readers, both of whom had been here for many
> years: William Plomer and Daniel George. Neither then
> or at any time has this company rejected a manuscript for
> commercial reasons 'notwithstanding the literary merit
> of the book'. Though of course the two must be relative
> to some extent.

Cape then said that they had found the reports on the book
by Plomer and George and that one was 'extremely negative'
and the other 'fairly negative'.
  Philip Larkin continued:

> If her publishers are correct, it is surprising that there
> was not someone at Cape prepared to invite Barbara Pym
> to lunch and say that while they had enjoyed publishing
> her books in the past and hoped to do so in the future,
> this particular one needed revision if it was to reach its
> potential value. It was the blank rejection, the implication
> that all she had previously written stood for nothing, that
> hurt.[20]

The rejection was, in fact, totally blank. The actual letters
that Barbara received from Wren Howard on 19 March and
3 April 1963, even now remain (to use Hilary's word) chilling.

Dear Miss Pym
  I feel that I must first warn you that this is a
difficult letter to write. Several of us have now read,
not without pleasure and interest, the typescript of your
novel *An Unsuitable Attachment*, and have discussed it
at considerable length, but have unanimously reached
the sad conclusion that in present conditions we could
not sell a sufficient number of copies to cover costs, let
alone make any profit.
  All costs have now increased so much that it is
necessary to sell many more copies than ever before to
break even. This also means that the investment involved
in publishing a new book is three or four times what it
used to be and our risk correspondingly increased.
  Our difficulties in publishing fiction have also greatly
increased by the disappearance of Smith's Circulating
Libraries and the reduction in Boots' Libraries, and by
the steady decline in the sales of novels in Common-
wealth markets. This is particularly marked in the case
of Australia. We are obliged, therefore, to be more than
ever cautious.
  You will, I am sure, appreciate how distasteful it
is for me to have to write to you in this strain after
publishing your novels and always having maintained
a particularly friendly author/publisher relationship, but

in fairness to one's company and to my colleagues I feel I cannot do otherwise.

and

Dear Miss Pym
    I have read and reread several times your letter dated March 21st and also the copy of my letter to you dated March 19th. I feel it would be impolite not to acknowledge your letter, though there is nothing more that I can add to what I originally wrote, for my letter seems to have anticipated most of what you yourself have written.
    I am truly distressed that you should feel that you have been unfairly treated and I most sincerely sympathise with your feeling of great disappointment. I have also again been carefully through the accounts of all six books, have checked the results and can now confirm that the losses incurred in publishing some of them exactly equalled the modest profit derived from the others. Thus, while we have not exactly lost any money, we have not made any as a result of publishing these six novels, and a publisher unhappily cannot afford merely to break even. He must, somehow, in order to survive, make some profit.[21]

As Philip Larkin said, the reader must make what he can of these two accounts. It was not only that Cape was summarily dismissing everything she had ever written – that was bad enough – but there was no expectation that they would ever publish anything she might write in the future. Usually, normal politeness would have suggested the inclusion of a phrase like 'we will, of course, be happy to consider any future novel', but there is no hint of that. She had been (to use her own phrase) 'off-loaded', the door was slammed in her face. The fact is that the writing had been on the wall for some time. In 1962 when he left Cape to go to Longmans, Jock Liddell had written to her:

I was grieved to leave our publisher and would hardly have done so while dear Jonathan was with us. But the rot had, I think, already started before he was taken from us – and dear Mr Victor Gollancz years

ago told me it would not be much of a House without
its Head. . . . Horror stories came to me from various
authors of my acquaintance.

Francis King told me most of the Cape staff and
some authors had seceded. He said that Tom Maschler
had said my travel books were very well written: 'but
who wants to read travel, unless the author is going
round with a lioness on a leash or something'. It would
be inconvenient for me to travel with a lioness. Miss
Manning and Miss Farrell came with even stronger
persuasions – and in the past John Guest had tried to
woo me to Longmans. . . . Like yourself I detest change
– but it seemed to me that J.A. [Jock was writing a study
of Jane Austen] would never appear with Cape, and I had
stifled one book already [a travel book] to stay with them.
And I think rather well of J.A. if I may be allowed to say
so – and it seemed the moment to stand firm. Cape *may*
settle down but it still seems upside down.[22]

and after Barbara wrote to tell him of her rejection he wrote:

I am very much disappointed in Wren Howard. When we
were young 3,300 copies was thought a good sale. . . . Not
long ago I ran into one of the most foolish young men
I know (I forget his name) and learned he was a new
Maschler novelist. I hope that you and Ronald Fraser
and Newby may all have immense successes with the
novels he wouldn't have. . . . You might send the book
to James McGibbon at Gollancz or Raleigh Trevelyan at
Hutchinsons. You may name me to either for what it is
worth.[23]

The really sad thing is that Barbara did not live long
enough to read some of the reviews that greeted *An Unsuitable Attachment* when it was finally published, in Britain and
America, some twenty years later:

The publisher must have been mad to reject this jewel.
The cut-glass elegance of her precise, understated wit
sparkles, her understanding of the human heart gleams
more softly but just as bright. *Washington Post*

and

An Unsuitable Attachment is a paragon of a novel,
certainly one of her best; witty, elegant, suggesting
beyond the miniature exactness the vast panorama of
a vanished civilisation. *New York Times*

Justice was – eventually – seen to have been done.

So began the long, unhappy period of frustration and rejection.
Brief, stark entries in her pocket diary for those first months
give an indication of how it was to be.

23 April	Posted *Unsuitable Attachment* to Heath [a literary agent]
3 May	Heath returned *Unsuitable Attachment*
30 May	Sent *Unsuitable Attachment* to Ivor Guest at Longmans
6 June	Had *Unsuitable Attachment* back from Longmans
10 July	Sent *Wrapped in Lemon Leaves* to Macmillan
1 August	*Wrapped in Lemon Leaves* came back from Macmillan.[24]

Obviously simply changing the title wasn't going to be the
solution to the problem. According to the diary, life went on:

18 August	St Cyprian's Clarence Gate. 11 o'clock. Fr Doyle Fr Parry Chivers to tea.
8 September	Migraine
9 September	Day at home, ill (started to write again).[25]

In October she wrote to Bob Smith:

We have had another burglary and are now going to
have a metal folding gate across the kitchen window,
which is where they get in. This time they took decanters
and candlesticks. We were innocent and trusting but I'm
not any more.
    I have started to write another novel, as I knew I
would eventually, but I don't get on very fast. In the

meanwhile Philip Larkin is reading the rejected one, but
I cannot imagine he would wish to introduce it to Faber
[his own publisher] in its present state, nor would I wish
it really. I begin to feel now that I might improve it some
time. My friend Peggy Makins (a woman journalist [who
wrote under the name of Evelyn Home]) gave me much
helpful advice, but said of course *she* loved it, being a BP
fan. Of course that isn't enough, though, as we know![26]

Philip Larkin sent her his comments on *An Unsuitable
Attachment* later that month.

Of course, I don't think you could write a novel that I
should not enjoy, and this certainly isn't it. I found it
continuously interesting and amusing – I'm afraid you
quite fooled me with who was to marry Ianthe! Faustina is
splendid – in my view just a little more sparring between
her and Sister Dew would have been permissible – and I
like the obsessional quality of Sophia's affection for her,
this seems very real. . . . The excursion to Rome is good
and I think successful, but I hope you won't repeat the
experiment too often, as I think one of your chief talents
is for recording the English scene. Your librarians made
me smile. Mervyn is a worthy addition to your gallery
of rogue males, so well presided over (in my opinion) by
Fabian Driver. Your 'library detail' doesn't square very
well with my experience, by the way! 'London,' would be
my choice [as opposed to 'London:' and then the date,
for a library entry, which is the form we used at the
Institute] . . .
    I have tried to keep my eye open for anything that
would suggest why Cape's should not publish it, and I
am bound to say that it still seems a mystery to me, as
people who like your books (and I cling to my belief that
there are a lot of them) will like this one. It isn't as if you
had suddenly written in a quite different *genre*. Judged
within your own canon, it may be that its effect is a little
less well organised, and a little weaker in impact, than,
say, *A Glass of Blessings* or *Excellent Women*. If this is
so, I should put it down to the fact that we become rather
less implicated with Ianthe and John than is necessary
to give the book centre. In fact I found myself not caring
very greatly for Ianthe, or John either, really. Partly she

is played off by Penelope, partly her decency and good breeding are stated rather than shown; her 'Which is a great country' on p. 43 made me want to bat her over the head, apart from seeming out of character: would she be as assertive as that? I don't myself think that the number of characters matters much: I enjoyed the book's richness in this respect. What I did feel was that there was a certain familiarity about some of them: Sophia and Penelope seemed to recall Jane and Prudence, and Mark Nicholas; Mervyn has something of Arthur Grampian, and of course we have been among the anthropologists before. What this adds up to is perhaps a sense of coasting – U.S.A. for free-wheeling, I believe – which doesn't bother me at all, but which might strike a critical publisher's reader – unsympathetic I mean rather than acute – as constituting 'the mixture as before' . . .

I should very much like to see it published. What do you feel about my suggestion of trying to interest Faber's? I am quite willing to draw their attention to it; my only hesitation is whether you would like to reserve what puny effort I can make in this direction for a later book . . .

I hope you will excuse the criticisms outlined above – really, I was casting around for reasons for Cape's refusal to publish. I should think it is probably a matter of money, like most things.[27]

Barbara replied gratefully.

I was so much encouraged and cheered by your letter about *An Unsuitable Attachment*. . . . I am so glad it did give you some amusement and I am grateful for your comments and criticisms, which will be a help to me when I come to rewrite it, if I do, and also in a general way for the future. I can't help feeling that it would be better to start at Faber's with a new book, though, or with this one improved in some ways. . . . You are quite right about Ianthe and John. Ianthe is very stiff and John had been intended to be much worse – almost the kind of man who would bigamously marry a spinster, older than himself, for the sake of £50 in the P.O. Savings Bank! . . .

I suppose it *was* money, really, they didn't think they could sell enough copies. However well they do out of Ian

Fleming and Len Deighton and all the Americans they publish, I suppose they can't afford any book that will not
cover its cost. (I don't think I *really* feel this!)

She ends this letter:

May I say 'Philip' [this, after two years' correspondence],
if that is what people call you, or should we go through
the academic convention of 'Philip Larkin' and 'Barbara
Pym'?[28]

Philip Larkin's friendship came at a very important time
for Barbara. From that letter analysing *An Unsuitable Attachment*,
right on, through the darker years, he was constant in his
encouragement and appreciation. Barbara was always liable
to lose confidence in her own powers (in life as well as in
writing) and badly needed the sort of intelligent, perceptive
and affectionate criticism and advice that he gave her. He also
cheered her up by sending her lively, funny letters, which told
her *just* the sort of ordinary, frivolous things she liked to know
about people.

My hand is liable to tremble a bit today as a result of *two*
parties yesterday – the Vice Chancellor's annual sherry
party at *noon*, of all times, and a much more informal
affair at the Building Officer's flat in the evening – hot
punch, Beatles records, twisting. There were about 70
guests! making it next to impossible to get at the food
table. Their large black cat curled up on my lap, which
flattered me a little.[29]

What was also important to her was the fact that his
letters were written from one creative person to another –
they confirmed her status as a writer, something that was
very precious to her.
On holiday on Sark he wrote:

As usually happens when I am far from my ms book, I
feel I could do one or two poems. Let's hope the feeling
survives. . . . [About the new Introduction to *Jill*] I think
it would be nice to do an anti-Twenties piece – no ortolans

or Diaghilev or Harold Acton or Sebastian Flyte, just
grammar school scholarship boys clumping about in STC
uniform and one bottle of wine a term (the ration). Don't
you agree? And no evening clothes, no Balls, champagne,
strawberries, dances, girls, etc. You would I expect have
known the *douceurs de vie* of all these things before 1940.
Actually, the more I read about the old days (*George* by
Emlyn Williams, for instance) the more sympathetic my
own time appears. But my hands have been tied by learning that my College SCR has elected me to membership
– I am of course very pleased by this, but it will hinder
me in writing this preface if I ever do.

I have bought a Panama hat, with a black ribbon,
for 32 × 6d – sufficient to send the sun behind an infinity
of cloud, where it looks like remaining. I think autumn
and winter are better than spring and summer in that
they are not *supposed* to be enjoyable.[30]

and they both enjoyed the more ridiculous and gossipy
aspects of academic life:

'Some problems' are likely to get worse as a result of
Robbins [a new Higher Education review] – really what
a ghastly prospect! Though the real agony is not 1,000
or 10,000 students, but always being about two years
behind with staff, buildings, money and so on. Talk
about climbing up the climbing wave. The University of
Wisconsin offers me a year as Writer in Residence, with
lectures, creative writing seminars, and 'informal coffee
hours' – could this be worse, do you think? I think perhaps
it could, though it is funny to see an article about this very
institution in one of the papers today. (I always say 'one
of the papers' to upset people who only take *The Observer*
– 98% of university people – the other 2% take nothing –
but I don't think it does. I take about five or six and love
them all.) . . . I shall look at the next *Africa* with great
interest [she had written 'We have plenty of "problems"
with the next *Africa* – trying to avoid having *two* rather
dull articles together, and nothing to put in "Notes and
News" but endless Conferences and new African Studies
Centres springing up in the most unlikely places']. We
have a South-East Asian Centre here, which is sheer
folly.

and

> This trip of mine is to ... Oxford ... to try to reopen
> friendly relations with my College ... I expect it will
> be all very boring and irritating ('Hull? Hull? North
> of Derby, is it?') but it would be nice to build up a
> connection in case I wanted to RETIRE there (grim
> thought). My predecessor did. . . .
>
> If you were in university life you would be familiar
> with the phrase 'crushing teaching load' – i.e. six hours a
> week, six months of the year – and would no doubt have
> arraigned it by now.[31]

A letter written in December of that year (1963) was
comforting, helpful and cosy.

> I am writing this at my 'home', which is what one
> always calls where one's surviving parent lives. . . . It
> was a great pleasure to get your letter, and a relief to
> learn that you were not offended by my criticisms. It
> might be as well to try something new or rewritten on
> Faber's, though I still think those who like your books are
> going to like this one, rewritten or not. I have ventured to
> lend it [the typescript] to a friend of mine who also enjoys
> your work (*her* favourite heroine is Catherine, curiously
> enough my least favoured). . . .
>
> Since I last wrote I have had the proofs of the revised
> *Jill*, which looks pretty ridiculous and fearfully badly
> written. It was for this that I wrote an introduction
> which turned out to be mostly about K. Amis: funnily
> enough, I met him in London last week for the first
> time in two years and was able, as they say, to get it
> cleared. . . . Did you read Kingsley's latest novel? It
> takes its place among all the other books that don't
> make me want to visit America. I thought his hero was
> quite a decent chap, considering what he had to put
> up with.
>
> I'm told that the 'economic figure' for novels is 4,000
> and has risen a lot recently.
>
> Life at Pearson Park [his flat in Hull] is not agreeable
> at present because of these horn-playing people who have
> come to live below me. They not only play horns, they
> *bang doors* as if they are perpetually quarrelling or are

new to houses with doors. One night I counted 38 such in 2 hours – or an average of almost once every three minutes. I have begun to wonder if I should be better off in a bungalow. There must be *some* limit to the things money can't buy.

I meant to ask some searching questions about the Institute as revealed in the Annual Report, but have forgotten now what they were. I did wonder whether there was something of a discrepancy between expenditure on the library (staff) and the library (books). This is the question laymen always ask: does it take £3,000 of staff to deal with £300 of books? But I expect they do a lot of other things too . . .

And now Christmas is coming again, as if we hadn't enough to put up with. It's nearly enough to extinguish the low solstitial flame of life – and will, one of these years. Have you begun another novel?

You are very welcome to use my Christian name (or forename, as librarians say austerely) – you see I have ventured to use yours.[32]

She replied:

There seem to be more staff in the [Institute's] Library than anywhere else – I suppose their purpose is to discourage Visitors.

I hope you survived Christmas . . . it is a rather exhausting ordeal for the churchgoer, particularly as we had two ranting sermons, not quite the few words of greeting and comfort one expects at that time. . . .

I have written seven or eight chapters of a new novel. Of course in the end it will turn out not to be any good, perhaps, but I may as well write something even if only for private circulation among a few friends. . . . Catherine used to be quite a favourite heroine of mine but she now seems less real to me than Wilmet and Prudence (my own favourites).[33]

The novel she was writing was *The Sweet Dove Died* and the inspiration for it came, in part, from a new friend, Richard Roberts, who was becoming increasingly important in her life.

Chapter Sixteen

After teaching for several years in Nigerian universities, Bob Smith had become an Africanist – though an historian rather than an anthropologist. Barbara, who was less than enthusiastic about Africa and Africanists, wrote to him:

> Of course I don't really like your knowing about Fage [an expert on African history] and the Ethnographic Survey series and things like that – before we know where we are I shall be seeing a book of yours through the press and many of the other sordid things I have to do at the Institute.[1]

But she did enjoy the occasions, when, on leave from Nigeria, he visited her at the Institute. Bob Smith recalls:

> Now I had an official entrée to the International African Institute . . . on summer afternoons I often climbed the stairs of that cobwebby building in Fetter Lane to Barbara's office in order to take her out to tea. Half seriously she would clutch a packet of cigarettes in case we met the Director, Daryll Forde, on the stairs as we returned, thus preparing an alibi ('I slipped out to buy these') which of course was never needed.[2]

In October 1962 she wrote to him:

> I think I enjoyed the time you were here this summer more than former years even – perhaps one appreciates one's few congenial friends more with the years.[3]

She now had a new friend. That summer Bob had intro-duced Barbara and Hilary to Richard Roberts, a tall, dark, broad-shouldered young man in his thirties. Apart from his good looks and an extrovert charm that was immediately pleasing, he also had the glamour of being rich. His father had been Speaker of the House of Representatives in the Bahamas and his mother still lived in Nassau in some grandeur. Barbara was fascinated by details of his life there – Lady Roberts's jewellery, the black butler and the peacocks. It was a new world and she immediately began to weave fantasies around the whole family.

> His life there is full of such rich material for fiction, but I suppose it is really beyond my range.[4]

At the end of 1962 Richard was in Athens (with an introduction to Jock) and Barbara reported back to Bob:

> The first thing you wanted to know was about Richard and Jock. The latter had told me of meeting R and his friend 'Michael from Bangkok', he thought they were nice but rather overawed by Elizabeth Taylor [the novelist, a great friend of Jock], who was there at the time. Richard dined with us at the end of November so we got a fuller picture from him of the 'literati' who flock to see Jock. . . . *He* thought Elizabeth seemed very bored, but knowing her I should say it was her usual manner which conceals her shyness. Hilary and I are very fond of Richard – *we* dined with *him* in December – we met Maurice Quick [an actor], a nice young man called John something [then sharing a flat with Richard], and a young Siamese action painter just over here, and it was all very cosy. Now Richard is in Nassau with his parents and is, I believe, intending to go to Mexico. He sent us a very pagan Christmas card and also a beautiful postcard from Nassau.[5]

In May 1963, at the end of the letter in which she told Bob about her rejection by Cape, she wrote:

> Richard Campbell Roberts has invited us to the opening of an exhibition of Thai paintings which he is arranging, on Monday next – 6 p.m. – cocktails – so he is evidently back in London and it will be nice to see him – he brings

a bit of joy into life because he is so much *not* of this grim everyday world.[6]

and in June

Richard's exhibition was splendid – masses of champagne but the pictures all much too expensive for *us*. Even prints or lithographs (or whatever) were 17 guineas each at the *lowest*. R. was very sweet and wearing a becoming summer suit of some dark silky material.[7]

Because of the gap in her life, now that she was no longer (at least for the present) a published novelist, what had been a 'cosy' relationship became something much more to her. The fact that he was eighteen years younger than she was and a homosexual, didn't really matter. In the notes for her new novel she writes

She (Leonora) thinks perhaps this is the kind of love I've always wanted because absolutely *nothing* can be done about it![8]

Here was someone from whom one did not demand 'a fond return of love' – simply to love him was enough. Like Ianthe, she simply let it 'sweep over her, like a kind of illness'.[9] But the eye of the novelist (the saga maker) was still alert, even at moments of deeply felt emotion.

Supper with Richard. We eat cosily in almost total darkness (one candle). On the mantelpiece many Easter cards and a telegram. One couldn't give him anything that he hadn't already got. Not even devotion and/or love. It gives one a hopeless sort of feeling. Roman Emperors (a Coles wallpaper) on the wall facing the bed which is large and covered in orange candlewick.[10]

Richard – whom she now called Skipper, the name used by his close friends – was friendly and naturally sociable and perhaps flattered by the attention of someone who had, after all, published six novels. Barbara was still a novelist first and foremost, writing a novel in her head (and in her notebook) even as she lived a scene.

> At Covent Garden with Skipper. He crunches ice as we drink orangeade in the Crush Bar – the great oil paintings, the flowers (real). A happy evening. If 'they' went to Covent Garden Leonora would like to feel the touch of his sleeve against her bare arm (but that would be as far as it would go). Close, intimate red and gold semi-darkness.[11]

The other world that Richard introduced her to was that of antique dealers and the saleroom; he had several friends in the antique trade and he had now opened a shop of his own, L'Atelier, near Sloane Street. Sometimes, in the middle of a tedious afternoon at the Institute, her hand would hover over the telephone. 'Shall I ring him?' she would say. 'No. Better not.' In her notebook:

> Walking in Bond Street I see a young man sitting alone in a grand antique shop, presumably waiting for customers. A woman admirer might be a great nuisance, always coming to see him.[12]

She saw a lot of him that summer, 'his car now knowing its way down Carlton Vale [from Sussex Gardens]'. Hilary was in Greece for three months (time off from the BBC for twenty-five years' service) and, without her sister's rather anxious eye upon her, Barbara was free to live those months in a kind of romantic haze. On 2 June:

> My birthday [her 51st] and dinner with Richard at his flat. Champagne and a lovely present. A Victorian china cup and saucer. 'The Playfellow' – a lady and her cat.[13]

She wrote to him – one letter, headed '18th August (Night)', which might have been written by a younger Barbara:

> My dearest Skipper
>   Thank you for sending back the letter. It was perhaps silly and capricious of me to ask for it, but I

was punished by the disappointment of finding that
an envelope addressed in your hand contained only my
own letter back again. So that will teach me ('Behaviour',
indeed!).

Anyway this little note will contain all the fondness
of the other letter, in a concentrated form like a cube
of chicken stock or Oxo. . . .

I hope you are reasonably well and happy – I really
mean *very* well and reasonably happy – no more of those
sad looks that cut me to the heart, Skipper dear. I would
send you Peruvian heliotrope if I knew where to get it.
But love anyway.[14]

and in her notebook:

4 September. (Oh what a month August was too!) Walking
in Hampstead with Skipper. Parked the car in Church
Row and went up by the Huguenot Cemetery – all beautiful in the dark, warm evening. In the little R.C. church
on Holly Mount, R. lights a candle but I don't somehow
like to and don't say anything either. It is a bit too much
like something in a B.P. novel. Later we walk to Windmill
Hill, Admiral's House, see Galsworthy's house etc., have
coffee in the High St. Talk and wander about peering into
people's uncurtained windows and even their letter boxes.
And on Thursday he is going to Venice.[15]

It was all vintage Romantic Pym, even down to the
graveyard. But she was older now, and perhaps wiser.
She wrote to Bob Smith:

Of course I have become very fond of him, as you must
have gathered, especially this summer, and he has been
very sweet to me. I wish he could be happier but perhaps
that is not in his nature. 'I love Bob, I love Richard, I
love Rice Krispies . . . ' says the brisk jolly voice from
the pulpit, and a ripple of laughter goes through the
congregation. Perhaps it is best in the end just to love
Rice Krispies?[16]

When Hilary returned from Greece, she was distressed to
see how emotionally involved Barbara had become and told her

affectionately but firmly 'to be her age!' Gradually the novelty wore off for Richard, and Barbara saw him less often.

> Yesterday afternoon R. called. . . . He had been burgled – now the lovely square gold watch and the platinum and diamond one (in the style of the 20s) left him by his father has gone. . . . We went to Sussex Gardens for a drink. R. was in his scarlet pullover and rather long navy raincoat. Very sweet, but not, perhaps, Skipper ever again. . . .
>
> He [R.] and I went up to the General's and had coffee and collected two pictures. Everyone said how well I looked – 'blooming' – but is that joy at seeing R. again or what over three weeks *away* from him has done?[17]

The happiness was melting away.

> *20 February [1965].* A sad day. Rang R. in the evening and he felt 'guilty' which I hate. He came to tea on Sunday in his very spoilt little Bahamian mood, full of euphoria, money and sex talk, teasing me and being unkind to Minerva. I get irritated with him.
>
> *24 May.* Fortunately all the fury and bitterness I sometimes feel has stayed hidden inside me and R. doesn't – perhaps never will – know!
>
> *25 May.* All miserable again and determined to 'end it all' between us – but how? And why?
>
> *29 May.* A letter from R. inviting us to dinner on my birthday. I phoned him and we talked. I must learn not to take 'things' so much to heart and try to understand – don't stop loving (can't), just be there if and when needed.[18]

Perhaps in an attempt to put their relationship on a different footing, Richard asked her to bid for some books at Christie's, while he was abroad. She enjoyed the atmosphere of the saleroom. In our lunch hours at the Institute we often went into the book sales in Chancery Lane, and the auctioneer's cry of '£10 at the table!' became one of our catch phrases.

> We did go into Hodgsons ... but we were afraid we
> might find ourselves buying all those 40 vols of Angus
> [Wilson] and Iris [Murdoch] if we stayed, so we slunk
> out again.[19]

Christie's was, of course, more formidable, especially as
she was bidding large sums.

> Went to Christie's to bid and got Sharpe's 2 vols of *Birds
> of Paradise* for £1,000! It *was* rather nerve-wracking but
> rewarding. . . . [20]

She wrote to Bob.

> Miss Pym is still frequenting the sale rooms – a week
> ago R. pushed me into the end of a sale at Sotheby's and
> made me bid for a book on the Bahamas for him, which
> I got.
>   The present fiction situation is extremely tiresome,
> even disagreeable (as Jock might say) but perhaps it will
> pass and I shall have the strength to write a Romance
> of the Sale Room – perhaps. *That* opens up a very rich
> field![21]

She was, painfully, learning to come to terms with her
relationship with Richard – though there was occasionally
a brief outburst of self-distaste.

> Rainer Maria Rilke 1873–1936
> Princess Marie von Thurn und Taxis 1855–1934
> (18 years difference between them, but *he* was a man
> of genius)[22]

She wrote to Bob:

> St Lawrence's goes on. . . . Last Saturday we had our
> annual bazaar, at which Richard made an appearance,
> rather against my wishes. It is rather like me meeting,
> or *not* meeting, his mother – only at the *very* opposite
> end of the scale, if you see what I mean![23]

and later:

I have had no word from him so I suppose I must make an approach myself, if I want to get all that rich assortment of jumble before October 15th. A somewhat farcical situation really.[24]

But in her next letter to Bob, the following month, the bitterness and the hurt were showing:

It would now seem that he has definitely 'offloaded' me, which I think he has been trying to do ever since he came back from Mexico earlier this year. There is now no communication between us at all, except that I asked him to dinner about three weeks ago, and he came, bringing jumble for St L's! We are friendly, of course, but no longer *en rapport.* . . . I shall certainly send him a birthday card next week, perhaps even a present, but if he doesn't want to see me, that's that. 'If it comes not as easily as the leaves to a tree, it had better not come at all' [Keats]. And how *does* he manage all these people in his life, poor boy. I did find it rather sad, but as time goes on, so *peaceful*, and that is perhaps all one asks for now . . .
    Life has its farcical moments and perhaps my sense of humour is greater than his. Perhaps my sardonic tongue has sent him away or he has just lost interest, the latter probably. How well I know that feeling of 'embarrassment' you speak of – racking one's brain for something to say! . . . Trying to understand people and leaving them alone and being 'unselfish' and all *that* jazz has only the bleakest of rewards – precisely nothing![25]

A year later, she still felt the humiliation.

The other day in a fit of boredom I nearly telephoned Richard for a bit of conversation but then I was afraid he might feel awkward and that I might not be able to think of anything to say, so I didn't. So *unflattering* to feel that a person really doesn't ever want to see you again – I don't think it's ever happened to me before *quite* like this! Now, alas, I am too old to change myself but shall just be more cautious in future – not allowing myself to get fond of anybody.[26]

Once again she had given her love to someone who had not
asked for it – 'like having something like a large white rabbit
thrust into your arms and not knowing what to do with it'[27]
– this time with her eyes wide open as to the impossibility
of it all, but none the less miserable for that. But as Robert
Liddell wrote:

> 'Nothing,' of course, 'could come of it.' But something
> did. It was the inspiration of her most deeply felt novel,
> *The Sweet Dove Died*. Though every book of hers must
> have made someone laugh aloud, I do not think she has
> ever drawn a tear from the reader. Nevertheless this
> book, which ends in tears, has an atmosphere of tender
> melancholy.[28]

As far back as 1965, when Richard was abroad, she
wrote in her notebook:

> After the dentist went to the Wimpole Buttery. A de-
> licious creamy cake tasting of walnuts. Now Skipperless
> one begins to understand 'compensatory eating'. Better
> surely now to write the kind of novel that tells of one
> day in the life of such a woman.[29]

The theme of the book was firmly in her mind – the
affection of an older woman for a younger man. She had
felt it before, of course, with Julian, but now it was no
longer 'Oh how absurd and delicious it is to be in love with
somebody younger than yourself! Everybody should try it',[30]
now the mood was autumnal. Her memory of a wet day in
Hampstead, going round Keats's house, 'austere and simple',
sent her to the verse which gave her book its title:

> I had a dove and the sweet dove died;
>   And I have thought it died of grieving:
> O, what could it grieve for? its feet were tied,
>   With a silken thread of my own hand's weaving . . .

Richard, of course, was not James, or even Ned, though
there were elements of him in both of them. What he really
provided was the mood that made her feel the need to write

it. She saw herself on two levels in the book: as Leonora, cool
and in control, her dignity intact even in pain and defeat, but
also, in part, as Meg, whose love for Colin is the caricature
of Leonora's love for James. The depth of feeling makes it
her most painful novel and the scene at the end when Ned
comes to give James back to Leonora and she rebuffs him, has
great power and tension, perfectly in tone with the rest of the
book, but making one aware that here she has attempted and
succeeded in something quite different. Ned, with his devious
nature, his voice as pervasive as a whining gnat, moving in a
dubious world, is, perhaps, her only villain, in the true sense
of the word, and gives the book a darker tone than any of her
others. The background of the book and some of the incidents
fell into place quite easily – the world of antiques and the saleroom, the opera and intimate little dinners, tea at Virginia
Water. And, of course, the episode of the furniture. Bob Smith,
who liked to keep his friends in different compartments, had
promised to lend certain items of his furniture, while he was
in Africa, to both Barbara and another friend, Joan Wales, so
that when Barbara and Hilary went to the furniture depository
(the one that Piers and Wilmet had admired on their walk[31]),
they found that 'another lady' had also been enquiring about
it. In some amusement Barbara wrote to Bob:

> I hear through Richard that Joan would like to have
> the furniture etc the first week in January, so that
> will be all right with us. Anyway, I have already given
> the marble-topped table a *good polish* and will clean up
> the other things. I shouldn't like anyone to say that we
> hadn't taken care of them. (My dear, you should have
> seen the state they sent them back in!)[32]

and later:

> And of course I was very glad to meet Joan her-
> self . . . and thought her very amusing and cosy – I
> should have been surprised if she had not been, seeing
> that she is a friend of yours and Richard's. Of course the
> whole situation is rather what one would like to treat in
> fiction, especially the negotiations about the furniture
> – Henry James or even Anthony Powell – only there

the protagonists (if that isn't too strong a word) could hardly be such nice women as we obviously are. I hope she liked *me*?[33]

Her first draft of the book was rather diffuse, with several extraneous characters and quite a few scenes set in the village where Phoebe had her cottage, which dissipated the build-up of tension and the unity of tone she finally achieved. She sent the draft to Philip Larkin who immediately realised its potential and also what alterations were needed to strengthen it.

The value of the book would be Leonora's slightly absurd 'managing' qualities turning to pathos and – what? . . . I think there's more potential *feeling* in this book than in any you have written. . . . I expect I am being irritating by trying to tell you how to write your book – what the 'real' story is, as DHL would no doubt say. Your writing always moves me one way or another, even when it's this tiresome way of rewriting it for you, without any of the hard work, of course. I think it could be a strong, sad book, with fewer characters and slower movement.[34]

Working on her new novel and rewriting her rejected one was, however, uphill work in the face of the discouraging climate of the publishing world at that time and it was merciful that she had no idea how long it would be before a novel of hers would be accepted.

Chapter Seventeen

Although Cape's rejection had diminished her confidence
in her own ability, she also saw quite clearly that the literary
climate had changed. She read books like *The Naked Lunch*,
Tropic of Cancer, which had finally been published in England
('60,000 copies sold on the 1st day of publication'), and the
novels of James Baldwin (' "powerful", very well written, but
so upsetting – one is really glad never to have had the chance
of that kind of life!'[1]) and realised that this was what publishers
wanted now. She wrote to Philip Larkin:

> I like writing, but am depressed at future prospects
> for my sort of book.... I did read it [*An Unsuitable
> Attachment*] over very critically and it seemed to me
> that it might appear naïve and unsophisticated, though
> it isn't really, to an unsympathetic publisher's reader,
> hoping for that novel about negro homosexuals, young
> men in advertising, etc.[2]

and to Bob Smith:

> I get moments of gloom and pessimism when it seems as
> if nobody could ever like my kind of writing again.... I
> get depressed about my writing, and feel that however
> good it was it still wouldn't be acceptable to any beastly
> publisher.[3]

He was sympathetic:

> *Your* forte was, goodness, I hope still is, to find richness
> and entertainment in the commonplace; you once told me

of an unperceptive ass who thought that *Excellent Women* was a depressing book about washing up.[4]

Philip Larkin was also encouraging:

> I am glad to hear *An Unsuitable Attachment* is coming on – I very much want to see Faustina on my shelves again. When it is finished I will certainly do my best to interest Faber's in it – I hope the Anglican fringe of the firm won't fade too rapidly now Eliot is dead.[5]

Emboldened by this, after a good deal of revising and polishing, she sent the novel to Faber and Faber. But they too rejected it.

> It came back, but with a nice letter from Charles Monteith. Now I feel as if I shall never write again, though perhaps I will eventually. Rather a relief to feel that I don't have to flog myself to finish the present one since probably nothing I write could be acceptable now.[6]

She thanked Philip Larkin for all his efforts on her behalf and said:

> I can quite see that it wouldn't be an economic proposition, and not the kind of book to impress a new publisher anyway. . . . I don't know yet whether I shall try the book anywhere else – at the moment I don't feel at all hopeful. . . . But I expect I shall go on. The ideal is perhaps to be 'at work' on a book but never to finish it.[7]

He replied sympathetically.

> I sent a long grumbling letter to Charles Monteith asking him what he thought would happen to the English novel if publishers wouldn't print stories about sane ordinary people doing sane ordinary things, and

while he acknowledged the point he remained ultimately
unmoved, though regretful. He mentioned the names of
two men at other publishers whom he thought might be
sympathetic, and if you like I will pass them on. . . . Do
try a few more people with it![8]

One of the people that Charles Monteith suggested was
Raleigh Trevelyan, then with Michael Joseph, and when, at
the end of 1965, the BBC broadcast *No Fond Return of Love* as
the serial in *Woman's Hour*, she felt 'it might be a propitious
time' to approach him. But he also refused it.

'A pleasant book, but hardly strong enough'! almost
exactly what Cape said about *Some Tame Gazelle* in
1936.[9]

There were some consolations, though, especially from
Philip Larkin.

I have been re-reading your novels in one fell swoop,
whatever that is – in order. . . . Once again I have
marvelled at the richness and variety of mood and
setting. . . . *STG* is your *Pride and Prejudice*, rich
and untroubled and confident, and very funny. John
Betjeman was here a few weeks ago and we rejoiced
over your work. I also harangued George McBeth of
the BBC about it, he having said incautiously that he
divided novels into two classes, readable and unreadable,
and having replied to my question 'Do you think William
Golding any good?' with 'I prefer to bypass that aspect of
his work'. Rather nice, don't you think?[10]

and

Yes, I read your books, in order, in succession, as
I do from time to time, and once more found them
heartening and entertaining – you know, there is never a
dull page: one never feels 'Oh, now I've got to get through
this before it becomes interesting again' – it's interesting

all the time. I do wish I could write an article pointing out their excellence, but I'm not good at novels. Do you think you 'derive' from any tradition – social comedy rather than Brontë stuff, I suppose? And yet at times they are so moving. Really, they are entirely original, and I wish I could say so.[11]

But even when all that was said, nobody seemed to want to publish her. Her letter to Bob Smith in October 1966 was pessimistic but brave:

I am feeling in better writing form myself now and have at last got my book back from Hughes Massie (the agent of Paul Gallico and Agatha Christie). In all the eight months that she had it, Miss Patricia Cork sent it to only *one* publisher and then only because I asked what was happening to it. This was Collins, who kept it a long time and perhaps almost decided to take it but in the end decided against it. I am now going to send it round on my own for a bit. In the meantime I am working on another one which is nearly finished. People urge me to go on and it is encouraging that you should again have mentioned it. So easy to sink into apathy and despair, but that is not really my nature.[12]

and later:

Yes, of course, I knew all my books were out of print. The author usually does know these things. It makes it all the more fun to search for second-hand copies, but it was nice of you to think of ordering a set. I always buy second-hand copies now. I have just sent a copy of *Less Than Angels* to an admirer in the Dept. of Anthropology, Univ. of Indiana, Bloomington! I think the Americans appreciate that book more than people here did.[13]

As well as the serialisation of *No Fond Return* on *Woman's Hour,* she had another piece of good news to tell Bob when she wrote to him in November 1967:

Some Tame Gazelle and *Excellent Women* are being reprinted ('in a modest edition') by a firm in Bath [Portway] that does reprints for Libraries, as there appears to be still some demand for them.[14]

It is ironic that the two books chosen for reprinting (by what, after all, was popular demand) should be those that were quintessential Pym, as far removed as possible from what publishers saw to be public taste.

Taking Philip Larkin's advice, she rewrote *The Sweet Dove Died* along the lines he had suggested, and began to send it out to various publishers. It was rejected by Chatto and

Longman's returned *The Sweet Dove* – 'well written' – but what's the use of that.

Sweet Dove rejected yet again (by Mcdonald).

It is 'virtually impossible' for a novel like *Sweet Dove* to be published now (by Constable).

My novel has had its umpteenth rejection (from Cassell). After lunch [I] go to Red Lion Square and I enter the portals of Cassell's to collect the nicely done-up MS. Where next? Up to Faber in Queen's Square.[15]

So it went from publisher to publisher. Several times, to escape the stigma of being a 'female novelist' she sent it out under the name Tom Crampton, but with no success.

There were tiny glimpses of comfort.

I fear Macmillan will not take *The Sweet Dove*, but only (they say) because it seems a risk commercially. I have never had a more flattering letter about my work (or even review) than the one James Wright wrote about it. He praised my 'perfection of taste' so you can see what is wrong, especially when you read the reviews in the Sundays any week.[16]

and

> I am feeling encouraged because *The Sweet Dove* was
> very nearly accepted by Peter Davies, and I sent it
> completely out of the blue with no indication that
> I had ever written anything else. One of the direc-
> tors (Mark Barty-King) wrote me a long letter, quoting
> five readers' reports, some of which were very flatter-
> ing. It was 'very accomplished' and 'a minor tour de
> force' but the general opinion was that it wasn't quite
> powerful enough or plotted enough to appeal to enough
> readers. I have had to write back and reveal my secret,
> but I don't suppose they can change their minds now.
> One of the less kind reports said that it was clever-
> clever and decadent – *that* made me feel about 30 years
> younger![17]

Comfort too from Philip Larkin's unwavering admiration.

> How *good* they [the novels] are! How much what one
> wants after a hard, or even a soft, day's work! How
> vivacious and funny and observant! And feeling, of
> course. It seems fearful that you should be trying not
> to be 'cosy' – I really don't think that that was the
> trouble with this particular book [*The Sweet Dove*], and
> really it is what one comes to you *for*, it's what people
> want, despite Tom Maschler and M. Drabble. However,
> the best of luck. If I could help by writing a 'foreword' –
> an 'appreciation' – of course I'd love to try, though I'm
> not much good at criticism. I have just written a poem,
> which cheers me slightly, except when I read it, when
> it depresses me. It's about the seaside, and rather a self
> parody.[18]

He too was experiencing difficulties.

> Poetry has deserted me – I had a sonnet in the
> Sheffield *Morning Telegraph* last Saturday, which is
> how some people *start*, I suppose. Perhaps we shall kick
> the lids off our tombs simultaneously.[19]

Bob Smith, too, was anxious that she should not compromise, should retain her own particular style and view of life:

> I am a bit worried that you are trying to be 'less cosy'. Oh what is one to say. I did so love your books and read them when I can over and over. The boring but consoling thing is that later, and it may be too late for material consolation, you are bound to be discovered and older men at Oxford as well as young men at Texas will get down to solid work on you and your opera, published and unpublished.[20]

In 1971 Bob Smith was able to give Barbara some practical help. His article, 'How Pleasant to Know Miss Pym', appeared in the literary magazine *Ariel* – it was the first critical study of her work to be published. In it Bob Smith made an eloquent plea for the kind of book which he described as 'books for a bad day'. But hers, he said, were something more. As well as providing a valuable record of their time, she has created 'her own domain':

> Her works are miniatures, exquisitely, nearly perfectly, done. But, beyond this, it is her wit and her sense of the ridiculous which make her books both delicious and distinguished. Above all, they must be ranked as comic novels, but the comedy is realistic and demonstrates again and again the happiness and merriment which can be found in the trivia of the daily round – that 'purchase of a sponge-cake' about which Jane Austen felt it proper to write to Cassandra.[21]

He ends with a rallying call:

> Meanwhile, bad days come to us all, and we cannot anticipate their ever not coming. Let us hope that Miss Pym will begin again to help us deal with them.[22]

She was hopeful that this might just catch the eye of some publisher, and so was Philip Larkin.

> I do hope it [*The Sweet Dove Died*] comes out: partly I am longing to see it, partly I want these purblind money

mad publishers (Messrs Ginn & Tonnick, Messrs Costa &
Brava) to realise how rare and valuable your books are.
It's absolutely scandalous that you've not been reprinted
in paperback. Messrs Cabin & Cruiser deserve to be on
the breadline – or the smoked salmon line at least.

I read Robert Smith's article ... and was glad to
read his sober and sensible praise. ... I must say I'd
sooner read a new BP than a new Jane Austen![23]

But nothing came of it.

Her friends were supportive and Hilary, who had been
fiercely indignant about her sister's rejection, was always
there, comforting and perceptive, someone with whom to
share the incidents and overheard remarks still jotted down
in the small spiral-bound notebooks. They had a busy social
life, entertaining their friends – Barbara was an excellent cook
– and taking holidays abroad together.

Her work at the Institute was demanding and although
she was only interested in the unintentionally comic aspects
of anthropology, she was glad to be dealing with proofs and
printers and reviews and felt that she was, even if only per-
ipherally, still in the world of books.

She read a great deal – Iris Murdoch and Charlotte M. Yonge
('echoes or rather foreshadowings of Ivy Compton-Burnett').
She was very moved by the Winifred Gérin life of Charlotte
Brontë, and went back to reread *Villette*, *Shirley* and *The Professor* ('not *Jane Eyre*'). And she 'found comfort' in Anthony
Powell's great novel sequence. In fact, they became almost
another Denton-like obsession and she made 'family trees' of
the linked novels, our afternoons were spent in devising *Music
of Time* quizzes, and she suggested that she might write a short
paper for a literary magazine on Mrs Widmerpool's bridge coat.
She sent Bob Smith, equally enthusiastic, the 'concordance'
she had made and he wrote back:

Thanks for the Anthony Powell concordance. I suppose
it is only in its first stage and there is no point in trying
to arrange it (alphabetically by characters or whatever)
until the series is complete. But I wondered why you
had not included the last two novels – e.g. nothing
about ... that intelligence colonel or those foreign liaison

officers, though P. Flitton is there. How silly of A.P. to go
off to India, and really, too, I wish he hadn't got mixed up
with the theatre. After all he is in his 60s and one must
have *The Music of Time* finished – though how can it
finish? Perhaps the best ending would be in mid-course,
things going on but not recorded.[24]

He also had the occasional literary curiosity that he knew
would amuse her:

I have been reading a delightful, though perhaps rather
bitchy new book by Fr Stephenson about Walsingham
and Fr H.P. There is a vignette of H.P. instructing the
Sunday school children on what to do when confronted
with an unbaptized person dying in a railway carriage.[25]

Although she was not actually writing a new novel (and
had given up 'tinkering' with the two unpublished ones) she
still made entries in her notebooks.

Mr Claydon in the Library – he is having his lunch,
eating a sandwich with a knife and fork, a glass of
milk near at hand. Oh *why* can't I write about things
like that any more – why is this kind of thing no longer
acceptable? . . . What is wrong with being obsessed with
trivia? Some have criticised *The Sweet Dove* for this. What
are the minds of my critics filled with? What *nobler* and
more worthwhile things?[26]

Mr Claydon was partly the inspiration for a new novel that
she was turning over in her mind. Her friends had often suggested that she should write about 'other things', novels that
might be 'more commercial' – detective stories, perhaps, or
even a biography. But she felt that she could only write her
own kind of book. Nevertheless, it seemed to her that quite a
few novels about academic life were being published. She was,
actually, fascinated by the spate of American academic novels
that had appeared – it seemed like another world – and she
thought that she might attempt such a thing herself. She
rejected the idea of an Oxbridge novel, choosing the more
'swinging' setting of a redbrick university. She had, indeed,

quite a lot of material to draw upon. Not only was she, through the Institute, in touch with a number of anthropologists in provincial universities, but she also had some splendid letters from Philip Larkin in Hull to draw upon.

> Wretched term has started again, and the place is full of replicas of Che Guevara and John Lennon, muttering away and plotting treason . . . great shambling boys from Dewsbury, all reading the *Guardian* . . .

> Well, we have had our sit-in, our baptism of fire. . . . It was a disagreeable experience: I suppose revolutions always are. I wish I could either describe it, or say something penetrating about it: on reflection it seemed to me not so much a *change* in our universities as forcible recognition that a change had taken place some time ago, when we expanded them so suicidally. The universities must now be changed to fit the kind of people we took in: exams made easier, place made like a factory, with plenty of shop-floor agitation and a real-life strike. Also disagreeable was the way the staff loved it, calling meetings and issuing press statements and wearing the 'campaign badge' and trying to climb on the bandwagon to get softer lives for themselves (nine cushions instead of eight).

> We are on the verge of term now: on Friday night I attend the dinner for new staff. Dropping in at the Registrar's office for a 'sneak preview' of the table plan (always a necessary precaution) I found I had been put next to a new girl in Italian called Borgia. Soon put an end to that! On Tuesday I have to address the freshers on 'Books' ('How to Kill, Skin and Stuff Them'), very much in the shadow of Marshall McLuhan. My new Library extension is rising slowly – I forgot if I said there was such a thing. Since about 1961 it's been the daysman of my thought, and hope, and doing.

> My library wasn't quite finished by 1st March, as planned, so we shan't be moving in until after the exams in May and June. It's an odd building, of a curious glaring drabness, with far too little staff space. No doubt the students will make it a pretext for some 'polarisation' (the latest word for sit-in) or other when the time comes. I believe 'sit-ins'

will replace Rag Week: same time, same general motives.
Thank God you aren't in a university! It's like a compre-
hensive where the kids have never left. Our president next
year is a bearded, sandalled, bare-footed, pectoral-crossed,
robed, singing militant who does research in Pure Maths
.... I feel deeply humiliated at living in a country that
spends more on education than defence:

> 'When the Russian tanks roll westward
>   What defence for you and me?
> Colonel Sloman's Essex Rifles? The
>   Light Horse of L.S.E.?'

Or possibly that mythical company known in the War as
'The King's Own Enemy Aliens': Pioneers, were they?

Last term was dreadful, with students threatening all
sorts of trouble, but this term ... has been just dull, with
them concentrating on not paying their rent.... As if
there were no glass in the windows! they shiver and shift
in their seats. Then suddenly they find a good cause and
withdraw their labour or take industrial action or something ... and are more at ease. Anyway, as long as they
keep off the Library I can't say I lose much sleep over it.

How exciting to hear that you're thinking of turning your
austere regard on redbrick academic life.... There's a
subject and a half if you like.... I should love to offer
to stand as technical adviser, but in fact even after 25
years I really know little about provincial university life.
As a librarian I'm remote from teaching, examining and
researching; as a bachelor I'm remote from the Wives'
Club or the Ups and Downs of Entertaining; as an
introvert I hardly notice anything anyway.[27]

By the end of October 1971 Barbara had finished the
first draft and wrote to Bob Smith:

The idea for it was inspired by that business of John
Beattie and Rodney Needham in *Africa* and the original version of Mrs Fisher's *Twilight Tales of the Black
Baganda* – there are also two characters in it rather
like Richard and his mother, exiles from the Caribbean.

> Perhaps my immediate circle of friends will like to read it.[28]

An academic wrangle in the pages of *Africa* provided the mainspring of the plot, a rather dashing female anthropologist, much in demand as a reviewer, was the inspiration for Iris Horniblow, Mr Claydon, the Institute's Library Assistant provided the sardonic tone of Dr Cranton, and the Hull University student unrest provided a climax for the novel. Sister Dew's old people's home was called Normanhurst, perhaps a memory of a large house with that name opposite Blytheswood in Oswestry. The novel was written in the first person, the narrator being the young wife of a university lecturer. 'It was supposed to be a sort of Margaret Drabble effort but of course it hasn't turned out like that at all.' She felt, in fact, that it was too 'cosy', too like her other, rejected books, so she wrote a second draft in the third person, trying to make it sharper and 'more swinging'. The heroine, Caroline, was a transitional figure, being by upbringing and temperament an excellent woman, fitting uneasily into the role of graduate wife. The novel had some splendid moments and some memorable characters – it also had a notable failure, Caro's daughter Kate (Barbara was never very happy with children). She 'tinkered with it' for some time, but was ultimately dissatisfied and laid it aside. She never revised it and it was only published posthumously as *An Academic Question*. But it proved to be a valuable exercise, since it kept her view of the world up to date, so that her future books were not set in a sort of time warp, as they might have been if she had written nothing at all during this period of social change. It was a step forward in her development and led the way to the different mood of her last two novels.

Meanwhile she had other things on her mind. At the end of April 1971 she had discovered a small lump on her left breast. Her doctor sent her to hospital for an examination and it was found to be malignant. In her notebook entry, her first reaction was literary:

> Morning at St Mary's Hospital, Paddington. O little lump – almost a subject for a metaphysical poem.

Her second was a novelist's observation:

> Conveniently opposite [the hospital] are an ABC café
> and a pub. I choose the latter (Private Bar). Two elderly
> ladies with light ale, coughing and cackling, and an Irish
> landlord.

The third is a sentence worthy (in such a context) of
John Aubrey or Anthony à Wood:

> Andrew Cruickshank said that in the 18th century
> there was moss growing round the high altar of St
> Paul's Cathedral.[29]

Unfortunately, Hilary, who had retired from the BBC that
year, was on holiday, travelling in Greece and couldn't be con-
tacted, but Barbara, with support from her friends, appeared
to take the news calmly and cheerfully – 'behaviour', as she
might have said. She was admitted to hospital very quickly
and was operated on immediately. From hospital she wrote
to Bob Smith:

> You will have guessed that it was cancer and that
> was why they took away the left bosom. I can't make
> out whether the other ladies here are breastless (like
> Amazons?) or have other things the matter with them.[30]

and later, when she was convalescing at Ailsa Currie's
cottage, she wrote to Philip Larkin:

> Since there are no longer hushed voices when one speaks
> of it I'll tell you that it was breast cancer, luckily caught
> when very small so I hope there won't be any recurrence,
> though I suppose one mustn't be over-optimistic. . . .
>   I have lately taken to reading Charlotte M. Yonge.
> I've found much enjoyment and richness, especially in
> *The Pillars of the House*, which is a very churchy one.
> What a wonderful length books were allowed to be in
> those days before the telly and all that![31]

He replied sympathetically:

You are lucky to have got such despatch from the NHS (I'm a craven BUPA subscriber). Anyway, I do hope you are fully restored, or on the way to it. . . . It sounds nice, reading Charlotte M. Yonge. I've been struggling through some of Trollope's political novels, with fair admiration. They are so *grown up*, to my mind, beside Dickens' three-ring circuses. My recollection of C.M.Y. is that no one has any *vices*, except perhaps quick temper or obstinacy. Very restful in these *Oz* filled days.[32]

Barbara made a good recovery from her cancer, not needing any additional treatment after the operation. She accepted philosophically the loss of her breast ('one minds much less about one's physical beauty and of course it doesn't show at all when one is dressed') and was fascinated and amused by the process of fitting the false one ('a very fine shape indeed'). She was away from the Institute for several months and found that she was 'gratifyingly missed'.

The July *Africa* has come out 4 pages shorter than intended. Also the mystique of the advertisements has not been fathomed by anyone else. . . . Hazel has been doing all my work, of course, though one or two things have been 'left'. Daryll has been fussing rather, but I think she knows how to deal with him![33]

She was also quick to pounce on the effect of her operation on the new vicar. ('Little does he know', she wrote on another occasion, 'who is drinking it all in!'):

Fr Jennings continues to minister to us somewhat unenthusiastically now. Mrs P.C. forced him to pray for me when I was in hospital and has asked him to visit me. Apparently he couldn't manage it this week because he was 'going away', but will come *next* week, by which time the 'invalid' will hardly be one. He is certainly building himself up into a character for a B.P. novel and I shouldn't be at all surprised if I didn't write it one day.[34]

If her thoughts turned often to the memory of her mother's death from cancer, she never spoke of them, even to Hilary.

She seemed to put the whole thing behind her ('unless anything unforeseen happens I am clear of *that*') and was able to
reply in a relatively cheerful vein to a melancholy letter from
Philip Larkin, reluctantly on holiday:

I have a theory that 'holidays' evolved from the medi-
aeval pilgrimage, and are essentially a kind of penance
for being so happy and comfortable in our daily lives.
You're about to point out the essential fallacy in this,
viz., that we aren't h. & c. in our daily lives, but it's too
late now, the evolution had taken place, and we do the
world's will, not our own, as Jack Tanner says in *Man
and Superman*. Anyway, every year I take my mother
away for a week, and this is it. God knows why I chose
this place [Kings Lynn]: well, there are certain basic
requirements – must be fairly near where she lives, must
have single rooms with private bathrooms and lift, must
for preference be near the sea . . . even so, one can make
grave errors, and I rather think this is one of them. . . .
   It's been a depressing day. For one thing, my hearing
aid has gone wrong again: it's a new one, and has gone
wrong before – I'm beginning to feel, as it cost £80, a
bit of a mug. (I forget if I've ever said that one of
the few blessings of my advancing age is a merciful
blurring of the sounds around me.) Then one *does* get
depressed sometimes, has anyone ever done any work
on why memories are always unhappy? I don't mean really
unhappy, as of blacking factories, but sudden stabbing
memories of especially absurd or painful moments that
one is suffused and excoriated by – I have about a dozen,
some 30 years old, some a year or even less, and once
one arrives, all the rest follow. I suppose if one lives to
be old one's entire waking life will be spent turning on
the spit of recollection over the fires of mingled shame,
pain or remorse. Cheerful prospect! Why can't I recall
the pleasure of hearing my Oxford results, having my
novel accepted, passing my driving test – things such
as these? Life doesn't work that way.[35]

It says a great deal about the easiness of their relationship,
that he, the most reserved of men, should have felt able to
write to her in such a way. He realised, of course, that she,

too, had had her own dark moments, and that she would be perceptive and understanding. And so she was, but with a bracing common sense, a kind of acceptance – ending, as she so often did, on an upbeat.

> I'm not sure that I agree about memories *always* being unhappy or uncomfortable ones. I find as I get older that I tend to steer clear of any kind of memories or push them away, unless I want to call them up for any special reason. But when I'm unhappy or depressed I do find myself remembering 'better times', those good reviews of my novels etc. but that doesn't make one any more cheerful – on the contrary, *Nessun maggior dolore* . . . and all *that* jazz! But now I want to pass my driving test and I want to publish another novel, and even to *write* another novel to my own satisfaction, so perhaps my mind is filled with all that, and I am lucky.[36]

She might also have told him of her own particular version of the old tag about Time being a great healer, which she had written over 30 years before.

> Her own heart or memory . . . must be like a kind of lumber room – full of old pictures with their faces to the wall, broken chairs, stuffed birds, and in one corner there might be an object shrouded in a dust sheet, something that had had to be hastily covered up so that one couldn't see it or think of it any more . . . And then years afterward one might lift a corner of the sheet and discover that one could fling it off quite carelessly. . . . Nothing to be afraid of any more.[37]

Now she was past the more impetuous and declared emotions of youth, she had found that one could come to terms with those thoughts and feelings which become deeper (and often more painful) with maturity, by 'refining' them – to use her own image, like mincing meat that was too tough. She had come to terms with many things in her own life, partly by a kind of stoical acceptance and partly by writing them out of her system, and she would do the same with her cancer.

Chapter Eighteen

When Barbara returned to work in the summer of 1971 she was very aware of an atmosphere of change and, indeed, decay. St Lawrence's Church had been made redundant and closed, the Kardomah in Fleet Street had gone ('where now will we be able to read and brood?'), Gamage's in Holborn was about to be closed and demolished ('Oh unimaginable horror!'), leaving hundreds of lunchtime idlers and browsers desolate. Sitting in the Kingsway Kardomah (a pale, unsatisfactory substitute for the one in Fleet Street) reading the *Church Times* ('even that has gone off – no Answers to Correspondents') she notes:

> The *only* places to have lunch now: Kingsway Kardomah, Holborn Kardomah (The Dutch House), Gay Fayre opposite the Prudential – very squashed but one could sit in the window there on a high stool and watch Gamage's being demolished.[1]

She might also have added the ABC teashop in Fleet Street (later to be renamed The Lite Bite, though retaining its green and orange and stripped pine décor), where, since it was opposite the Law Courts, Barbara often observed, with amusement and sympathy, distraught litigants being comforted by their relations with nice strong cups of tea and sausage and chips.

St Dunstan's Chambers was also decaying fast. The Fleet Street/Fetter Lane area was being either rebuilt or redeveloped (we lived in a permanent haze of brick dust) and the leases of the buildings were gradually falling in. In the end only the Institute remained in the depressing building.

I still try to get the odd day working at home [editing or correcting proofs] and don't stay too late in the dilapidated and decayed Institute building. Now that the advertising firm above us have left the place is empty except for us and you can hear the mice scuttling overhead in the evenings (c. 5.30).[2]

The Institute moved and there were the usual acrimonious wrangles over rooms and status. ('I long to write a novel about the office move and the strange passions aroused and the unpleasantness about who was to go where.'[3]) She wrote to Bob Smith:

At last we are moving the Institute to 210 High Holborn, then this building is to be demolished and so is Gamage's – a whole period of civilisation gone!... The new offices are nice but far less spacious ... and we shall all be rather cramped. Hazel and I have a room rather like the one here but smaller. Of course the new place will be more convenient – nearer to the British Museum, SOAS, Bourne and Hollingsworth, Marks and Spencer and other desirable places.[4]

Philip Larkin had been spending six months at All Souls, working on the new edition of *The Oxford Book of 20th Century Verse*, reviving old memories of Oxford:

First of all I did experience a remarkable return to youth – I bought a college scarf (not an All Souls one, there are no such things) and *nearly* bought a pipe, but reason remounted her throne in time.... In fact I worked quite hard: Bodleian stack in the morning, Upper Reading Room in the afternoon (do you remember the 75 stairs, and how the last half dozen were steeper than the rest?).[5]

After Hilary's retirement from the BBC, both sisters decided that they would like to live somewhere near Oxford and Hilary finally found a cottage in the village of Finstock. Barn Cottage had not actually been a barn, but a wheelwright's shop belonging to the adjoining cottage, and was picturesque, with large oak beams and an open fireplace. It had been well converted and was very comfortable, with a sitting room, kitchen, spare room and bathroom downstairs and two large bedrooms upstairs. There was a double garage and a garden at the side and Barbara's room led out on to the flat roof of the garage, which, since the cottage was on a corner right in the centre of the village, commanded a splendid view in all directions.

Finstock was, at that time, an unfashionable village, still ungentrified and not particularly picturesque – though the Cotswold stone of the buildings gave it some distinction. Its only claim to fame was the occasion in 1927 when T. S. Eliot was received into the Anglican Church in a secret ceremony at Holy Trinity, the rather austere Victorian church on the main road at the top of the village. The Oxfordshire countryside around was very beautiful, with the Wychwood Forest nearby and elegant parklands surrounding the many small manor houses that are the glory of that part of the Cotswolds.

Barbara was now fifty-nine.

> Next year I shall be an OAP or a senior citizen – special terms for hairdos if you go between 9 and 10 a.m. on a Monday or Tuesday.[6]

She hoped to go on working until she was sixty, so she needed to find some sort of room in London to live in during the week.

> I might advertise myself in the *Church Times* . . . (gentle-woman, Anglican, quiet, 'business lady', etc) . . . A pity one can't offer oneself to the advertisers who ask for '4th girl share super Chelsea flat'.[7]

She was fortunate to find a room in Balcombe Street just off Baker Street, in a house belonging to a friend of Henry Harvey's sister. Not only was the rent very modest (£5 a week), but her hostess (it would have been impossible to think of her as a landlady) was a charming, vague eccentric and interesting company. Barbara had a good-sized bedsitting room and 'use of kitchen'. Sharing a kitchen and using it only at certain set times, gave her the pleasure of planning 'splendid woman' food, cooking rather 'dainty' things that didn't leave a lingering smell. It was all a delightful game and at lunchtime she would have a happy 'surge' round the small branch of Sainsbury's (long since vanished) not far away in Drury Lane, coming back with her string bag full of small tins and 'portions for one'.

She travelled back to Finstock each weekend, leaving the office early on Fridays to catch the five o'clock train from Paddington to Charlbury, where Hilary met her. As she was at home all the time, Hilary had become involved in village and church affairs and Barbara helped at weekends.

> The church is not very high ('Series 2') but there is quite an enthusiastic congregation of people who have come fairly recently to the neighbourhood. Hilary and I are a bit jaded and cynical about things like bazaars but try not to show it.[8]

Daryll Forde had retired from University College in 1969 and, since then, had been concentrating all his formidable energies on the Institute, so Barbara was busier than ever. After working together for so long (he had quite unexpectedly taken her to lunch at the Athenaeum to celebrate her twenty-five years at the Institute) they got on well now that he had mellowed a little with age. 'His helmet now,' she used to quote, 'an hive for bees shall be', and henceforth he became Helmet, or Old Helmet. She wrote to Bob Smith:

> It's rather nice having him around more, 'stimulating' as you say, and I feel that we are the two old people cleaving together. . . . The Institute continues to flourish. I have had a nostalgic time lately throwing away a lot of old correspondence from our files, some of it dating from the thirties when our first research fellows went out into the field. Those were the days – really gallant ones, when they all got malaria and other horrible things and were expected not to marry.[9]

Now that she was the most senior member of staff at the Institute (apart from Daryll Forde) she worked very much in her own way, to suit herself. As long as *Africa* and the various publications all appeared on time (and they always did) she was left alone in her own little kingdom – our smallish room

still vaguely labelled EDITORIAL. We worked in short, sharp,
concentrated bursts, with little breaks when we drank tea
and read the *Daily Express* and the *Daily Mirror* and chatted.
Sometimes she would make an entry in her notebook, just
occasionally she would type a bit of novel on the back of
some old galley proofs (a valuable source of free stationery).
Sometimes she wrote to Bob Smith in Nigeria ('In hic exilium')
as a reviewer – and then continued the letter as a friend:

> Many thanks for your review of Malowist's book – I
> am sure the length will be just right. Fancy no [Polish]
> dictionary in Lagos! It has been difficult getting reviews
> for the July number but they are starting to come in
> now. *Africa* reviewers are a good and conscientious body
> of men, with a few exceptions.
>
> ....
> Now, having removed the carbon, I can use up this
> valuable bit of airletter to thank you for your letter. It
> was mysteriously without an ending, a blank half page
> and no signature – presumably you thought you had
> finished it or were suddenly interrupted by a Yoruba
> historian coming to argue about Old Oyo.[10]

High Holborn was a rather uninspiring part of London ('all
the shops are now Travel or Photocopying or Employment
Agencies, with the occasional Sandwich Bar'[11]). But there
was the Rendezvous, a few doors along from the Institute,
where we had lunch (Luncheon Vouchers value 25p), and
a few yards in the other direction, a branch of the public
library. We were on the fringe of Bloomsbury ('scene of so
many and distant past glories') and sometimes at lunchtime
we sat (as Viola did) in Lincoln's Inn Fields or wandered round
the Soane Museum.

She was now resigned to the fact that there seemed
to be no market for her novels.

> What can my notebooks contain except the normal
> kinds of bits and pieces that can never(?) now be worked
> into fiction. Perhaps in retirement, and even in the year
> before, a quieter, narrower kind of life can be worked
> out and adopted. Bounded by English literature and the
> Anglican Church and small pleasures like sewing and
> choosing dress material for this uncertain summer.[12]

But she could never give up writing. She had always thought of herself as a novelist and she would go on having ideas and wanting to write about them.

> Have thought of an idea for a novel based on our office move – all old, crabby characters, petty and obsessive, bad tempered – how easily one of them could have a false breast! But I'd better not write it till I have time to concentrate on it (look what happened to the last).[13]

But, of course, she couldn't resist it.

> I am writing, quietly in bed in the early morning, a novel about four people in their sixties working in the same office.[14]

And once again the notebooks are full of thoughts and observations:

> There could be talk in the office about elderly people being found dead with no food in the house.
>   I have fallen through the net of the Welfare State, she thought, picturing this more as a coarse serviceable hair net than a net to catch trapeze artists.
>   If only, Letty thought, Christianity could have had a British, even an English origin![15]

She came back from visiting the library in her lunch hour, happily bearing leaflets about Help With Heating and the Dangers of Hypothermia and suddenly she felt herself able to comment on the climate of the times once again. The 'swinging sixties' had given way to the more anxious seventies and she could cope with that so much better, feeling that she had something to write about again. She knew about getting old, and she observed the whole process with delighted irony – the social services jargon, the careful euphemism of 'Senior Citizens', the bus passes and cut-price perms, tightly curled grey hair and white Crimplene cardigans – as well as with a compassionate insight into the darker side, the loneliness, the frustrations and the despair.

Life at the Institute was sad now. In May 1973 Daryll Forde had died quite suddenly of a heart attack at the age of seventy-one. Barbara went to his memorial service at the London University Church in Gordon Square:

> D.F. was *not* a believer so it wasn't very Christian though the Chaplain gave a kind of blessing at the end. It consisted of readings and music with an address by a colleague. Afterwards some of us were invited to have a drink in what was described as an 'anteroom' but really it was a kind of vestry with crucifixes and hymnbooks lying around and, on a hanger, a very beautiful *white* cassock or soutane, such as Roman priests in the tropics wear – that rather puzzled me.[16]

The Institute was, as she said, rather like a rudderless ship. No new Director could be found. The Institute's work was changing. Now that there were more universities in Africa it was not so easy to get finance for the various projects. Before he died, Daryll Forde sold the Institute's library – a unique and valuable collection – to the University of Manchester, and we all felt that with its going the heart had also gone from the Institute. However, two 'Acting Co-Directors' were appointed and the work went on.

Philip Larkin was moving house too:

> It's an ugly modern detached little house, fearfully dear (expect I was diddled) in a quiet and 'sought after' district near the University. It has a respectable garden at the front and a vast one at the back: both take a great deal of my time. At the same time it is jammed up to a twin house on the next 'plot': our back doors are about 20 feet apart, as on a council estate. . . . I had a new front door that began swelling the moment it was hung, and has never been usable – indeed it seems to have discovered the secret of the creation of matter. There are four bedrooms but only one room downstairs, except for the kitchen. Neighbours are (?) a Humber pilot on the open side (children, washing, two cars) and an old lady on the blind side, but she is going – a board is up. Nobody has any money these days. I wish I had stuck out for £2,000 less. Still what's £2,000 these days?[17]

Barbara had now evolved a routine, enjoying both town and country.

> *January 1974.* In Charlbury churchyard the older graves
> have sunk right into the turf – worn cherubs' heads just
> visible above the grass.

> *March. Balcombe St.* Woke early. 'The Trout' on
> Radio 3 and reading *The Clever Woman of the Family*
> [by Charlotte M. Yonge] in bed.[18]

Now she knew, at least during the week, all about older
people living in bedsitters – though she had the haven of
Finstock and the company of Hilary and the cats at the
weekend.

In April she had a slight stroke, caused by excessive
calcium in the blood. She was not physically disabled, but,
most distressingly, it led to a kind of dyslexia, which made it
difficult to read or write properly.

> Dr Burke examineed me (© studdens) and suscepts excess
> of parathroughoid gland in the neck ... hopefully home
> cerca Wednesday.[19]

With great determination she taught herself to read and
write again and by May she was able to write an almost
normal letter to Bob Smith.

> Things are going on well for me and I am now able to write
> letters, though not very well – I make mistakes, mostly
> in individual letters, as you can see from my corrections.
> Reading is a bit better too – though not easy or fluent. It
> is difficult to cope with this but I am addapting [sic] – at
> the moment I am reading a Romantic novel which in a
> curious way counts as 'work'. Before my affliction I had
> promised to ack [sic] as one of the judges for the Romantic
> novel awards, so this may be my salvation! Otherwise I'm
> reading a novel by Charlotte M. Yonge which in its way
> is equally romantic.
>   I have to go to hospital again to have my parathyroid
> gland removed as this is apparently the cause of the
> excessive calcium in my blood.[20]

And to Philip Larkin:

I was in the Radcliffe the whole of April. . . . The problem of being old is with one on such occasions, though. When I thought my days were numbered I did feel that it was perhaps better to die in one's sixties. I feel if I were disabled or incapacitated I wouldn't be able to bear it – wouldn't be 'splendid' as women are expected to be – men too, no doubt.

I haven't done any writing lately but think I will try again soon – at least to put words down on paper. Perhaps the only hope of getting published is a romantic or gothic novel?

When I was first ill I had difficulty in reading and writing. . . . Imagine the irony of *that*!

Once again many thanks for the book [*High Windows*]. I shall take it into hospital. The Churchill this time, where they say you get bacon for breakfast![21]

After her operation she was told that she must retire.

Ironical to think that I used to look forward to retirement as the time when I would really be able to get down to *writing*![22]

Inspired by her reading of the genre, she tried to turn *An Unsuitable Attachment* into a Romantic novel, but, not surprisingly, with little success. She was quite glad to have left the Institute. There was a new Director who had made a great many changes, which involved getting rid of many of the older members of staff and, in general, running things down. She found the atmosphere disagreeable and unsympathetic. I took over her editorial work and she agreed to help me out by doing the subject and tribal indexes for *Africa* and the occasional bibliography at home. She said that she found it good discipline, and the payment, though meagre, was a useful supplement to her Institute pension, which was negligible (£1,000 a year).

She did enjoy her retirement party – when she told her doctor about it he told her not to get too emotionally excited. She told Bob Smith:

> My [lunchtime] retirement party went off quite well and
> I didn't burst into tears or anything shaming like that.
> There was wine and lots of nice food. John Middleton
> made a speech and everyone (almost) that I liked was
> able to come. . . . I was presented with a cheque but
> my real 'present', the new Oxford Dictionary, which I
> had chosen, rather typically hadn't arrived as it was
> re-binding and I haven't had it yet.[23]

With her cheque she bought a handsome heavy gold ring set
with a large topaz – 'almost as big as an Edith Sitwell ring!'
  She settled down happily in Finstock, doing a little mild
indexing, enjoying village affairs and hospitality, and 'reading
novels *in the morning*'. She drew her usual ironic picture of her
situation for Bob Smith:

> Well here I am really a 'pensioner' and every govern-
> ment is saying they will *do* something for me – £10
> extra at Christmas and an increase next April from
> Mr Healey. My basic rate is £11.25 a week and I go
> up the hill to Finstock post office to collect it. Margaret
> (the postmistress) also murmured something about 'beef
> tokens'. I find I am not too proud to accept any handout,
> but at the moment seem to have plenty of money. Of
> course there are fewer opportunities to spend it here.[24]

  She was glad to have the job of reading novels for the
Romantic Novelists Association awards. Not only did she
find it interesting to observe the technique (and wonder if
she might use it herself), but it also reassured her about her
own status as a professional, published writer. She wrote to
Philip Larkin in December:

> I have . . . read about 10 novels. They are extremely
> varied in type – some historical, others more purely
> 'romantic' in a modern setting. The one thing they lack
> is humour or irony – and of course one does miss that.
> But in a way they do seem to reflect some aspects of
> life that may be valid for the fortunate ones! As much
> as Doris Lessing or Edna O'Brien, or even B. Pym.[25]

He replied:

I'm so glad you're enjoying retirement. We have talked before of the dangers of self-indulgence [drinking before eleven in the morning], and to them I expect (for me) would be added the dangers of depression. Already I find it incredible to be over 50 and 'nothing done', as I feel. In March I shall have been here 20 years. . . . In fact I feel somewhat in the doldrums these days: of course *work* goes on, but I am quite unable to do anything in the evenings – the notion of expressing sentiments in short lines having similar sounds at their ends seems as remote as mangoes on the moon.[26]

She answered sympathetically:

I hope you are feeling more like writing and perhaps generally in better spirits with the coming of spring. I do feel like writing sometimes and am gradually trying a novel, doing a bit every morning when I can. . . . I do find that I am *not* reading all those heavy works that people always say they will read in their retirement [he had suggested Motley's *History of the Dutch Republic*].

I have got Betjeman's new poems. . . . Not very good value for money (you get *more* with Larkin), but of course one is glad to have them. I lately read T. S. Mathews' biography of [T. S.] Eliot and apparently he often thought he would never write another line so it must be the sort of thing that all writers feel – but one does rather wonder if Shakespeare ever experienced it. But surely everyone must get the 'so little done' feeling as age creaks on? Here I am sixty-one (it looks worse spelled out in words) and only six novels published – no husband, no children.[27]

He, in his turn, wrote encouragingly:

Didn't J. Austen write six novels, and not have a husband or children?[28]

On the 23 April (and both would have appreciated the agreeable coincidence of the date), Barbara and Philip finally – after fourteen years' correspondence – met in the bar of the Randolph Hotel in Oxford. The meeting had been the subject of several letters between them.

I'm sure I should recognise you, but would *you* know *me*? I'm tallish (5.8½ in the old measurements) with

darkish brown hair cut short. I shall probably be wearing
a beige tweed suit or a Welsh tweed cape if colder. I shall
be looking rather anxious, I expect.[29]

I'm sure we shall recognise each other by progressive
elimination, i.e. eliminating all the progressives. I am
tall and bald and heavily spectacled and deaf, but I can't
predict what I shall have on.[30]

The Spirit of Irony, never far from Barbara on such
occasions, arranged that these two shy, reserved people
should be joined by a complete stranger, a jovial red-faced
man, the kind who attaches himself to people in hotel bars,
who chatted to them for what seemed like hours.

Barbara and Philip both enjoyed the meeting, each knowing
precisely what to expect of the other. When she got home
Barbara wrote to him:

After I left you I . . . made my way to the station –
having a few minutes to spare I went into the refreshment
room and found myself sitting by a strange woman eating
curry at 4 o'clock, a late lunch or an unusual tea.[31]

Their correspondence continued comfortably, with their
usual exchange of idiosyncratic news. He had previously
described how he got his gold medal for Poetry 'through the
post. It turned up when I was shaving one morning. Alas for
my dreams of entering high society! "We are told you are the
best poet in our Empire, Mr Larkin" – fat chance.' Now he
described being 'O.B.E.'d'.

A strange occasion at once homely and scaring. Awful
lot of standing about. I can now, in theory at any rate,
be married in the Chapel of the Order in St Paul's, but
it needs a special licence. I think I have now 'reached my
ceiling'. A local industrialist has bullied me into writing
words for *a choral work to celebrate the Humber Bridge,*
and this haunts the troubled midnight and the noon's
repose. I wish a thousand times over I'd said no. What
can one *say* about such a thing? And say *in advance?*
That seems to me the worst of 'public poetry': it's not
the *public* element, it's having to write *in advance* of

Princess Anne's wedding or whatever it is. I take comfort
in Beaumarchais' assurance that what is too silly to be
said can be sung.
    Is there any news of your new novel? I don't know
if G[wendoline] Butler [a writer whom Philip Larkin had
recently met and found to be a Pym enthusiast] could
succeed where I have failed, but it might be worth trying.[32]

She replied:

It [the novel] is slowly progressing but I don't seem
inclined to hurry as there seems so little chance of it
getting published. Or perhaps I've just reverted to my
natural indolence and anyway Professor Forde always
used to say 'Barbara has no sense of urgency'. Of course
he didn't mean it as a compliment.[33]

The novel ('austere and plain though it may be'), which
at that stage was called *Four Point Turn*, was progressing, but
slowly. This was partly because she was taking her time with
it, almost putting off the moment when it would be finished
and she would, once again, have to face the dreadful discour-
agements involved in trying to get it published. Partly, she was
still not well.

'Asphasia' at a drinks party on Sunday morning. When
talking I couldn't remember the name of Dr Kissinger!
That rendered me tongue-tied and speechless so that I
couldn't speak at all. It didn't last long but must have
been disconcerting for those involved. I wasn't offered
another glass of sherry but perhaps that was just coincidence! Later a slight feeling of pins and needles in my
right hand which seems to go with it. On Friday night
after watching a terrible telly programme I was conscious
of seeing jagged coloured shapes all the time when away
from the TV, but that soon passed. Was that anything to
do with what I am now calling The Kissinger Syndrome?
Is that why I am now incapable of finishing this novel
which is so near its end?[34]

In January 1976 the novelist Elizabeth Taylor died and
Barbara wrote to Bob Smith:

> Very little notice seems to have been taken of her
> but I am hoping when her novel comes out there
> may be an appreciation in some of the TV book pro-
> grammes. . . . Still, what does it matter, really, such
> writers are caviar to the general, are they not, and
> fame is dust and ashes. . . . [35]

There were other deaths – both Rupert Gleadow and
Gordon Glover had died within months of each other. She
wrote to Bob Smith:

> Two of my contemporaries have died – both men. I
> should have been a widow twice over by now if I had
> married either.[36]

One of her contemporaries, however, had come back into
her life. Henry Harvey had retired and come to live in a
cottage at Willersey in Worcestershire, not thirty miles away.
He was now divorced from his second wife and lived alone
(except for a large white cat called Offa), seeing friends, his
two sons and, once or twice a year, Elsie and members of his
family from Finland, and showing many domestic skills, like
jam making and vegetable growing. Now it really was a case
of 'mild kindly looks and spectacles', since their relationship
was one of easy and comfortable friendship and they took
occasional weekend holidays together. 'Fancy,' she said to
me, 'Belinda and the Archdeacon going on a Winter Break
together!'

Meanwhile she had reached the final stages of revising
Four Point Turn. She wrote to Bob Smith in March 1976:

> I am reading a biography of Hawker of Morwenstow
> but hope I'm not getting into one of those people who
> never have time to read a novel. I'm in the middle of
> typing one, but the prospects are gloomy for all kinds
> of books. Jock says Duckworth haven't set up his [book
> on] George Eliot yet, though they think highly of it. And
> he is writing a novel which he is going to dedicate to me,
> but will it ever see the light of day?
>   I don't like X Trapnell [in Anthony Powell's *A Dance
> to the Music of Time*] at all and regret that he is such a

major character in the later books. I sometimes feel that there are such beautiful bits that one could re-read just for the pleasure of coming on them, if nothing else.[37]

Philip Larkin had been visiting Anthony Powell and knew that she would want to hear about it:

Visited Anthony Powell near Frome for lunch. . . . He showed us the estate – a kind of assault course through brambles and midges – but not the house, which would have interested me more. Many ancestral portraits and Burke's *Peerage, Landed Gentry* etc within easy reach.[38]

He proposed visiting her at Finstock 'about tea time'.

It would be a great pleasure to see you again and I should like, if I may, to introduce Monica Jones, an old friend of mine and a devoted admirer of your books.[39]

On one of his visits Barbara had a rare pleasure, when they walked up to the church to see the memorial to T. S. Eliot.

So two great poets and one minor novelist came for a brief moment (as it were) together. . . . What is the point of saying (as if for posterity) what Philip is *like*. He is so utterly what he is in his letters and poems. In the best, like 'Faith Healing', 'Ambulances', and even Jake Balokowsky, my biographer. 'Life at graduate level' as he once said about my novel *No Fond Return of Love*.[40]

He read the new novel and wrote immediately, saying that he parted from it reluctantly:

It would be wrong to say that I *enjoyed* it in the simple sense of the word, because I found it strongly depressing, but I seem to recall that some Greek explained how we can enjoy things that make us miserable. It's so strange to find the level good-humoured tender irony of your style unchanged but dealing with the awful end of life: I admire you enormously for tackling it, and for bringing it off so well. The book brings out more clearly the *courage* that all your characters can call on and have to call on, at

some point or other in their stories. I think the tales of
both Letty and Marcia are brilliantly told, and sad almost
beyond bearing: Marcia's battiness is splendidly caught,
quite devastating. The 'twists' of her leaving her house to
Norman, and the engagement of Marjorie are fascinating
and one wants to know more about them. Touch of Jessie
Morrow in Beth Doughty? It all sounds true: I can hardly
believe it hasn't happened.

The two women are 'bigger' than the men, and
Marcia is bigger than Letty, and yet there's sadness
in Letty's life too, if more quietly expressed. One is
relieved by the faint hint at the end that she may
have a little respite from dreariness before the close of
her life. Edwin is a more familiar *type* than Norman – I
liked Norman – should have liked to think he would live
in Marcia's house (Monica thinks he wouldn't: the sight of
it made him realise that a bedsitter was what suited him
best). The pathos of the half-relations – *almost* calling –
is plainly announced early on, with Letty and the silent
table-mate. And the occasional Pym torpedo: 'Yet, now
that she had left him the house, he was prepared to think
she might have been almost beautiful.'

What now? I do hope you try it on some publishers:
I wish I could be of practical help. Does your romantic-
novel work give you any contacts? If an introduction by
me would help, I will try to write one (though my brain
has virtually packed up). And could you ask whether a
subsidy would make any difference, and, if so, what it
would have to be? Do please try. Or I will try if you like.
Let me know.

I think the title *Four Point Turn* a little smart for
so moving a book: it needs something sadder, more compassionate. The book isn't long – I make it about 48,000
– should it be longer, for commercial purposes?[41]

Barbara had already tried the novel on several publishers
(and had it rejected) when Philip Larkin sent a copy of the
typescript to Pamela Hansford Johnson. She liked it and
promised to recommend it to Hamish Hamilton, which led
to an ironic situation.

Writing to Pamela Hansford Johnson to tell her that
Hamish Hamilton had already rejected my novel when

he had just written to her saying he was 'eager to read it'! The embarrassment of being an unpublished novelist knows no bounds and what price the memory of publishers![42]

Philip Larkin, back from a visit to All Souls ('no shade on the guest room lamp') was indignant.

Most disappointed at your news. Considering the tumult of unreal and indecent rubbish (I am going only by reviews!) that pours from the presses these days it seems ridiculous that your book should be turned down. What sort of people act as publishers' readers? Like Piers's colleagues, perhaps?[43] I always remember the rejection of Kingsley's first novel – treasure, in fact, the reader's report – the one before *Lucky Jim* – the report, after outlining *why* it was completely unpublishable (no plot, no action, no characters, etc.), finished with 'Above all, it is completely devoid of *humour*'! In fact it was very funny.[44]

She worked at the novel, though without much hope, as she wrote to Bob Smith that Christmas:

I'm trying to make it a bit longer as H[amish] H[amilton] said the prospects of publication at that length (48,000) were 'bleak'. Personally, I don't think anyone will take it, whatever length it is, but I may as well try a few more publishers. It is rather odd, trying to make a novel bigger when in the past one has always had to shorten.[45]

1977 opened on a depressing note. The first entry in her notebook was decidedly irascible:

Yesterday a small congregation for the First Sunday after Epiphany – and ought not the Christmas decorations to have been taken down? A lapsed Catholic is no good to man or beast.[46]

She went on 'improving' her novel and wrote to Bob Smith:

I made two more chapters – Edwin going to a memorial
service and the three of them, with Father G., having
lunch after Marcia's funeral at the crematorium. Then
I added a few more 'bits', remembering that you had
wanted more of Norman, I described his Christmas in
more detail and the first morning of his holiday, though
I did not dare penetrate too far into the bedsitter.[47]

She did all this for her own satisfaction, to 'get it right',
and not simply to add a few chapters before sending it out on
the round of publishers. As she had written to Henry Harvey
a few months before:

Novel writing is a kind of private pleasure, even if
nothing comes of it in worldly terms.[48]

She had, after fifteen years, painfully achieved a philosophical attitude towards her novels: a combination of a
courageous acceptance of the status quo with the tenacious
hope that *one* day, if she persevered, she would be published
again.

Chapter Nineteen

On 21 January 1977 the *Times Literary Supplement* published a list, chosen by eminent literary figures, of the most underrated writers of the century. Barbara was the only living writer to be named by two people, Philip Larkin and Lord David Cecil. Philip and another friend, the writer Paul Binding, telephoned that evening to give her the good news. The following day there was a piece about it on the front page of *The Times*, where, as Barbara noted wryly, 'Cape apparently said they "might consider a reprint" (*That'll* be the frosty Friday!)'[1]. Radio Oxford did an interview with her and there were many letters from friends.

Lord David Cecil wrote her a kind note:

I learn to my horror that your books are out of print and that some are unpublished. I do hope that my words and Philip Larkin's will do something to remedy this lapse. Everyone I lend them to from my 82 year old sister to my son-in-law of 29 enjoys them enormously. May I say again how much I admire your books, with what pleasure I read and re-read them.[2]

and a week later he wrote again:

I gave up my weekend to read *Less Than Angels*, enjoyed every moment of it. No other living novelist writes books that amuse one as yours do; they enlarge my imagination too, by introducing me to new worlds. . . . All is vitalized and transfigured by your particular vein of humour and keen observation. I was also impressed by the way you did for once introduce death – that of poor Tom Mallow – and yet kept the Comedy atmosphere and this without going in for that, to me, displeasing phenomenon called 'black humour'.[3]

It was all a wonderful – and completely unexpected – surprise, which did, as she said, a lot for her morale. But she had learned to be wary ('And hope, once crush'd, less quick to spring again') and not to expect anything of Fortune. She wrote to Philip Larkin expressing her delight and gratitude, adding a sardonic comment on *The Times* piece and refusing to expect too much:

> Funny Cape's 'might consider . . .'. I can imagine some minion being phoned up on a Friday evening when everyone else had gone home! A pity they had already rejected *Four Point Turn*. Of course I haven't had a word from them.
>   I am struggling to get that novel into a fit state to send to Macmillan (as Pamela Hansford Johnson recommended) but I have no very high hopes.[4]

She sent it off at the beginning of February.

> The girl who acknowledges it addresses me as Mrs Pym. This puts me into a different category altogether.[5]

On St Valentine's Day she was sitting at her sewing machine when Alan Maclean telephoned from Macmillan, to say that

> they would *love* to publish the novel. Can hardly believe it can be true but he said he would confirm by letter (with $8^{1}/_{2}$p stamp) [first class].[6]

The letter that she wrote to Philip Larkin was practically incoherent with joy:

> I haven't *dared* to write to anyone until I actually saw it in print. . . . But now I have the letter before me, and it

seems from this that you know (perhaps?), so this is just to say my inadequate thanks. . . . If it hadn't been for you, and sending it to Pamela H.J. . . . not to mention all those *years* of encouragement. What can I say that would be at all appropriate? I hope anyway (12.10) that you are having a *good lunchtime drink.* We are about to have one – poor Hilary has a bad cold so hers will be whisky – mine sherry.[7]

His reply was almost as disjointed.

Super news! I am drinking (or, come to think of it, have drunk) a half-bottle of champagne in honour of your success. Monica and I are really happy about it: we look forward to publication day as if it were our own. Have you heard from Pamela Howe of Bristol BBC? She says BBC Radio 4 will read *Ex.W.* on 'Story Hour' next autumn too. Oh, I am so pleased: I want a real Pym year.

Apart from the champagne, I have rung up a lady to collect some *jumble* tomorrow for some 'church players' – I've never done this before, so it's *also* in honour of you.

TLS has okayed my Pym article ('Something to Love'), and I rather dread your seeing it; would you like to see it in proof, or would you prefer it to come as a surprise, 'pleasant or unpleasant as the case may be'? (O. Wilde). Perhaps the latter would be better.

Title: *Last Quartet* is better than *Four Point Turn*, but I still wish for something less literary, more striking, more . . . oh I don't know. Titles are so very personal, one hesitates to plunge: *For the Dark, The Way into Winter, Doors Into Dark* something about *age*, something *poetic.* These are all terrible, but my feeling persists. *Last Quartet* sounds a shade like Julia Strachey or Isobel Strachey or someone like that. . . . Oh dear, please excuse me, it must be the Moet et Chandon, or the jumble, or something.

My life: a conference with the chief cataloguer and the head of the clerical division on the question of why there is a 15 week delay in getting cards into the catalogue. Work without responsibility is the privilege of the helot (a completely original epigram, so please laugh).

Oh dear, the M et C is making this rather an absurd

letter, but I'm so delighted to think of you having 'a
new publisher' and proofs and everything . . . my most
luxuriant felicitations.[8]

She replied in her most buoyant and most typical vein,
though not without a certain ironic comment:

Isn't it splendid that good news, when you're older,
sends one to the drink. . . .
   Of course what I really wanted to know was what
kind of jumble. I dare say you'd have some old books
from that Library of yours?
   Yesterday I met and had lunch with . . . Alan Maclean
and James Wright from Macmillan. . . . *They* like *Quartet
in Autumn* – a sort of compromise . . . of various ideas –
what do you think?
   One of the funniest things has been the reaction
of Tom Maschler in Cape who has been writing me
some quite cordial letters and I gather that he and
Alan Maclean have spoken about me on the telephone.
Hilary and I invented a Maschler pudding – a kind of
milk jelly.[9]

All her loving and faithful friends sent letters of congratulations. Jock Liddell wrote from Athens:

I am absolutely delighted and hardly know whom to
congratulate most on your return to the shelves – you
and Hilary, of course, and Macmillan for securing an
author who ought to do more to console them for the
loss of Miss Manning – lured away by Lord Weidenfeld
with the promise of a CBE I believe. . . . Now someone
can write a thesis on 'Barbara Pym – the silent years'.
Ultimately I think our kind of books date the least – and
the once 'up-to-date' is speedily 'out-of-date'.[10]

Philip Larkin's article, which duly appeared in the *TLS*,
helped to establish Barbara as a major novelist, showing
the richness and complexity of thought and emotion that
lay underneath the apparent smooth and comic surface of
her work. She wrote him a pleased and grateful note and he
replied:

Thank you for the card: I'm glad the article wasn't too awful. I had a nice letter from Lord David Cecil (not a usual correspondent), saying how widely loved your books are among all sorts and conditions, a fact he had established by lending his own copies. . . . I should like to think of you correcting proofs all through the [Easter] holiday, or even writing something new.[11]

Macmillan proposed publishing *Quartet in Autumn* in the September, to coincide with the BBC *Storytime* reading, and they also wished to publish *The Sweet Dove Died*, which James Wright had so much enjoyed in 1970. At last Barbara's confidence was restored:

Who is that woman sitting on the concrete wall outside Barclay's Bank reading the *TV Times*? That is Miss Pym the novelist.[12]

In May, during a motor tour of Dorset with Hilary, Barbara finally met her other champion.

Tea with Lord David Cecil. A comfortable, agreeable room with green walls and some nice portraits. They are so easy to talk to, the time flew. We had Lapsang tea, brown toast, redcurrant jelly and ginger cake. He told me he had been inspired to write after reading Lytton Strachey's *Eminent Victorians* (just as I had been inspired by *Crome Yellow*). He said that Anthony Powell and I were the only novelists he would buy without reading first . . . he said he thought comedy in the novel was out of fashion now – not well thought of – we agreed on this.[13]

He was very enthusiastic about *Quartet in Autumn*:

The subject came home to me since I also am retired – though in much luckier circumstances than the members of your quartet – but still aware of a great deal of change and some decay both in myself and the world around me. This inevitably makes my response to the book a little more 'autumnal' than it has been to your previous ones. Some sadness mingles with much amusement – and

admiration. I particularly admire the way you have kept
up-to-date, so that the book does not seem a harking back
to the past and yet by writing about older characters you
have avoided falling into the trap, which has undone so
many older authors, of trying to write convincingly about
a younger generation. Also, and in spite of its autumnal
tone, the book remains delightful, alight with so many
gleams of acute, amused, original observation.

P.S. I long to know if Letty did go in the end to live with
Marjorie in the country. I cannot help feeling she would
have been happier there in spite of the dead rabbit and
hedgehogs. But perhaps this is because I have grown to
like living in the country so very much more than in a
town.[14]

Lord David was to take part in a BBC TV film about
Barbara that Will Wyatt was making for the *Book Programme*.
Philip Larkin had been asked, but had refused, partly because,
as he said, he hated 'being TV'd' and partly because he was
the chairman of the Booker prize judges and, since *Quartet in
Autumn* had been entered, he felt he must appear impartial.

The television team filmed Barbara by the church. ('I seem to
remember,' she wrote to Philip Larkin, 'that you were taken in
a churchyard – it makes a good background for all shades of
belief, and after all it's what we all come to.') Since it was
decided that the programme was to be called *Tea with Miss Pym*
a table had been laid in the garden and Barbara and Lord David
were 'discovered' chatting over the tea cups. They agreed that
the whole thing might easily have lapsed into farce, rather like
the Mad Hatter's Tea Party, especially since the tortoiseshell
cat Minerva insisted on leaping on to the table, trying to put her
paw into the milk jug. Barbara had certain reservations about
how it would all turn out, as she described it to Philip Larkin.

I enjoyed it all very much, my only fear being that I
may have said rather foolish things or not said anything
I meant to say – e.g. I couldn't remember what I read,
who were my favourite authors etc. I did at least save
myself once when a question about my treatment of men
characters suggested that I had a low opinion of the sex.

My instinctive reply sprang to my lips 'Oh, but I *love* men,'
but luckily I realised how ridiculous it would sound, so
said something feeble, but can't remember what.[15]

Lord David wrote to her:

I see in the *Radio Times* ... that our programme is
to appear ... on Friday 21st October at 11.25 p.m. I
had always thought this was the hour reserved for the
late-night Horror Films. I trust the BBC does not include
ours under this category!

P.S. I think I am rather glad Jane Austen died when
she did. For me, she is the last fine flower of 18th century
civilisation. To have her coming to terms – or failing to
come to terms – with the Victorian age offends against
my sense of the fitness of things.[16]

When the programme appeared Philip Larkin commented:

How pretty and luxuriant the garden looked. I thought
you were jolly good – unflappable and 'cool'. I especially
liked your quelling reply to the chap when he asked
when you thought of your novels – 'I may be thinking
of one now' – 'and you'd be in it' – was the unspoken
implication.[17]

In August she and Hilary had driven to the BBC in
Whiteladies Road in Bristol, scene of so many memories for
both of them, where Barbara did an interview with Pamela
Howe to be broadcast on *Woman's Hour*. It was a terrible day,
with heavy rain, thunder and flooding. Barbara went off with
Pamela Howe's umbrella

and she got mine, not discovered until we were miles
apart! This could well provide a ridiculous episode for a
novel.[18]

In addition there was a feature article about her in *Harpers'/
Queen*, and interviews for *The Times* and the *Guardian*, and
Cape were reissuing some of her early novels. Caroline
Moorhead, who interviewed her for *The Times*

told me how hard it was to find writers to write about these days so perhaps I have been a godsend to somebody![19]

She had already been approached by an Italian postgraduate student, Tullia Blundi, who was writing a thesis on her novels – the first, as it turned out, of many.

Quartet in Autumn was published on 15 September to almost universal praise. Comments like 'This quietly powerful novel', 'The wit and style of a twentieth-century Jane Austen', 'Barbara Pym has a sharp eye for the exact nuances of social behaviour', 'An important novelist' and 'An exquisite, even magnificent, work of art' were almost enough to make up for all the years of waiting and misery. Philip Larkin sent her an enormous congratulations card, inside which he had drawn a dragon, labelled 'Maschler', pierced to the heart by a spear.

The timing had been exactly right. The original *TLS* piece and Philip Larkin's article had prepared people's minds and had led them to expect a major novel and *Quartet in Autumn*, as well as the 'good-humoured tender irony' of style that Philip Larkin had found in it, also had a spareness and (to use Barbara's own word) austerity, which was the result of the refining of emotion through pain. Her years in the wilderness had not been wasted. She had always maintained her habits of observation and recording and with the years her eye had sharpened ('How sharp the nicest women are') especially as society every day provided her with more and more objects for appraisal. To her gift of comedy she now added an insight that was born of a deep compassion and the way that the one enhanced the other so delicately gave her a unique quality that was at last appreciated.

It was the reviews, in a way, that gave her the most pleasure. They were the outward and visible sign that she was a published author again. She wrote to Bob Smith enumerating them. One gave her especial pleasure:

I had a letter from the Editor of the *Church Times* saying that although they didn't now normally have space for novel reviews he was going to review mine in November (the new one and the reprints) if only because I had given so many splendid free commercials for the *Church Times*.

I have had quite a lot of letters . . . including several from people who say they have always liked my novels and thought I was dead! A very nice, generous letter from Jock in Athens, who thinks *Quartet* very fine, even if it is 'darker' than my others.[20]

Jock had written:

I do admire the progress and development it shows . . . and I think you are brave and clever to beat out this new track – the same and yet not the same.[21]

and

I have read *Quartet* with increased pleasure and admiration, mixed with sorrow for the way in which the Church and the World have gone down. As I said to dear Bob on All Saints Day, it was sad to think of Edwin going to an Evening Mass, however sung – when he ought to be at Solemn Evensong at Margaret St, with a procession after the Third Collect and a Colonial pontiff (alas not © Robert Ibadan) blessing right and left and clouds of incense.[22]

He did, indeed, call 'this fine, uncomfortable book', 'her strongest finest work'.[23] This seems to be the universal opinion. It is not her best-loved novel, it *is* too uncomfortable for that, but its sparer structure and more classic form gives it an added strength. It is, after all, the climax of her work, the culmination of both periods of her writing. Most of her friends and the admirers of her earlier novels found it difficult at a first reading. It seemed spare to the point of sparseness, the melancholy of the subject was painful, the humour dark indeed. But this, of all Barbara's books, repays rereading. Each time one comes across new observations, nuances and – above all – humour, and each time the ending becomes more upbeat (as all Barbara's endings are, though some end on a question). The 'infinite possibilities for change', a hope she had always kept, had actually happened to her in a way she could never have imagined.

She sent a copy of *Quartet in Autumn* and of the two Cape reprints, suitably inscribed, to Philip Larkin and he replied:

I am just awaiting the last 15 minutes of an Allinson's breadmix (yes, I know the [bakers'] strike's over, but I am finishing a packet), and have heaps to do otherwise, but I must thank you most *warmly* for the three lovely books, and for troubling to write something different in each one. It really is a deep joy for me to contemplate them – not *unmixed* joy, because I want to set my teeth in the necks of various publishers and shake them like rats – but a great pleasure none the less. I take a selfish pleasure in seeing my name on them, but it could really have been any number of names. I think especially of my sister, who was talking of you back in the fifties, and of course Monica, and people one happens on like Gwen Butler, and the people who write to you – it's so nice to think that good writing wins through in the end. I hope your books all sell like billy-o (Brewer is silent on the origin of this phrase). . . . I saw the *Guardian* (bought by chance in St Andrews) and agree that it was v. good, and sank teeth in the neck of Maschler and Co. I saw the *Sunday Times*, quite perceptive, except for not seeing that it was the *noise* that drove Letty out.

Have got the loaf out and it looks all right, perhaps a trifle overdone. It sounds quite different knocked on the top from knocked on the bottom. Is this a good sign?

It's really awful being back, so much work and worry, and I don't have the resilience I like to think I once had. You will probably have to cheer *me* through 15 years . . . [24]

Barbara's *annus mirabilis* was not yet done. In October *Quartet in Autumn* was short-listed for the Booker prize, along with novels by Paul Scott, Paul Bailey, Penelope Lively, Caroline Blackwood and Jennifer Johnston – Barbara noted that she wanted Paul Scott to win ('then Paul Bailey and then B.P.'). She did go to the ceremony ('a once-in-a-lifetime opportunity to mingle in the Literary World'). It was held at Claridge's and at dinner she sat next to the Literary Editor of *The Times*, Ion Trewin, and opposite Francis King, whose novels she greatly admired.

Philip spoke on what they had looked for in the novels . . . . Then he mentioned two of the near misses, mine and Caroline Blackwood's, before coming to the winner, Paul Scott.[25]

In typical fashion she describes each of the participants, ending up with:

B.P. in her 65th year. Tall, short hair, long black pleated skirt, black blouse, Indian with painted flowers (C & A £4.90).[26]

'What a marvellous evening it was,' she wrote to Philip Larkin.

Words are beginning to fail me ... but you must know what a deep pleasure the whole thing was – even to the meeting with Tom Maschler! (charming, of course). I thought your speech was splendid.
Alan talks of more reprints, perhaps he and 'Tom' can fight it out between them! Dutton in the USA have taken *Q. in A.*
Don't bother to answer this. . . . It's only just a heartfelt expression of thanks from the most over-estimated novelist of 1977.[27]

He did reply:

Wasn't Bookernacht bewildering! I do hope you enjoyed it. Fancy meeting Maschler – more than I have. I never saw the table plan at all. I'm sure all sorts of famous people were there. A little man came up to me and said: 'I'm Lennox Berkeley', and I nearly said 'I loved all the dances you arranged', then remembered that was Busby Berkeley, and this chap was some sort of Kapelmeister.
I hope all your books are selling like crazy: have you had the proofs of *Dove* yet? Any more reprints emerging from Cape? It all makes me *very* happy. The *TLS* is going to print my in-a-funk-about-death poem ['Aubade'] in their Christmas number (23rd December). The death-throes of a talent.[28]

He sent her a copy of the poem and she replied:

I have read it many times with, I was going to say, increasing pleasure and enjoyment – words which may seem inappropriate but that's the feeling it gives me. I know it will be among the ones I like best – 'Faith Healing', 'Ambulances', 'The Building' and of course 'Jake Balokowsky'. But when I wake in the small hours I don't think of death, I always try to switch my thoughts to something frivolous like clothes or planning a novel. And it's not so much death that would worry me as an incapacitating illness or something like that. . . .

Talking of 'Jake Balokowsky' reminds me that I have had a letter from Rota, the antiquarian bookseller, acting on behalf of an American university (he doesn't say which) wanting to buy some or any of my manuscripts or typescripts. . . . Ought one to bequeath one's MSS to some English university (much to their dismay)? I imagine you must always be having requests for the scraps of paper you keep by your bed to write down things. What do you do about it?[29]

Philip Larkin felt very strongly that English MSS should not go abroad – as, indeed, did Barbara. He listed the alternatives for her:

1. *Do nothing:* A comforting alternative, too often over-looked. Tell Rota you don't want to part with what you have and forget about it.
2. *Deal with Rota:* Just send him the list you sent me, and await events. . . . Rota would take a commission, I expect. The papers would almost certainly go to USA.
3. *Try to find a purchaser in the U.K.:* I should be happy to make enquiries on your behalf, without commission! You may think first of the Bodleian, or what we used to call the British Museum. They have the most money, and also the most calls on it. I really have no idea what a collection like this should fetch in the UK. It would of course be much more valuable with the *un*published material you speak of, letters, diaries and so on, but I quite understand you don't want to part with those. My tentative figure for what you describe would be something like £1000–£1200, but this kind of estimating is very tricky even if you are in the trade. . . . Of course my own Library would be very willing to pay as much for them, but you may not want them so far off in a place where you have no connections.

4. *Give them away in your lifetime:* No trouble. Any Library would be delighted. You might think of St Hilda's too.

5. *Give them away after your death:* No trouble except for adding the codicil or whatever. In this case you could add the notebooks etc and make a real Pym archive. It also gives you 'full enjoyment' of them during your life.

6. *Sell or give to people:* I ought to mention this, as it certainly is a possibility, although 'private ownership' is not smiled on by people like me.

Perhaps that is enough horns for one dilemma! I see I haven't explained 'ought' [to fetch some money]: simply that nobody has any money these days and very few librarians 'believe' in modern literary mss: I remember the awful time I had trying to sell L. P. Hartley's papers.[30]

She eventually decided to do nothing.

I suppose 'draft' [of a MS] is more appropriate than 'version' but the way I wrote, and still do, was to work straight on to a typewriter with a handwritten draft or a few notes or even nothing. If whole chapters exist in handwriting it is because I didn't have a typewriter available at the time, was away or ill in bed (the first version of *Quartet* was written in bed with my breakfast in Balcombe Street – 1973–4). . . .

I honestly don't care about the *money* – after all it would be money for nothing as it were – and wouldn't like any of my MS handwritten material to go to the USA to be pored over by earnest Americans (not even Jake Balokowsky). . . .

And now my literary remains are all in a large cardboard box in my bedroom – more like novel by J. I. M. Stewart than *The Aspern Papers!* [After her death Hilary gave all her papers to the Bodleian.][31]

1978 was another busy year. *Quartet* (which was reprinted twice) had already been sold to the USA and Sweden and now Dutton's also proposed publishing *Excellent Women*, while Cape reissued *Some Tame Gazelle* and *Less Than Angels*. Barbara was asked to speak to various groups, including the Romantic

Novelists Association (for whom she had an especial affection, since they had wanted her literary services when nobody else did). She was also commissioned to write a piece for *The Times*:

> Caroline Moorhead asked me to do whatever I felt like so I produced a half-joking half-serious defence of the poor novel.[32]

The BBC planned a serial reading of *Quartet* and Barbara did a broadcast in the Radio 3 series *Finding a Voice*. In July she was also given the accolade of popular fame by appearing on Roy Plomley's radio programme *Desert Island Discs*. Philip Larkin had also been 'done' and they compared notes. As one of her eight records she chose Philip reading 'An Arundel Tomb'.[33]

> The other discs (records, I call them) are mostly rather romantic music and the book Henry James' *The Golden Bowl* (which I have already stumbled through once).[34]

He replied:

> I taped it (no doubt illegally) so that I shall always have it. I thought you spoke very sensibly and amusingly, and though your music was a little *foreign* for me I very much warmed to 'In the Bleak Midwinter'. It was a great honour to be included [referring to his own reading], though I could hardly bear my tedious voice slogging on.[35]

In this letter he delightedly enclosed a newspaper cutting announcing the engagement of a Richard George Larkin and an Elizabeth Ann Pym, both of Derbyshire!

The Sweet Dove Died was published in June to great critical acclaim. 'A highly distinctive and – ultimately – charitable novel', 'Leonora is the product of sharp observation, sympathy without sentimentality, and teasing wit', 'Miss Pym's quiet, steely grip on her creatures in this faultless novel is as scrupulous as it is deadly'. Pre-publication sales had been good and the book was in the *Sunday Times* bestsellers list.

The public were in the mood to admire *The Sweet Dove Died*.
Like *Quartet in Autumn* it was a moving book, full of complex
emotions and attitudes, and with the same spare, refined con-
struction. Because it, too, had a small cast of characters, their
interactions were seen to be more intense and deeply felt. As
the theme of age in *Quartet in Autumn* had been apt for the
time, so the theme of *The Sweet Dove Died* – the ambivalent
relationships between Leonora and James and James and Ned
– was relevant to current fashionable attitudes, even though
it had been written some years before.
  Bob Smith sent his congratulations from Nigeria:

People do seem to be getting your message these days.
Perhaps this is what will distinguish the 1970s from
those, in so many respects, brutal 1960s.[36]

Lord David Cecil wrote:

Leonora is particularly brilliantly evoked. You make it
gradually clear that she is *not* a nice character; yet you
do justice to her better qualities; and above all you never
seem angry with her – on the contrary you enjoy her as
an interesting, elegant and rare example of the human
species. . . . I was asked at short notice to say something
about the book on a programme called *Kaleidoscope*.
Since I could not go to London I was interviewed on the
telephone, which was a new experience and a flustering
one. I did not feel afterwards that I had done the book
justice. I was particularly put out by the interviewer –
who meant to be very friendly – asking me if I thought
the book was about 'unreal' life. This seemed to me such
an idiotic way of talking that I was irritated. Any life
that exists is 'real' and the life that you describe exists
as much as any other. I fear I showed my irritation. I
have seen several reviews of the book – all favourable I
am glad to say, but all discussing the milieu you portray
as if it had something to do with the merits or demerits
of the book. They did not talk about whether the story
was convincing or entertaining or well-written – in fact
it is all these things – but mostly about what social class
the characters came from.[37]

Jock Liddell commented:

Leonora sounds so enviable, if she knew her luck . . . and
of course there are the unexpected felicities all the time.
I wonder what Anthea Wedge's [literary] remains were
like.[38]

Philip Larkin, who hadn't seen the new version, revised
along the lines he had suggested, was delighted with it.

I've read it . . . consumed with eagerness to know *what
happens next.* . . . Well, another sad book, and notable
additions to your gallery of male monsters, though
James is really too feeble to be called a monster.
However, there *are* feeble monsters. It is clever how
you slowly bring the reader round to Leonora's side,
whom one starts by rather disliking, and nice of you
to give Miss Foxe a happy destiny. The antiques make
admirable symbols for a world of delicate and perhaps
old fashioned emotions (o.f. in their expression rather
than their quality, I mean). The parallel of Meg and
Colin is good without being laboured.[39]

She replied jubilantly.

Thank you so much for the kind things you said about
The Sweet Dove. It has been gratifyingly well received,
enough balm to soothe and heal all those wounds when
only you and a few kind friends thought anything of my
works. Francis King has written beautifully in *Books and
Bookmen*. It's interesting that some people definitely like
SDD better than *Quartet* – Francis King, notably. But
Lord David and Robert Liddell prefer *Quartet* and the
earlier ones. My next, if it ever gets finished, will probably
be a let down for everyone – a dull village novel, with no
bi- or homo-sexuality.[40]

Ever since she and Hilary had moved to Finstock she had
wanted to write another book set in a village ('When I wrote
Some Tame Gazelle I didn't know *nearly* as much about village
life as I do now') and she had said:

> I have always wanted to write something about this place
> and its environs and I have started to think and make a
> few notes and bits. There is so much rich material, of
> course, if only I could do it.[41]

It was to be quite different from *Some Tame Gazelle*. Village
life had changed since the 1930s. Now the church was no
longer the centre of village life.

> The doctor's surgery is crowded but the vicar's study
> is empty. And there could be a sort of rivalry between
> them when it comes to dealing with life's difficulties.[42]

Her hero (if Tom Dagnall may be called that), although
a clergyman, is a far cry from the lively, richly egotistical,
Archdeacon. Although Tom is not a 'modern' vicar – indeed,
he is by inclination more of a historian than a clergyman – he
is a product of a less confident church – a church that Barbara
was increasingly dissatisfied with.

> A dire Good Friday service – the Bible (the gospel
> narrative) lamely paraphrased and meditations, so far
> from the old days when the preacher for the Three Hours
> Service would draw such a large congregation that extra
> chairs had to be brought in.[43]

The heroine is no excellent woman but an anthropologist,
casting a cold, scientific eye upon the inhabitants. But even
the anthropologist is uncertain, aware in the end that people
cannot be classified and tabulated, and she turns eventually
to the idea of writing a novel, since only in fiction, with its
subjective view of life, can real people be found.

The picturesque setting is rigorously stripped of sentimentality. The patch of purple in the woods is not a clump
of violets but the discarded wrapping of a chocolate bar;
the villagers eat frozen food and watch television, only the
newcomers make jam and join the local history group. The
de Tankerville mausoleum in the churchyard, the symbolic
ending of the old order in Miss Vereker's collapse, and the
death of Miss Lickerish, when the cat leaves her cold lap,

are all overt expressions of a pervasive feeling of mortality, as if Barbara is feeling the decay as well as the change. She had written:

> It is left to me to find the dead bird, the dried up hedgehog body, the mangled rabbit.[44]

Although it contains much irony and humour there is also an elegiac quality about *A Few Green Leaves*. It was what Robert Liddell has called 'Barbara's farewell to her readers'.[45]

Chapter Twenty

In October 1978, to her 'surprise and pleasure', Barbara was made a Fellow of the Royal Society of Literature. She told Bob Smith:

> I haven't yet been able to go up and sign the book . . . but I *have* paid my subscription and that surely must be the main point. Jock is one and Elizabeth Taylor was – it's interesting to study the list. Philip Larkin is a Companion of Lit. of which there are only 10 at one time.[1]

He had described the ceremony rather ruefully.

> I duly got my C.Lit. but it seemed rather a casual affair. We stood around for about an hour, then we were herded into a room where the D of Kent and the President and the Chairman sat on the platform and all the guests stood around in an uneasy horseshoe. The D of K made a 'light' speech (called me 'the Satchmo of poetry' if you can believe it) and handed us enormous folded boards, like chess boards, far too large to go in the small suitcase I had for overnight stay. Like all RSL occasions I've attended it seemed for them rather than for us – no one introduced me to the Duke, or really paid much attention at all, except bores who wrote children's books etc. 'Nobody was there', in the sense of anyone I'd heard of, except the recipients, and John Heath-Stubbs.[2]

Earlier that year Barbara had been at the Rawlinson College Feast at St John's in Oxford. 'We may,' she wrote to Philip Larkin, who was also to be there, 'catch a glimpse of each other ("across a crowded room", of course). I thought I had better warn you, though in a novel one would prefer the man to be taken by surprise and even dismayed!'3

She also went to a Feast at University College ('You will soon,' commented Philip Larkin on a postcard, 'have had more college feasts than I've had hot dinners') and drawing on both of these occasions she wrote a short story for the *New Yorker*, which she called – of course – 'Across a Crowded Room'. The romantic title was ironic since, in typical Pym fashion, the encounter she describes left the middle-aged woman painfully aware that the man in question barely remembered her. It is a delicately balanced piece, written in the full flow of her new confidence and is one of the most satisfying of all her short stories. Her readers were also given one last glimpse of the unspeakable Ned from *The Sweet Dove Died*.

She was also invited to write a short story for the Christmas issue of the *Church Times* and – never one to waste anything – she wrote 'The Christmas Visit' about Mark and Sophia Ainger (and Faustina), now in a country parish. It gave her great satisfaction to produce the characters (especially Faustina) in public, as it were, at long last.

The strands of her life were coming together. She had always kept up an affectionate correspondence with Jock Liddell and, indeed, kept all her friendships in good repair. She still saw many friends from the WRNS and from the Institute as well as others like Honor Wyatt, Bob Smith (now home from Africa), John and Elizabeth Barnicot (living quite near at Henley) and, of course, Henry Harvey. She records a visit to Henry's cottage.

> *17–19 August.* Spent at Willersey staying with Henry. Elsie was there too. Strange situation dating back over 40 years. A long walk up the hill in lovely country. Three elderly people walking – not together but in a long line separately, Elsie stopping to pick flowers.4

Henry Harvey, commenting on Barbara's description of the occasion, said that they were walking one behind the other simply because the path was so narrow, but it remains, nevertheless, a splendid example of the 'little polishing' by which Barbara transmuted what, to someone else, was a prosaic occasion into a moment full of subtle and allusive meaning.

Barbara had been feeling increasingly unwell for some time and in January 1979 she went to consult her doctor 'about my increasing bulk, which seems unnatural'. She was sent into the Churchill Hospital in Oxford for tests.

The analysis of the fluid from my abdomen shows that there is something (malignant) though the X-rays didn't indicate what. . . . Mr Webster says it is probably 'an ovarian problem'. He says the drug will work – it is a poison and may make me feel sick. It is a long-drawn-out treatment, may last months – injections every three weeks.[5]

Her doctor, judging her character correctly

Asked me to consider now how I wanted my end to be, whether at home, in hospital or hospice, or private nursing home.[6]

She was, then, fully aware that she didn't have very much longer to live. She faced up to the situation with a cheerful stoicism and a practical acceptance of the situation which her friends found brave and moving. She wrote brief letters to all her friends, the one to Philip Larkin was typical.

After all, I have lived eight years since my breast cancer operation in 1971 so I suppose you could say that I *have* survived. . . . Of course 'they' won't tell you how long you've got – it may be several years yet and as I don't want to live to be very old (what one says in middle age anyway!) it is really not so bad. Hard to know what to tell people really, but what with all these programmes about cancer on TV one feels it's best to be honest. But in some ways you feel a bit foolish, looking and seeming quite well (What, you *still* here?)[7]

They drained off the fluid and she felt more comfortable, but she found the radiotherapy distressing, and the outpatients clinic, as she wrote to Bob Smith, was 'a rather dire place, but luckily I manage to get some amusement and "material" out of hospital visits as you know'. Her notebook entry, as usual, went into greater detail. As always, just by the act of noting down an experience she was more able to cope with it, perhaps, in a way, externalising it.

> Waited nearly half an hour in a cubicle, sitting on a bed (shoes off) or lying gazing up at the ceiling. If you think wouldn't it be better if I were just left to die you remember the fluid and how impossible it made things. . . .
> All humanity is in the Out Patients, those whom we as Christians must love.[8]

The last remark, although it has sardonic overtones, is, nevertheless, a reminder that her faith was still strong, she *was* a Christian and she was facing death in a Christian way, with all the inner strength that such an affirmation implied.

She also had a strong motive for 'struggling on'.

> In the afternoon I finished my novel [*A Few Green Leaves*] in its first, very imperfect draft. May I be spared to retype and revise it, loading every rift with ore![9]

For a while the therapy helped and she was able to enjoy her new, hard-won literary fame. She told Philip Larkin:

> Penguin are going to do *Excellent Women* and *A Glass of Blessings*, Cape tell me, though not till next April or thereabouts. This is an enormous pleasure to me. I have had super American reviews for *Excellent Women* and *Quartet in Autumn* including a long one in the *New Yorker* from John Updike (did you ever read *Couples?*). *The Sweet Dove* comes out there this month. The advance cover has a springlike or greenery yallery cover with a design of doves (Miss Pym, the ornithologist).[10]

He was delighted.

How *splendid* about Penguin! That must mean that they think they'll sell 40,000 of each – you're really in the big time. All the others will follow (the other titles, I mean) – no one can read you without wanting to read more. I can just see all your novels, each with some enigmatic female on the front à la E[lizabeth]. J[ane]. Howard, ranged temptingly on station bookstalls. I really am delighted – shall buy the whole lot and send them to Chas. Monteith on All Fools' Day (he's chairman of the board now!).[11]

She went to the Hatchards Authors of the Year Party with Hilary where she met, among others, Patience Strong (and her agent), Steve Race, Iris Murdoch, Olivia Manning, Jilly Cooper and the Revd. W. Baddeley (Vicar of St James's, Piccadilly). 'The Duke of Edinburgh was there but I don't think he reads my books.'
She wrote to Bob Smith:

'Literary Life' – well, yes, I suppose I am in it to some extent. I was invited to a party by Hatchard's . . . mostly 'showbiz' people (after all they do write books). Then last week I went to a luncheon of the Romantic Novelists Association. A nicer collection of women you couldn't possibly meet. But most of the time I am here, struggling to write another novel. The American reviews continue to be good and I have earned a lot of money which is surprising. But I had a lot of years to make up for!
    Thank you for sending me *The Lagos Consulate* (printed in Hong Kong, like *SDD*). I haven't read it yet, though I looked at the author's acknowledgements, the first thing I always do with books of African interest! Rather sad that nobody at the IAI helped you. . . . It all seems so far away now, that life. I see Hazel, of course – went to stay with them at the end of March.[12]

Life went on.

A fine Easter, sunshine and things burgeoning. I live still![13]

Both Tom and Minerva had died in the fullness of time, but a little tabby cat, whom they called Mother, because she was heavily pregnant, adopted them and duly gave birth to four kittens. They kept Mother and one of the kittens – a black one, whom they named Justin.

She was able to go for one more 'weekend break' with Henry, this time to Derbyshire ('sensible shoes', she notes in her diary). She was a little uncertain if her health was up to it, so she 'didn't drink much'. She notes fondly that Henry demanded that the bottle of Orvieto he ordered should not be *too* cold and she was delighted to discover in one of the public lounges a private showing of somebody's holiday slides – 'I fled though Henry would have stayed.' The young Barbara would have been thrilled to know that she featured in *his* diary, where he notes ($23 \times 3 \times 79$) that he picked her up at Finstock and drove her to Grindleford (Maynard Arms Hotel) via Towcester. Lunch in [D.H.] Lawrence's Eastwood. The other days they 'drove round in Derbyshire and got lost in a huge colliery trying to find Newstead. We looked in other hotels to see what people were eating.'[14]

In May:

Summer at last! (What one has stayed alive for?!)[15]

Typing *A Few Green Leaves*, adding bits here and there ('more about Tom's church . . . Adam Prince at the end of the holiday – a short section or vignette'), she knew that it was more in her early, less formal style, than the two books that had brought her her new fame. 'Some people may be disappointed in it,' she wrote, 'others will like it.'[16]

She and Hilary spent a few days' holiday with friends at Snape in Suffolk and visited Aldeburgh – a happy peaceful time, doing nothing very much, wandering about the beach collecting pebbles. Her eye was as sharp as ever for 'material'. On the way back they stopped for tea at a hotel where a conference was going on.

Perhaps salesmen from Birmingham. Youngish men, rather too fat. Tea very expensive (£1.40). Chateaubriand

Steak on the à la carte menu was £11.50! It would be a
good setting for a romance, an unexpected meeting, or a
short story about a conference or seminar.[17]

She also started to plot out a new novel about two
women

starting with their college lives (not earlier). One from
a privileged background, the other from a more ordinary
one (but not working class) and the subsequent course
of their lives. This would be a chance to bring in World
War II.[18]

The American reviews of her novels gave her great joy.
John Updike had written:

Excellent Women, arriving on these shores in a heyday
of sexual hype, is a startling reminder that solitude may
be chosen, and that a lively, full novel can be constructed
entirely within the precincts of that regressive virtue,
feminine patience.

Two other American novelists were equally enthusiastic.
Louise Field Cooper (one of Barbara's favourite writers)
said:

Barbara Pym knows everything there is to know about
the quiet, very funny small eventful, poignant lives
of the people in her books, and when we have finished reading them so do we and are all the happier
for it.

Shirley Hazzard described her work as:

Penetrating, tender, and for these times, greatly dar-
ing. There is a thrill of humanity through all her
work.

While *Newsweek* ended a long review:

Her books work: they are taut with art.

The American public suddenly found that they had an insatiable appetite for her work. Several years after her death, the author Anne Tyler wrote:

> Whom do people turn to when they've finished Barbara Pym? The answer is easy: they turn back to Barbara Pym.

To her amazement and amusement she learned that she was being 'taught' in American universities – a far cry from her days at Oxford, where 'Literature came to a full stop with Matthew Arnold'. She wrote to Philip Larkin to say that she had been asked to 'lecture' in Carlisle, Pennsylvania, 'but won't go'. Even if she had been well enough it was not a prospect that would have attracted her – although she would have loved to have been an ironic fly on the wall to 'drink it all in'. She knew that Philip felt much the same, since he had written to her a few months before:

> The director of a sort of research institute in Washington ... urged me strongly to go there for a year or even four months, but I'm not greatly attracted. I suspect all the Fellows spend their time 'leading discussions' and 'contributing to seminars' and the like. Over my head. Over my dead body.[19]

By August she was feeling ill again.

> Mark Gerson came to photograph me – a nice easy to get on with person. Luckily it took my mind off my poor physical state. Very blown out and feeling disinclined to eat and rather sick. I wore my loose black cotton dress and a red scarf....
>
> I feel awful on waking, but bit better now sitting in the sun writing this, also trying to finish off my novel. Shall I write more in this notebook?
>
> Perhaps what one fears about dying won't be the actual moment – one hopes – but what you have to go through beforehand – in my case this uncomfortable swollen body and feeling sick and no interest in food or drink.[20]

She went back to the clinic but the progress of the disease could not be stopped. In October she wrote:

As I am not feeling well at the moment (more fluid) I find myself reflecting on the mystery of life and death and the way we all pass through this world in a kind of procession. The whole business as inexplicable and mysterious as the John Le Carré TV serial *Tinker, Tailor, Soldier, Spy*, which we are all finding so baffling.[21]

She was now more or less confined to bed. She wrote to Bob Smith that she was

feeling sick, so not getting much nourishment. A few nips of brandy, Lucozade, weak tea, toast – hardly enough to sustain me.
    Later The doctor has just been and cheered me up . . . he says that champagne is better than Lucozade.
    A simply lovely day here – sun so powerful that I had to draw the curtains in my bedroom. Hazel has brought Tom to Wadham (I suppose young people are all brought to Oxford by car these days). So he is embarking on what should be the happiest days of his life.[22]

I used to call on her when I was visiting my son in Oxford and found her cheerful and prosaic about her condition and always with some splendid Pym anecdote or 'happening'. Because of the cancer treatment her hair was very thin and she wore a kerchief knotted round her head, which we decided looked like the photographs of the Olivier girls in the *Life of Rupert Brooke*, that she had found so fascinating. Sometimes Tom came too, to bring her news of undergraduate life in Oxford, and she gave him an idea for an Oxford short story: a shy young undergraduate has finally persuaded a rather glamorous and popular girl at the same college to come to lunch, and just as all seems to be going well they are interrupted by a visit from two elderly female friends of his mother. He wrote the story for her.

Bob Smith sent her letters full of the sort of detail she loved.

At Faith House the General Secretary, rather rarely seen, is a youngish cleric, on the hearty side and *married* (has this ever before been the case in the C[hurch] U[nion]?). Then there's a cosy lady typing-secretary who gives me coffee and a terrifyingly intelligent and earnest nun. I work in the 'Douglas Room', a sort of board-room where I'm often interrupted and put out (in both senses) when it's needed for a meeting.[23]

She was able to send Philip Larkin copies of the two final reissues from Cape:

The whole six really look quite handsome in their bright jackets and looking at them perhaps I can quote St Hilda's motto – *Non frustra vixi*.[24]

and they continued to exchange those details of the minutiae of life that they both found so fascinating. He replied to a letter of hers:

As for who cleans my windows, I can only answer with Desdemona (was it?) 'Nobody, I myself.'[25]

and

Oxford was its usual self: heavenly for 24 hours, then I couldn't get away fast enough. It's always the same. I had really come down as a guest at an All Souls Chichele dinner ('after eating in honour of Chichele we stood round and talked rather bichele'), and this was all right, except that the food was uninspiring. Apparently the bill of fare is chosen by the bursar ('no gourmet he', as *Time* would say) and honestly one course could only be described as 'game rissole': an absurd cylinder made up of all the game people had left on their plates for a week or two. 'Croquette de gibier' or some such cosmetic.
    Do you expect your proofs soon? If someone asked me to define happiness I might well say correcting proofs: it's really nicer than getting the published work, which is always something of an anticlimax in my experience,

and of course contains all the misprints one overlooked at the proof stage.[26]

Barbara had sent the manuscript of *A Few Green Leaves* to Macmillan, not really satisfied with it, but knowing that she could now do no more. When I saw her just before Christmas she asked, in her usual practical way, if I would see it through the press for her.

Hilary had been looking after her with great devotion and they still shared so much – reminiscence and jokes and affectionate fun – but Barbara felt that she did not want to be 'a burden' and arranged to go into Michael Sobell House, a hospice in Oxford. She had been taken round it in a wheelchair – 'Oh, the richness!' she told me, her eyes lighting up as they always did at the prospect of 'material', and when she went into the hospice, just after Christmas, she took her notebook with her. When he went to see her there, Henry Harvey found her wit and her courage undiminished, joking about the wig she now had to wear. It seemed fitting, somehow, that almost the last visit Belinda had should be from the Archdeacon – (just as Belinda had imagined it over forty years before) – Life imitating Art, as it so often did with Barbara.

She died, as Hilary said, with her customary consideration for others, just *after* breakfast on the morning of 11 January.

After her death, the interest in her work, already gathering force in her lifetime, increased. All her novels were published in the United States and they have now been translated into French, Italian, German, Dutch, Portuguese, Hungarian, and Russian. They are still in print in hardback and paperback. Scholars have written books and theses about her work, and her novels form part of the curriculum in both English and American universities. 'Miss Pym the novelist', indeed.

One of my favourite quiz games on television was one in which panellists were asked to guess the authorship of certain passages and then to discuss various features of the author in question. There were no prizes for guessing, no moving belt of desirable objects passing before their eyes, just the pleasure of recognising the unmistakable voice of Henry James or Graham Greene, or whoever it might be. I think that's the kind of immortality most authors would want – to feel that their work would be immediately recognisable as having been written by them and by nobody else. But, of course, it's a lot to ask for.[27]

Notes

Abbreviations
AAQ: *An Academic Question*
AUA: *An Unsuitable Attachment*
CH: *Crampton Hodnet*
EW: *Excellent Women*
FGL: *A Few Green Leaves*
G&F: *Gervase and Flora*
GOB: *A Glass of Blessings*
HFN: *Home Front Novel*
J&P: *Jane and Prudence*
LTA: *Less Than Angels*
NFRL: *No Fond Return of Love*
QIA: *Quartet in Autumn*
SDD: *The Sweet Dove Died*
STG: *Some Tame Gazelle*
SVS: *So Very Secret*
YMIFD: *Young Men in Fancy Dress*
B.MSS: MSS numbers of the Barbara Pym papers now in
          the Bodleian Library
p.c.:   personal communication to the author

Chapter One

1. *STG.*
2. Diaries (B.MSS 107).
3. *J&P.*
4. *STG.*
5. cf *J&P.*
6. cf *STG.*
7. *STG.*
8. *EW.*
9. *EW.*

10. Notebooks (B.MSS 88).
11. *Finding a Voice*, radio talk by BP, broadcast on BBC Radio 3, 4 April 1978.
12. *YMIFD.*
13. Ibid.
14. Ibid.
15. Ibid.
16. Ibid.
17. Ibid.
18. Ibid.
19. Ibid.
20. Ibid.
21. Aldous Huxley, *Crome Yellow*, Chatto & Windus, 1921.
22. *YMIFD.*

Chapter Two

1. Diaries (B.MSS 101).
2. Ibid.
3. Ibid.
4. *J&P.*
5. *EW.*
6. *J&P.*
7. Diaries (B.MSS 101).
8. Ibid.
9. Ibid.
10. Ibid.
11. Ibid.
12. Ibid.
13. *J&P.*
14. Diaries (B.MSS 101).
15. Ibid.
16. Ibid.
17. Ibid.
18. *CH.*
19. Diaries (B.MSS 101).
20. Ibid.
21. Ibid.
22. Ibid.
23. Ibid.
24. Ibid.

25. Ibid.
26. Ibid.
27. Corresp. with Rupert Gleadow (B.MSS 149–50).
28. Ibid.
29. Diaries (B.MSS 101).
30. Corresp. with Rupert Gleadow (B.MSS 149–50).
31. Ibid.
32. Ibid.
33. Diaries (B.MSS 101).
34. Ibid.
35. Ibid.
36. Corresp. with Rupert Gleadow (B.MSS 149–50).
37. Ibid.
38. Ibid.
39. Ibid.

Chapter Three

1. p.c. Henry Harvey.
2. Ibid.
3. Diaries (B.MSS 101).
4. Ibid.
5. Letter to Henry Harvey 1933.
6. Diaries (B.MSS 101).
7. Ibid.
8. Ibid.
9. Ibid.
10. Ibid.
11. Ibid.
12. Ibid.
13. Ibid.
14. Ibid.
15. Ibid.
16. Ibid.
17. Diaries (B.MSS 102).
18. Diaries (B.MSS 103).
19. p.c. Elizabeth Barnicot.
20. p.c. Henry Harvey.
21. Diaries (B.MSS 102).
22. Ibid.
23. Ibid.

24. Ibid.
25. Ibid.
26. Ibid.
27. Ibid.
28. Ibid.
29. Ibid.
30. Ibid.
31. Ibid.
32. Ibid.
33. Ibid.
34. Corresp. with Robert Liddell (B.MSS 154–7).
35. Diaries (B.MSS 102).
36. *J&P*.
37. Diaries (B.MSS 102).
38. Corresp. with Rupert Gleadow (B.MSS 149–50).
39. Diaries (B.MSS 102).
40. PEN Club meeting in celebration of Barbara Pym, 1985.
41. Ibid.
42. p.c. Henry Harvey.
43. Pen Club, 1985.
44. Ibid.
45. Diaries (B.MSS 103).
46. Diaries (B.MSS 102).
47. Ibid.
48. Ibid.
49. Diaries (B.MSS 103).
50. Ibid. (This was to become *Some Tame Gazelle*.)
51. Ibid.
52. Ibid.
53. Ibid.
54. Ibid.

Chapter Four

1. Corresp. with Robert Liddell (B.MSS 154–9).
2. Ibid.
3. Diaries (B.MSS 103).
4. Corresp. with Robert Liddell (B.MSS 154–9).
5. Ibid.
6. Ibid.
7. Letter to Robert Liddell (B.MSS 154–7).

8. Corresp. with Robert Liddell (B.MSS 154–7).
9. Ibid.
10. Letter to Robert Liddell (B.MSS 153).
11. Corresp. with Robert Liddell (B.MSS 154–7).
12. Ibid.
13. Letter to Henry Harvey 1935.
14. Ibid.
15. Diaries (B.MSS 103).
16. Letter to Henry Harvey 1936.
17. Diaries (B.MSS 103).
18. Corresp. with Robert Liddell (B.MSS 154–7).
19. *EW.*
20. Diaries (B.MSS 103).
21. Letter to Robert Liddell (B.MSS 153).
22. Corresp. with Cape (B.MSS 163).
23. Diaries (B.MSS 103).
24. Corresp. with Robert Liddell (B.MSS 154–7).
25. Letter to Henry Harvey 1936.
26. Diaries (B.MSS 103).
27. *G&F.*
28. Letter to Robert Liddell (B.MSS 153).
29. PEN Club 1985.
30. Letter to Robert Liddell (B.MSS 153).
31. Diaries (B.MSS 103).
32. Letter to Henry Harvey 1936.
33. Letter to Robert Liddell (B.MSS 153).
34. Corresp. with Robert Liddell (B.MSS 154–7).
35. Ibid.
36. *G&F.*
37. p.c. Henry Harvey.
38. B.MSS 7. Published posthumously under the title *Gervase and Flora.*
39. Corresp. with Robert Liddell (B.MSS 154–7).
40. Ibid.
41. Ibid.
42. *G&F.*
43. Ibid.

Chapter Five

1. Diaries (B.MSS 102).
2. Ibid.

3. Corresp. with Rupert Gleadow (B.MSS 149–50).
4. Diaries (B.MSS 102).
5. Diaries (B.MSS 103).
6. Ibid.
7. Corresp. with Robert Liddell 1938.
8. Ibid.
9. Ibid.
10. Ibid.
11. Ibid.
12. Ibid.
13. Diaries (B.MSS 106).
14. Diaries (B.MSS 107).

Chapter Six

1. Diaries (B.MSS 103).
2. Ibid.
3. Corresp. with Julian Amery (B.MSS 147).
4. Diaries (B.MSS 103).
5. Ibid.
6. *CH.*
7. Diaries (B.MSS 103).
8. Diaries (B.MSS 104).
9. Diaries (B.MSS 146).
10. *HFN.*
11. Ibid.
12. *SVS.*
13. Diaries (B.MSS 107).
14. Diaries (B.MSS 146).

Chapter Seven

1. Diaries (B.MSS 104).
2. Ibid.
3. Ibid.
4. Ibid.
5. Letters to Henry and Elsie Harvey 1938.
6. Ibid.
7. Ibid.

8.   Ibid.
9.   Ibid.
10.   Corresp. with Robert Liddell (B.MSS 154-9).
11.   Ibid.
12.   Ibid.
13.   Letters to Henry and Elsie Harvey 1939.
14.   Letter to Robert Liddell 1936.
15.   Letters to Henry and Elsie Harvey 1939.
16.   p.c. Henry Harvey.
17.   Letters to Robert Liddell 1938.
18.   Ibid.
19.   Letters to Henry and Elsie Harvey 1938.
20.   Letters to Robert Liddell 1938.
21.   Diaries (B.MSS 105).
22.   Letters to Elsie and Henry Harvey 1939.
23.   Diaries (B.MSS 105).

Chapter Eight

1.   Diaries (B.MSS 105).
2.   Ibid.
3.   Ibid.
4.   Ibid.
5.   Ibid.
6.   Ibid.
7.   Ibid.
8.   Elsie's mother had escaped from Russia in an open boat in 1917.
9.   PEN Club 1985.
10.   Diaries (B.MSS 105).
11.   Diaries (B.MSS 105-6).
12.   *Huston Post*.
13.   Miss Moberley, who first appeared in the Finnish novel, was her generic name for difficult, bullying old ladies.
14.   *CH*.
15.   Corresp. with Robert Liddell (B.MSS 154-7).
16.   Ibid.
17.   Ibid.
18.   Diaries (B.MSS 107).
19.   Diaries (B.MSS 106).
20.   Ibid.
21.   Diaries (B.MSS 106).

22. Diaries (B.MSS 107).
23. Ibid.
24. Diaries (B.MSS 106).
25. Diaries (B.MSS 107).
26. Ibid.
27. Ibid.
28. Letter to Robert Liddell 1940.
29. Diaries (B.MSS 107).
30. Ibid.
31. Ibid.
32. Ibid.
33. Ibid.
34. Ibid.
35. Ibid.
36. Diaries (B.MSS 146).
37. Diaries (B.MSS 107).
38. Diaries (B.MSS 106).

Chapter Nine

1. Letter to Henry and Elsie Harvey 1942.
2. Letter to Henry Harvey 1942.
3. Ibid.
4. Letter to Henry and Elsie Harvey 1942.
5. Letter to Henry Harvey 1943.
6. Ibid.
7. Diaries (B.MSS 109).
8. Letter to Henry Harvey, 1943.
9. Diaries (B.MSS 108).
10. Ibid.
11. Diaries (B.MSS 108).
12. Ibid.
13. Ibid.
14. Notebooks (B.MSS 40–82).
15. Ibid.
16. Diaries (B.MSS 108).
17. *EW*.
18. Diaries (B.MSS 108).
19. Ibid.
20. Letter to Henry Harvey, 1942.
21. Diaries (B.MSS 108).

22. Ibid.
23. Ibid.
24. Diaries (B.MSS 109).
25. Diaries (B.MSS 108).
26. Ibid.

Chapter Ten

1. Diaries (B.MSS 109).
2. Ibid.
3. Ibid.
4. Ibid.
5. Ibid.
6. Ibid.
7. Ibid.
8. Ibid.
9. Ibid.
10. Ibid.
11. Ibid.
12. Ibid.
13. Ibid.
14. Ibid.
15. Ibid.
16. Ibid.
17. Ibid.
18. Ibid.
19. Ibid.
20. Notebooks (B.MSS 40–82).
21. Diaries (B.MSS 109).
22. Ibid.
23. Letter to Henry Harvey, 1944.
24. Ibid.
25. Ibid.
26. Ibid.
27. *EW.*
28. Diaries (B.MSS 110).
29. Ibid.
30. Ibid.
31. Ibid.
32. Ibid.
33. Ibid.
34. Ibid.
35. Ibid.

36. Corresp. with Robert Liddell (B.MSS 154–7).
37. *AUA.*
38. Diaries (B.MSS 110).
39. Ibid.
40. Ibid.
41. Ibid. also *GOB.*
42. Diaries (B.MSS 110).
43. Ibid.

Chapter Eleven

1. Corresp. with Robert Liddell (B.MSS 154–7).
2. Ibid.
3. *EW.*
4. Corresp. with Robert Liddell (B.MSS 154–7).
5. Letter to Henry Harvey, 1945.
6. *EW.*
7. Corresp. with Robert Liddell (B.MSS 154–7).
8. Letter to Henry Harvey, 1946.
9. *STG.*
10. Letter to Elsie Harvey, 1938.
11. Letter to Henry Harvey, 1945.
12. Letter to Henry Harvey, 1946.
13. *LTA.*
14. Letter to Henry Harvey, 1946.
15. Ibid.
16. *AAQ.*
17. *NFRL.*
18. Corresp. with Robert Liddell (B.MSS 154–7).
19. Ibid.
20. Ibid.
21. Letter to Henry Harvey, 1946.
22. Corresp. with Robert Liddell (B.MSS 154–7).
23. Letters to Henry Harvey, 1946.
24. Corresp. with Robert Liddell (B.MSS 154–7).
25. Letter to Henry Harvey, 1952.
26. *EW.*
27. Letter to Henry Harvey, 1944.
28. Letter to Henry Harvey, 1946.
29. Letter to Elsie Harvey, 1938.
30. Diaries (B.MSS 109).
31. *EW.*
32. *LTA.*

Chapter Twelve

1. Notebooks (B.MSS 40).
2. Robert Liddell, *A Mind at Ease*, London, Peter Owen, 1989.
3. Robert Smith, 'How Pleasant to Know Miss Pym', *Ariel*, 1971.
4. Corresp. with Robert Smith (B.MSS 162).
5. *EW*.
6. Diaries (B.MSS 116).
7. Corresp. with Robert Liddell (B.MSS 154–7).
8. Notebooks (B.MSS 40).
9. *NFRL*.
10. *AAQ*.
11. Corresp. with Robert Smith (B.MSS 162).
12. Ibid.
13. Ibid.
14. Corresp. with Robert Liddell (B.MSS 154–7).
15. Robert Liddell, *A Mind at Ease*.
16. Corresp. with Philip Larkin, 1964.
17. Corresp. with Robert Smith (B.MSS 162).
18. *EW*.

Chapter Thirteen

1. Corresp. with Robert Liddell (B.MSS 154–7).
2. Notebooks (B.MSS 44).
3. Notebooks (B.MSS 46 *et seq.*).
4. Notebooks (B.MSS 46).
5. Corresp. with Robert Smith (B.MSS 162).
6. Ibid.
7. Correspondence with Lord David Cecil (B.MSS 148).
8. *J&P*.
9. Ibid.
10. *J&P*.
11. Corresp. with Robert Smith (B.MSS 162).
12. Notebooks (B.MSS 45).
13. Ibid.
14. *LTA*.
15. Corresp. with Robert Smith (B.MSS 162).
16. p.c. John Middleton.
17. *LTA*.
18. Notebooks (B.MSS 48).
19. Ibid.

20. Notebooks (B.MSS 49).
21. Notebooks (B.MSS 48).
22. *The Denton Welch Journals,* edited by Jocelyn Brooke, Hamish Hamilton, 1952.
23. Notebooks (B.MSS 69).

Chapter Fourteen

1. Rachel Ferguson, *We Were Amused,* Jonathan Cape, 1958.
2. Ibid.
3. Ibid.
4. Notebooks (B.MSS 51).
5. Rachel Ferguson, *The Brontës Went to Woolworths,* Ernest Benn, 1931.
6. Notebooks (B.MSS 46).
7. Ibid.
8. Ibid.
9. Corresp. with Robert Liddell (B.MSS 154–7).
10. *GOB.*
11. *NFRL.*
12. Corresp. with Robert Smith (B.MSS 162).
13. *NFRL.*
14. Corresp. with Robert Smith (B.MSS 160–1).
15. Corresp. with Robert Liddell (B.MSS 154–7).
16. Corresp. with Robert Smith (B.MSS 162).
17. Ibid.
18. Corresp. with Robert Smith (B.MSS 160–1).
19. Ibid.
20. Corresp. with Robert Smith (B.MSS 162).
21. Notebooks (B.MSS 55).
22. Ibid., cf also *AUA.*

Chapter Fifteen

1. Corresp. with Robert Smith (B.MSS 162).
2. Corresp. with Philip Larkin (B.MSS 151–2).
3. Letters to Philip Larkin, 1961.
4. Notebooks (B.MSS 55).
5. Ibid.
6. Corresp. with Philip Larkin (B.MSS 151–2).
7. Ibid.

8. Ibid.
9. Ibid.
10. Letters to Philip Larkin, 1963.
11. Corresp. with Philip Larkin (B.MSS 151–2).
12. Ibid.
13. Ibid.
14. Letters to Philip Larkin, 1963.
15. Notebooks (B.MSS 57).
16. Corresp. with Robert Smith (B.MSS 162).
17. Diaries, 1958 (B.MSS 124).
18. Letters to Philip Larkin, 1963.
19. Corresp. with Philip Larkin (B.MSS 151–2).
20. Philip Larkin, Introduction to *An Unsuitable Attachment*.
21. Corresp. with Cape (B.MSS 164).
22. Corresp. with Robert Liddell (B.MSS 154–7).
23. Ibid.
24. Diaries (B.MSS 129).
25. Ibid.
26. Corresp. with Robert Smith (B.MSS 162).
27. Corresp. with Philip Larkin (B.MSS 151–2).
28. Letters to Philip Larkin, 1963.
29. Corresp. with Philip Larkin (B.MSS 151–2).
30. Ibid.
31. Ibid.
32. Ibid.
33. Letters to Philip Larkin, 1964.

Chapter Sixteen

1. Corresp. with Robert Smith (B.MSS 162).
2. Robert Smith, 'Remembering Barbara Pym', in *Independent Women*, edited by Janice Rossen, Harvester Press, 1988.
3. Corresp. with Robert Smith (B.MSS 162).
4. Ibid.
5. Ibid.
6. Ibid.
7. Ibid.
8. Notebooks (B.MSS 60).
9. *AUA*.
10. Notebooks (B.MSS 59).
11. Ibid.
12. Ibid.

13. Ibid.
14. Letters to Richard Roberts, 1964.
15. Notebooks (B.MSS 60).
16. Corresp. with Robert Smith (B.MSS 162).
17. Notebooks (B.MSS 60).
18. Notebooks (B.MSS 61).
19. Corresp. with Robert Smith (B.MSS 162).
20. Notebooks (B.MSS 61).
21. Corresp. with Robert Smith (B.MSS 162).
22. Notebooks (B.MSS 61).
23. Corresp. with Robert Smith (B.MSS 162).
24. Ibid.
25. Ibid.
26. Ibid.
27. *EW*.
28. Robert Liddell, *A Mind at Ease*.
29. Notebooks (B.MSS 62).
30. *The Lumber Room* (unfinished, 1938).
31. *GOB*.
32. Corresp. with Robert Smith (B.MSS 162).
33. Ibid.
34. Corresp. with Philip Larkin (B.MSS 151–2).

Chapter Seventeen

1. Letters to Philip Larkin, 1964.
2. Letters to Philip Larkin, 1963.
3. Corresp. with Robert Smith (B.MSS 162).
4. Corresp. with Robert Smith (B.MSS 160–1).
5. Corresp. with Philip Larkin (B.MSS 151–2).
6. Notebooks (B.MSS 62).
7. Letters to Philip Larkin, 1965.
8. Corresp. with Philip Larkin (B.MSS 151–2).
9. Letters to Robert Smith, 1965.
10. Corresp. with Philip Larkin (B.MSS 151–2).
11. Ibid.
12. Letters to Robert Smith, 1966.
13. Ibid.
14. Letters to Robert Smith, 1967.
15. Notebooks (B.MSS 66–70).
16. Letters to Robert Smith, 1970.
17. Ibid.

18. Corresp. with Philip Larkin (B.MSS 151–2).
19. Ibid.
20. Corresp. with Robert Smith (B.MSS 160–1).
21. Robert Smith, 'How Pleasant to
    Know Miss Pym'.
22. Ibid.
23. Corresp. with Philip Larkin (B.MSS 151–2).
24. Corresp. with Robert Smith (B.MSS 160–1).
25. Ibid.
26. Notebooks (B.MSS 71).
27. Corresp. with Philip Larkin (B.MSS 151–2).
28. Corresp. with Robert Smith (B.MSS 162).
29. Notebooks (B.MSS 69).
30. Corresp. with Robert Smith (B.MSS 162).
31. Letters to Philip Larkin, 1971.
32. Corresp. with Philip Larkin (B.MSS 151–2).
33. Corresp. with Robert Smith (B.MSS 162).
34. Ibid.
35. Corresp. with Philip Larkin (B.MSS 151–2).
36. Letters to Philip Larkin, 1971.
37. *The Lumber Room.*

Chapter Eighteen

1. Notebooks (B.MSS 70).
2. Corresp. with Robert Smith (B.MSS 162).
3. Letters to Philip Larkin, 1972.
4. Corresp. with Robert Smith (B.MSS 162).
5. Corresp. with Philip Larkin (B.MSS 151–2).
6. Corresp. with Robert Smith (B.MSS 162).
7. Letters to Philip Larkin, 1972.
8. Ibid.
9. Corresp. with Robert Smith (B.MSS 162).
10. Ibid.
11. Letters to Philip Larkin, 1972.
12. Notebooks (B.MSS 70).
13. Ibid.
14. Letters to Philip Larkin, 1973.
15. Notebooks (B.MSS 71).
16. Corresp. with Robert Smith (B.MSS 162).
17. Corresp. with Philip Larkin (B.MSS 151–2).
18. Notebooks (B.MSS 72).

19. Ibid.
20. Corresp. with Robert Smith (B.MSS 162).
21. Letters to Philip Larkin, 1974.
22. Notebooks (B.MSS 73).
23. Corresp. with Robert Smith (B.MSS 162).
24. Ibid.
25. Letters to Philip Larkin, 1974.
26. Corresp. with Philip Larkin (B.MSS 151–2).
27. Letters to Philip Larkin, 1975.
28. Corresp. with Philip Larkin (B.MSS 151–2).
29. Letters to Philip Larkin, 1975.
30. Corresp. with Philip Larkin (B.MSS 151–2).
31. Letters to Philip Larkin, 1975.
32. Corresp. with Philip Larkin (B.MSS 151–2).
33. Letters to Philip Larkin, 1976.
34. Notebooks (B.MSS 73).
35. Corresp. with Robert Smith (B.MSS 162).
36. Ibid.
37. Ibid.
38. Corresp. with Philip Larkin (B.MSS 151–2).
39. Ibid.
40. Notebooks (B.MSS 75).
41. Corresp. with Philip Larkin (B.MSS 151–2).
42. Notebooks (B.MSS 76).
43. *GOB.*
44. Corresp. with Philip Larkin (B.MSS 151–2).
45. Corresp. with Robert Smith (B.MSS 162).
46. Notebooks (B.MSS 76).
47. Corresp. with Robert Smith (B.MSS 162).
48. Letters to Henry Harvey, 1976.

Chapter Nineteen

1. Notebooks (B.MSS 76).
2. Corresp. with Lord David Cecil (B.MSS 148).
3. Ibid.
4. Letters to Philip Larkin, 1977.
5. Notebooks (B.MSS 76).
6. Ibid.
7. Letters to Philip Larkin, 1977.
8. Corresp. with Philip Larkin (B.MSS 151–2).
9. Letters to Philip Larkin, 1977.

10. Corresp. with Robert Liddell (B.MSS 158).
11. Corresp. with Philip Larkin (B.MSS 151–2).
12. Notebooks (B.MSS 77).
13. Ibid.
14. Corresp. with Lord David Cecil (B.MSS 148).
15. Letters to Philip Larkin, 1977.
16. Corresp. with Lord David Cecil (B.MSS 148).
17. Corresp. with Philip Larkin (B.MSS 151–2).
18. Notebooks (B.MSS 77).
19. Letters to Philip Larkin, 1977.
20. Corresp. with Robert Smith (B.MSS 162).
21. Corresp. with Robert Liddell (B.MSS 158).
22. Ibid.
23. Robert Liddell, *A Mind at Ease.*
24. Corresp. with Philip Larkin (B.MSS 151–2).
25. Notebooks (B.MSS 79).
26. Ibid.
27. Letters to Philip Larkin, 1977.
28. Corresp. with Philip Larkin (B.MSS 151–2).
29. Letters to Philip Larkin, 1978.
30. Corresp. with Philip Larkin (B.MSS 151–2).
31. Letters to Philip Larkin, 1978.
32. Ibid.
33. The eight records she chose were: 1. 'In the Bleak Midwinter'. 2. Czardas from *Die Fledermaus*. 3. Waltzes from *Der Rosenkavalier*. 4. A Greek song: 'Sto Perigiala'. 5. Chopin Variations. 6. 'Vissi d'arte' from *Tosca*. 7. An organ piece by Messiaen. 8. Philip Larkin reading 'An Arundel Tomb'.
34. Letters to Philip Larkin, 1978.
35. Corresp. with Philip Larkin (B.MSS 151–2).
36. Corresp. with Robert Smith (B.MSS 160–1).
37. Corresp. with Lord David Cecil (B.MSS 148).
38. Corresp. with Robert Liddell (B.MSS 158).
39. Corresp. with Philip Larkin (B.MSS 151–2).
40. Letters to Philip Larkin, 1978.
41. Notebooks (B.MSS 80).
42. Ibid.
43. Notebooks (B.MSS 73).
44. Notebooks (B.MSS 71).
45. Robert Liddell, *A Mind at Ease.*

Chapter Twenty

1. Corresp. with Robert Smith (B.MSS 162).
2. Corresp. with Philip Larkin (B.MSS 151–2).
3. Letters to Philip Larkin, 1978.
4. Notebooks (B.MSS 80).
5. Ibid.
6. Ibid.
7. Letters to Philip Larkin, 1979.
8. Notebooks (B.MSS 81).
9. Ibid.
10. Letters to Philip Larkin, 1979.
11. Corresp. with Philip Larkin (B.MSS 151–2).
12. Corresp. with Robert Smith (B.MSS 162).
13. Notebooks (B.MSS 81).
14. p.c. Henry Harvey.
15. Notebooks (B.MSS 81).
16. Ibid.
17. Ibid.
18. Notebooks (B.MSS 82).
19. Corresp. with Philip Larkin (B.MSS 151–2).
20. Notebooks (B.MSS 82).
21. Ibid.
22. Corresp. with Robert Smith (B.MSS 162).
23. Corresp. with Robert Smith (B.MSS 160–1).
24. Letters to Philip Larkin, 1979.
25. Corresp. with Philip Larkin (B.MSS 151–2).
26. Ibid.
27. *Finding a Voice*, radio talk by BP broadcast on BBC Radio 3, 4 April 1978.

A Publishing History

	Written	Hard Cover UK	Publication USA
Some Tame Gazelle	1935–50	Cape, 1950 reissued, 1978	Dutton, 1983
#*Civil to Strangers*	1936–8	Macmillan, 1987	Dutton, 1987
#*Gervase and Flora*	1937–8	Macmillan, 1987	Dutton, 1987
* *Crampton Hodnet*	1939–40	Macmillan, 1985	Dutton, 1985
#*Home Front Novel*	1939–40	Macmillan, 1987	Dutton, 1987
#*So Very Secret*	1940–1	Macmillan, 1987	Dutton, 1987
Excellent Women	1949–51	Cape, 1952 reissued, 1978	Dutton, 1978
Jane and Prudence	1950–2	Cape, 1953 reissued, 1978	Dutton, 1981
Less Than Angels	1953–4	Cape, 1955 reissued, 1978	Dutton, 1980
A Glass of Blessings	1955–6	Cape, 1958 reissued, 1977	Dutton, 1980
No Fond Return of Love	1957–60	Cape, 1961 reissued, 1979	Dutton, 1982
* *An Unsuitable Attachment*	1960–5	Macmillan, 1982	Dutton, 1982
The Sweet Dove Died (Revised for publication by Barbara Pym in 1977)	1963–9	Macmillan, 1978	Dutton, 1979
* *An Academic Question*	1970–1	Macmillan, 1986	Dutton, 1986
Quartet in Autumn	1973–6	Macmillan, 1977	Dutton, 1978
A Few Green Leaves	1977–9	Macmillan, 1980	Dutton, 1980

* Revised for publication by Hazel Holt
#Revised for publication in one volume (*Civil to Strangers*) by Hazel Holt

Index

Compiled by Hilary Walton